"This rich collection of essays combats the shallowness of much of our thinking and rhetoric about evangelicalism. *Whatever Happened to Evangelicalism?* brings the best in contemporary scholarship to bear on the timely question of what it means to be evangelical. It deserves a wide reading and thoughtful discussion."

—Donald A. Yerxa
Editor, *Fides et Historia*
Emeritus Professor of History, Eastern Nazarene College

"*Whatever Happened to Evangelicalism?* provides an excellent bird's-eye view of the evangelical movement that has spanned centuries and continents. It is informative, up to date, and thought provoking, since it is more than just a narrative but a bold and critical self-examination. By revisiting the roots of the movement it anchors 'evangelical' firmly on the kingdom of God. It successfully corrects misconceptions of the term 'evangelical' and identifies some key problems of contemporary evangelicalism, especially in the realm of politics. It sounds a timely clarion call to 'gospel people' to rise above the world of politics and to follow the way of Christ. This is an important book for Christian clergy and laypeople alike and a book of interest to readers who want to know what evangelicalism is all about."

—Maureen Yeung Marshall
Professor Emerita of Biblical Studies, Evangel Seminary, Hong Kong

"What is an evangelical? Are evangelicals fundamentalists? Are they Pentecostals? Do they care about God's kingdom on earth or just about individual salvation? Are they social and political conservatives? Can they be found in mainline denominations? This book answers these questions via a remarkable collection of voices: a scientist, a Catholic, Nazarenes, and Baptists. Each essay provides scholarly knowledge that is accessible to general readers. The essays advanced my understanding of evangelicalism and reminded me that evangelicals are engaged with contemporary society, both Christianly and ethically. This book is especially recommended for people who do not call themselves evangelical but who are curious about one of the most significant Christian movements of the last three centuries, a movement whose influence today is global. If you have stereotypes about evangelicalism, be ready to think differently."

—George Wiley
Emeritus Professor of Religion, Baker University, Baldwin City, Kansas

"In a time when words like 'Christianity' and 'evangelical' have become degraded by false practitioners, this collection of essays—rather than conceding key terms—offers fresh interpretations of the language used to define authentic followers of Jesus Christ. Deeply learned, yet quite accessible, this volume offers a global post-Christendom vision of how believers can bear witness with humility and hope in the transforming power of the gospel. This will be especially useful for doctor of ministry students, scholars, and practitioners in the body of Christ."

—Molly T. Marshall
President and Professor of Theology and Spiritual Formation
Central Baptist Theological Seminary

# WHATEVER HAPPENED TO EVANGELICALISM?

WHATEVER HAPPENED TO EVANGELICALISM?

AL TRUESDALE
EDITOR

THE FOUNDRY
PUBLISHING

Copyright © 2017 by Beacon Hill Press of Kansas City

Beacon Hill Press of Kansas City
PO Box 419527
Kansas City, MO 64141

ISBN 978-0-8341-3657-1

All rights reserved. No part of this publication may be reproduced, stored in a retrieval system, or transmitted in any form or by any means—for example, electronic, photocopy, recording—without the prior written permission of the publisher. The only exception is brief quotations in printed reviews.

Cover Design: Rob Monacelli
Interior Design: Sharon Page

The following versions of Scripture are in the public domain:
Douay-Rheims (DRA)
The King James Version (KJV)

The following copyrighted versions of Scripture are used by permission:
The Holy Bible, English Standard Version® (ESV®). Copyright © 2001 by Crossway Bibles, a publishing ministry of Good News Publishers. All rights reserved.

The Good News Translation (GNT), second edition, copyright © 1992 by American Bible Society. All rights reserved.

The New American Standard Bible® (NASB®), copyright © 1960, 1962, 1963, 1968, 1971, 1972, 1973, 1975, 1977, 1995 by The Lockman Foundation.

The Holy Bible, New International Version® (NIV®). Copyright © 1973, 1978, 1984, 2011 by Biblica, Inc.™ Used by permission of Zondervan. All rights reserved worldwide. www.zondervan.com.

The New King James Version® (NKJV). Copyright © 1982 by Thomas Nelson, Inc. All rights reserved.

The New Revised Standard Version Bible (NRSV), copyright © 1989 National Council of the Churches of Christ in the United States of America. All rights reserved.

The Revised Standard Version (RSV) of the Bible, copyright © 1946, 1952, and 1971 National Council of the Churches of Christ in the United States of America. All rights reserved worldwide.

The Tree of Life Version (TLV). © 2015 by the Messianic Jewish Family Bible Society.

Library of Congress Cataloging-in-Publication Data
Names: Truesdale, Albert, 1941- editor.
Title: Whatever happened to evangelicalism? / Al Truesdale, editor.
Description: Kansas City, MO : Beacon Hill Press, [2017] | Includes bibliographical references.
Identifiers: LCCN 2017041839 | ISBN 9780834136571 (pbk.)
Subjects: LCSH: Evangelicalism.
Classification: LCC BR1640.A25 W43 2017 | DDC 270.8/2—dc23 LC record available at https://lccn.loc.gov/2017041839

The Internet addresses, email addresses, and phone numbers in this book are accurate at the time of publication. They are provided as a resource. Beacon Hill Press of Kansas City does not endorse them or vouch for their content or permanence.

CONTRIBUTORS

Timothy J. Crutcher, PhD/STD
Professor of Theology and Church
  History
Southern Nazarene University
Bethany, Oklahoma

Floyd Cunningham, PhD
Academic Dean
Professor of the History of Christianity
Asia-Pacific Nazarene Theological
  Seminary
Taytay, Philippines

Timothy R. Gaines, PhD
Assistant Professor of Religion
Trevecca Nazarene University
Nashville

Svetlana Khobnya, PhD
Lecturer in Biblical Studies
Nazarene Theological College
Manchester, United Kingdom

David Rainey, PhD
Senior Research Fellow in Theology
Nazarene Theological College
Manchester, United Kingdom

Jason J. Simon, M.Div.
Executive Director
The Evangelical Catholic
Madison, Wisconsin

J. B. (Jim) Stump, PhD
Senior Editor
BioLogos
Grand Rapids, Michigan

Al Truesdale, PhD
Emeritus Professor of Philosophy of
  Religion and Christian Ethics
Nazarene Theological Seminary
Kansas City

Michael K. Turner, PhD
Associate Professor of the History of
  Christianity and Wesleyan Studies
Associate Director, Methodist House
  of Studies
Memphis Theological Seminary
Memphis

David Wheeler, ThD
Senior Pastor
First Baptist Church
Portland, Oregon

*So then, like prudent pilots, let us set the sails of our faith
for the course wherein we may pass by most safely,
and again follow the coasts of the Scriptures.*
—Ambrose, Bishop of Milan, *Exposition of the Christian Faith*,
bk. 1, chap. 6, sec. 47

---

*The history of Christianity is the history of the truth of Christ
contending constantly against the truth as men see it.*
—Reinhold Niebuhr, *The Nature and Destiny of Man*, vol. 2, chap. 2, sec. 3

CONTENTS

Introduction	13
1. Defining "Evangelical": An Overview (Al Truesdale)	17
2. The Good News of the Inaugurated Kingdom of God (Svetlana Khobnya)	35
3. Proclaiming the Good News of Christ through Tradition (David Rainey)	53
4. The Evangelical Revivals of the Eighteenth Century (Timothy J. Crutcher)	71
5. The Modern Evangelical Movement in North America (Michael K. Turner)	89
6. Evangelicals and Contemporary Science (J. B. [Jim] Stump)	109
7. Evangelicals and the Next Christendom (Floyd Cunningham)	125
8. Evangelical Proclamation and Teaching in the Twenty-First Century (David Wheeler)	151
9. Voting, Values, and Vocation: The Shape of Evangelical Politics (Timothy R. Gaines)	167
10. Evangelicalism in Catholicism (Jason J. Simon)	185
Conclusion	203
Appendix A	207
The Nicene-Constantinopolitan Creed	207
The Definition (Creed) of Chalcedon	209
The Apostles' Creed	210
The Athanasian Creed	211
Appendix B	215
Documentary Resources	215
Notes	217

INTRODUCTION

THE WORD "evangelical" lies near the center of the Christian faith, but often it is misunderstood and misused. With the potential of so much confusion, clarification is needed. That is our purpose in writing this book. We will explore the biblical, creedal, historic, and contemporary sources, meanings, and implications of this word. Our hope is that we can not only foster better understanding but also encourage faithful Christian discipleship.

Political candidates, pundits, and journalists often use "evangelical" to categorize large segments of a population. Political and social criteria are slung in every direction, while careful biblical and theological standards are disregarded. Fed up with confusing generalizations, in February 2016, Russell Moore, president of the Ethics & Religious Liberty Commission of the Southern Baptist Convention, announced he no longer wanted to be called an evangelical—at least not until the United States' 2016 election cycle was over.[1] Instead, he preferred the title "gospel Christian." "The word 'evangelical,'" he protested, "has become almost meaningless this year, and in many ways the word itself is at the moment subverting the gospel of Jesus Christ."[2] Thomas Kidd places the blame principally upon evangelicals themselves. Too many of them are responsible for the "watering-down and politicization of the term 'evangelical.'"[3]

As if confusing generalizations used by pundits and politicians were not enough, during the 2016 election cycle some "evangelicals" fell to arguing among themselves. One well-known evangelical blogger accused a

Christian university president of joining the "whores of Moloch." He was referring to apostate Hebrews who sacrificed their children to the Ammonite and Phoenician god "Moloch" (Lev. 18:21; 20:2-5, DRA). The university president's alleged apostasy? He had endorsed a presidential candidate who had voiced qualified support for Planned Parenthood.[4] Not surprisingly, David Kirkpatrick, writing in the *New York Times Magazine*, labeled such mayhem an "evangelical crackup."[5]

Even the word "Christian" guarantees no safeguard against abuse. Years ago, a prominent and somewhat frustrated Presbyterian pastor in Kansas City told me, "I no longer want to hear people tell me they are 'Christians.' What I want to know is, 'Are you a committed disciple of Jesus Christ?'"

Confusion of language plagues much of Christendom. For example, Christian Torajans, who live in the remote highlands of the Indonesian island of Sulawesi, augment their Christian funerals by slaughtering valuable water buffalo. They believe the buffalo will accompany the deceased into the next world as a form of money, thus guaranteeing sufficient wealth during their sojourn.[6] But we need not fly to the highlands of Indonesia to find "confusion of language." Today, a host of preachers in the United States have sprinkled stardust on God and magically transformed him into a guarantor of financial success, happiness, and physical well-being, all while generating megariches and luxury for themselves.[7] In the nineteenth century, Danish Christian Søren Kierkegaard complained the term "Christian" had become so corrupted that many Danes thought the cows should be called Christian. After all, they had been born in a "Christian" country.[8] Later, Dietrich Bonhoeffer protested that the "cost" of God's grace and the benefits of religion had become so "cheap" that they were being peddled to people at bargain-basement prices. A superficial form of Christianity was quite sufficient for obtaining "remission of sins."[9]

Theologian Romano Guardini lamented misuse of sacred Christian grammar. In the modern era, he said, "We live among sullied words and blurred thoughts." But rather than surrender Christian grammar to its abusers, Guardini insisted that it is "imperative that we clarify our thinking and speaking again and again."[10]

Guardini is correct. Though protecting our Christian vocabulary and its accompanying form of life is demanding, we must never abandon either one to a jungle of confusion and abuse. Apart from our vocabulary—all of it—we don't know who we are as Christians. Unless we respect and embody our language in our lives we can easily be subverted by "every wind of doctrine" (Eph. 4:14, NRSV) and sucked into the vortex of non-Christian values. Subvert or abandon our language and before long we will become completely disoriented about the integrated meaning of Christian faith and discipleship, witness and mission. And the range of Christ's lordship will be squeezed into an ever-diminishing and clouded corner.

Misuse or surrender of Christian vocabulary can happen in different ways:

- We can cave to an unredeemed world's insistence that our speech and convictions conform to its expectations (Rom. 12:1-2; 1 Pet. 1:13-25).
- Impaired speech can occur within the church if we fail to admonish and teach everyone in Christian wisdom, with the goal of presenting all Christians "perfect in Christ" (Col. 1:28, KJV).
- Misuse can happen if we rashly impose preconceived ideas and expectations upon the Scriptures and Christian doctrine.
- Misuse can happen when definitions and use of Christian language begin at narrow sectarian branches of the church. No single part of the body of Christ is an adequate steward of Christian grammar. Neither is what one segment "knows" superior to another's share of Christian wisdom. No part of Christian grammar is the sole property of any one branch of the church. If we err here, we should not be surprised to find ourselves tangled in webs of misunderstanding and conflict. "Discord," Cyprian warned, "cannot attain to the kingdom of heaven."[11]

- Misuse can occur if we fail to listen attentively wherever, in Christ's church, the Holy Spirit is speaking. Paul taught that in the church each member benefits from the diverse gifts the Holy Spirit administers throughout the Lord's body (1 Cor. 12:7-30).

The Scriptures and the historic Christian family must endlessly mentor us. The latter includes the ecumenical creeds (Nicene, the Definition of Chalcedon, Apostles', and Athanasian; see appendix A).[12]

As mentioned earlier, this book aims to explore the word "evangelical" (and "evangelicalism") and so foster better understanding and encourage faithful Christian discipleship. Chapter 1 provides an overview and sets the stage for what follows. Chapter 2 explains how, in the New Testament, the "good news" (Greek, *euangelion*) is news about the inauguration of God's kingdom in the person of Jesus Christ. The third chapter probes the meaning of the gospel as seen in the writings of the early apostolic fathers (inheritors of apostolic responsibility), the ecumenical creeds, and the sixteenth-century Reformers. In the fourth chapter we will learn about the great eighteenth-century evangelical revival in Great Britain and North America. Chapter 5 traces the growth of North American evangelicalism in the nineteenth and twentieth centuries. Chapter 6 will examine the relationship between Christian faith and modern science. In chapter 7 we will learn about the global context and how shifting the leading edge of Christian expansion to the Majority World (developing countries located primarily in the Southern Hemisphere) is affecting the shape of evangelicalism. Chapter 8 addresses evangelicalism from the perspective of parish ministry. Chapter 9 explores the contours of an evangelical life. Finally, chapter 10 is about evangelical Catholicism.

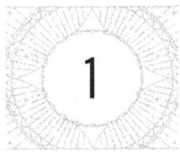

DEFINING "EVANGELICAL"
AN OVERVIEW

AL TRUESDALE

TRYING to "locate" Christians known as evangelicals socially or politically—as journalists often do—is futile. Evangelicals transcend economic, educational, ethnic, class, political, and denominational boundaries. Nevertheless, many believe there is an identifiable "common core."[1] What unites evangelicals is more important than their differences.

When describing themselves, many evangelicals rarely use the word "evangelical." They focus on the core convictions of the triune God, the Bible, faith, Jesus, salvation, evangelism, and discipleship.

To explore the contours of "evangelical," we must approach the word from different perspectives, and we will do so in subsequent chapters. This chapter, however, (1) examines some challenges associated with defining evangelicals, (2) introduces some prominent definitions, and (3) lays a foundation for understanding why "gospel" and "kingdom" are inseparable.

CHALLENGES

First, providing a definition for the word "evangelical" is one thing, but trying to define or identify it as a movement in Christianity is quite another. The word derives from the Greek word *euangelion* (yoo-ang-ghel-ee-an). It simply means "good news" or "good message." Our English word "gospel," which translates *euangelion*, comes from two Old English words: *gōd* (good) and *spel* (news). In the New Testament we first encounter the word in Matthew. "Jesus went throughout Galilee, teaching in their synagogues and proclaiming the good news of the kingdom" (4:23, NRSV). Matthew uses *euangelion* (or its cognate) five times, three of which explicitly reference the kingdom of God (4:23; 9:35; 24:14). Mark begins with the "good news of Jesus Christ" (1:1, NRSV). After John the Baptist was put in prison, Jesus went into "Galilee, proclaiming the good news of God" (1:14, NRSV). He said, "The kingdom of God has come near. Repent and believe the good news" (Mark 1:15, NIV; cf. Matt. 4:23; Luke 4:18). *Euangelion* is used ninety-eight times in the New Testament (never in the fourth gospel) to articulate the many dimensions of the good news of the kingdom of God.

Second, defining "evangelical" as a distinct movement within the Christian faith can be a bewildering exercise. Evangelicals transcend narrow political identification and social and economic philosophies. They range from those on the political right to a new generation of evangelicals who loosely identify as "progressive evangelicals."[2] As Wes Granberg-Michaelson correctly observes, "One size doesn't fit all."[3] There is no recognized founder or founding document.[4] Evangelicals affirm the historic ecumenical creeds (Apostles', Athanasian, Nicene, and the Definition of Chalcedon). However, there is no single evangelical creed, and no uniform agreement on how the Christian faith should be practiced. Sharp disagreements over the sacraments go all the way back to the sixteenth-century Protestant Reformation. Consequently, evangelicals disagree about the meaning of the Lord's Supper and baptism, including when and how one should be baptized.

We will search in vain for a unifying doctrine of the church, an agreed-upon form of worship (liturgy), accord in how the church should be governed (polity), or agreement about the role of women in Christian ministry. And although evangelicals "evangelize," they disagree sharply about who should be "evangelized." Is salvation meant for everyone or only for those whom God has "predestined" for salvation? Even the nature of Christ's atonement for sin on the cross is a source of constant debate. Moreover, there is disagreement over the measure of personal transformation a Christian can expect in this life. Should Christians think of themselves primarily as converted sinners saved by grace, endlessly battling against a countervailing "flesh"? Or should they, through the Holy Spirit's power, expect victorious Christian living in which the "flesh" is overcome?

The principle of *adiaphora* (Greek, "indifferent things" or "matters of indifference")[5] has often been employed to distinguish between what is commanded as essential for maintaining the integrity of the faith and what is permissible ("In necessary things, unity; in doubtful things, liberty; in all things, charity"[6]). But the principle faces strong headwinds because evangelicals often have a difficult time distinguishing between the two. It's an age-old problem. The apostle Paul dealt with it in Romans 14:1-23.

And now, as the final chapter of this book demonstrates, a thriving, Spirit-led part of the Roman Catholic Church in America, and elsewhere, identifies itself as evangelical.[7]

All of this might remind us of what American songwriter Bob Dylan sang in the 1960s, "The times they are a-changin'."[8]

Third, some scholars debate whether "evangelical" should be treated as a noun or as an adjective. Does the term refer to an identifiable entity with an "essence"? Or does it refer to descriptive "traits" that more or less accurately describe diverse groups of Christians at certain times and places? Or is it a mixture of both?[9]

Fourth, a discussion of evangelicalism must occur within the context of a genuinely global story. "When using the term 'evangelical,'"

Mark Noll, professor of history (now retired) at the University of Notre Dame and a leading historian and interpreter of evangelicalism cautions, "It is now imperative to consider the entire world. . . . More evangelicals now live in Nigeria and Brazil, when taken together, than in the U.S." For example, in the Majority World, "African developments are more important than anything occurring in the old evangelical homelands."[10] If "evangelical" has a core meaning that offers ongoing viability, it must be one that provides space for the plethora of cultural distinctions that currently enrich Christianity's global story.

Fifth, when attempting to delineate any part of the Christian family we risk compromising three of the four marks of the church—*one, catholic,* and *apostolic* (Nicene Creed; see appendix A). Whatever an adequate definition of "evangelical" might be, and whatever its contributing emphases, let's remember that evangelicals are simply part of orthodox Christianity.

SOME PROMINENT DEFINITIONS

As we examine the following representative definitions we should heed a warning by Mark Noll. Evangelicalism is not a fixed "ism." It has "always been made up of shifting movements, temporary alliances, and the lengthening shadows of individuals." At best, our efforts "provide some order for a multifaceted, complex set of impulses and organizations."[11] Referring to its institutional variety, British religious historian David Bebbington says evangelicalism is a "wine that has been poured into many bottles."[12] Today the "bottles" include many more cultural contexts than existed when the phenomenon appeared in the eighteenth century.[13]

Bebbington's Definition

Among the several definitions of "evangelical," one of the most respected was developed by David Bebbington. He examined the variations of British evangelical religion that had occurred during the eighteenth and nineteenth centuries and found that the character of evangelicalism had emerged and changed in response to British high culture. His highly influential work appeared in 1989 as *Evangelicalism in Modern Britain: A History from the 1730s to the 1980s*.[14] Bebbington discovered that those who could be identified as evangelicals "gave exclusive pride of place to a small number of leading principles."[15] But in spite of the continuity of "certain hallmarks" over time,[16] the history of evangelicalism shows that some evangelical principles considered to be most prominent in one period of its history gave place to others in other periods.[17] Evangelicalism is identifiable but not fixed in a hierarchy of priorities.

Bebbington identified "four qualities that have been the special marks of evangelical religion." Together they form "a quadrilateral of priorities that is the basis of evangelicalism."[18] The four "hallmarks" are (1) *"conversionism,* the belief that lives need to be changed;" (2) *"activism,* the expression of the gospel in effort;"* (3) *"biblicism,* a particular regard for the Bible;" and (4) "what may be called *crucicentrism,* a stress on the sacrifice of Christ on the cross."[19] The four are, according to Bebbington's analysis, the "defining attributes of evangelical religion."[20] Those who have "displayed all the common features that have persisted over time"[21] are the evangelicals.

Scholars commonly refer to these "four qualities" as the Bebbington quadrilateral. The quadrilateral provides a basis for understanding evangelicalism in England and the United States from the eighteenth through the twentieth century. Even as observers modify the quadrilateral, it remains what Kelly Cross Elliott of Abilene Christian University calls a "venerable standard."[22]

Mark Noll characterizes Bebbington's definition as a "noun" because it attempts to define the "essence" of evangelism.[23]

A "New" Definition

In the April 2016 issue of *Christianity Today,* National Association of Evangelicals president Leith Anderson and LifeWay Research executive director Ed Stetzer reported the results of a new research-driven attempt to define "evangelical."[24] The "new" definition was influenced by Bebbington's quadrilateral. With the help of a group of evangelical scholars, Bebbington's four characteristics were turned into a list of seventeen questions that bridge *belief, belonging,* and *behavior.* Among those in the research sampling, four belief statements emerged as constituting a common set of "evangelical" beliefs: (1) "the Bible is the highest authority for what I believe";[25] (2) "it is very important for me personally to encourage non-Christians to trust Jesus Christ as their Savior"; (3) Jesus Christ's death on the cross is the only sacrifice that could remove the penalty of my sin"; and (4) "only those who trust in Jesus Christ alone as their Savior receive God's free gift of eternal salvation."[26] Those who agreed with the four were "likely to *self-identify* as evangelicals."[27]

Anderson and Stetzer recognize the statements place some Christians under the "evangelical" umbrella who might never call themselves "evangelical." Conversely, there might be some self-described evangelicals who do not strongly agree with all four belief statements.[28]

Larsen's Contribution

In *The Cambridge Companion to Evangelical Theology,* Timothy Larsen defines an evangelical as (1) "an orthodox Protestant" (2) "who stands in the tradition of the global Christian networks arising from the eighteenth-century revival movements associated with John Wesley and George Whitefield;" (3) who has a preeminent place for the Bible in her or his Christian life as the divinely inspired, final authority in matters of faith and practice;" (4) "who stresses reconciliation with God through the atoning work of Jesus Christ on the cross;" and (5) "who stresses the work of the Holy Spirit in the life of an individual to bring about conversion and an ongoing life of fellowship with God and service to God and others, including the duty of all believers to participate in the task of proclaiming the gospel to all people."[29]

Noll identifies Larsen's definition as one that bridges "adjective" and "noun."

Seven Defining Affirmations

An important definition of "evangelical" appears in the Statement of Faith of the National Association of Evangelicals (NAE). The NAE connects nearly forty denominations, thousands of churches, schools, nonprofits, businesses, and individuals.[30] Its Statement of Faith includes seven affirmations: (1) "We believe the Bible to be the inspired, the only infallible, authoritative Word of God." (2) "We believe that there is one God, eternally existent in three persons: Father, Son and Holy Spirit." (3) "We believe in the deity of our Lord Jesus Christ, in His virgin birth, in His sinless life, in His miracles, in His vicarious and atoning death through His shed blood, in His bodily resurrection, in His ascension to the right hand of the Father, and in His personal return in power and glory." (4) "We believe that for the salvation of lost and sinful people, regeneration by the Holy Spirit is absolutely essential." (5) "We believe in the present ministry of the Holy Spirit by whose indwelling the Christian is enabled to live a godly life." (6) "We believe in the resurrection of both the saved and the lost; they that are saved unto the resurrection of life and they that are lost unto the resurrection of damnation." (7) "We believe in the spiritual unity of believers in our Lord Jesus Christ."[31]

Noll's Evangelical Traits

One of the most inclusive accounts of evangelical "traits" or "convictions" appears throughout Mark Noll's influential manifesto *The Scandal of the Evangelical Mind*. For him "evangelical" is an adjective, not a *noun*. This means the traits might not always characterize evangelicals. The traits Noll identifies appear along the way as he lauds the contributions of some and laments the failures of others.[32]

According to Noll, contemporary evangelical thought "is best understood as a set of intellectual assumptions arising from the nineteenth-century synthesis of American and Protestant values, and then filtered through the trauma of fundamentalist-modernist strife."[33] The traits Noll identifies include (1) "adherence to the Bible as the revealed

Word of God"; (2) certainty that Scripture consistently reveals God as the "author of nature" and the "sustainer of human institutions";[34] (3) the "need for a supernatural new birth"; (4) "spreading the gospel through missions and personal evangelism"; (5) the "saving character of Jesus' death and resurrection";[35] (6) the "indwelling presence of the Holy Spirit" in Christians; (7) the importance of "personal sanctity" and the "possibility of growing in grace throughout human life";[36] (8) evangelicals are "not prone to write off marginalized races or the poor";[37] (9) the "universal need for salvation in Christ"; (10) the "supernatural character of the incarnation";[38] (11) the "supernatural character" of the Christian faith; (12) the "objectivity of Christian morality"; (13) the "timeless validity of Scripture";[39] and (14) regeneration and sanctification by the Holy Spirit.[40]

These traits are laudatory and essential for the Christian faith. However, they are inherently reliant upon something more primary and determinative—the kingdom of God.[41] No combination of Christian convictions, no matter how constitutive, imperative, and glorious, is complete until solidly placed within the orbit of and explained with reference to the kingdom of God.[42]

THE "GOSPEL" OF THE KINGDOM OF GOD

In the New Testament, "gospel" is not a stand-alone word. Evangelicals too often err by attempting to define and preach the gospel without first anchoring it in the big picture of the kingdom of God inaugurated in Jesus Christ (see Matt. 10:7; 12:17-29; Luke 8:1; 9:2). Not surprisingly, unnecessary and obstructive doctrinal disputes often follow. When not defined by and consistently indexed to the kingdom of God, "gospel" can birth other kingdoms—nationalistic, denominational, economic, or even racial—that oppose or misrepresent the kingdom of God. Separated from the kingdom, "gospel" loses its prophetic, judging power (see the third dimension of the kingdom below).[43]

Jesus and the Kingdom

The Gospels do not say Jesus came preaching the "gospel," but that he came preaching the "gospel of the kingdom of God" (see Matt. 4:23; Mark 1:14; Luke 4:43; John 3:3). The "good news" proclaimed in his teaching, healings, parables, and violations of the Jewish boundary laws was that the kingdom of God was "at hand." It was appearing in him. All the hopes of Israel and God's promises for the nations—his covenantal faithfulness—were achieving their fulfillment in Jesus the Messiah (Matt. 12:17-29; 2 Cor. 1:19-22). In the Messiah, God was ending exile, dealing with sin, undoing the powers of darkness, and ushering in the age to come.

Hence, it is a mistake to treat "gospel" as an independent term that defines and encompasses salvation. This essential part of our Christian grammar must be restored to its rooting in the kingdom of God. Otherwise, "gospel" will never be, for us, as comprehensive, generative, and demanding as it is in the New Testament. "Gospel" in our understanding, teaching, and lives must approximate its magnitude as revealed in the person, ministry, and atonement of Jesus Christ.[44]

Jesus said, "[The] gospel of the kingdom will be preached in the whole world as a testimony to all nations, and then the end will come" (Matt. 24:14, NIV). But the Gospels expose a sharp division between what Jesus believed and taught and what many—including his disciples—expected the kingdom to be.

New Testament scholar N. T. Wright contrasts expectations of the average first-century Galilean with the actual proclamation of Jesus Christ. While awaiting the kingdom, the average Galilean wasn't seeking to secure a place in heaven after death. Rather, Jews in Jesus's day were living under centuries-old foreign rule. They asked, "If Israel is truly God's chosen people, why, after all this time, are we still living under pagan rule?" When expecting the kingdom of God, the people waited for God's reign to be established forcefully and decisively over the distorted world they faced daily—accented by the maddening Roman tax structure. The people believed that God would establish his rule and vindicate Israel's hopes. He would terminate oppression by bringing peace and justice to all his creation. However, although the expectation was fairly general, there was no uniform agreement on how God would accomplish this.

On the other hand, many Jewish leaders, including the powerful chief priests, had learned to "game the system" for personal benefit. They dutifully did the bidding of the occupiers. Herod Antipas (20 BC–AD 39, son of Herod the Great), slayer of John the Baptist (Matt. 14:1-12), wealthy and arrogant Roman puppet, unashamedly conspired with his Roman overlords.

Wright explains that Jesus taught and acted upon two vital points. *First,* Jesus believed the creator God had purposed from the beginning to address and deal with his creation's problems *through* Israel. Israel was not just an example of a nation under God. It would be his instrument for redeeming the world. *Second,* Jesus believed Israel's vocation would be fulfilled by history reaching a great climactic moment. Israel would be saved from its enemies, and the creator God—the covenant-making God—would finally establish his love and justice forever. Mercy and truth would embrace not only Israel but also the whole world.

In Christ, God was doing what Israel had hoped for, but in astonishing, often offensive, disappointing, and unrecognizable ways. Jesus's deeds electrified popular expectations and horrified Israel's religious and political power brokers. However, instead of satisfying popular expectations, "out of [Jesus's] deep awareness, in loving faith and prayer [to] the one he called 'Abba, Father,' he went back to Israel's Scriptures and found there another kingdom-model, equally Jewish if not more so."[45] Now, Jesus proclaimed, the long-expected kingdom was "at hand" (Mark 1:15, KJV). In his person and presence, God was unveiling his age-old plan, "bringing his sovereignty to bear on Israel and the world as he had always intended, bringing justice and mercy to Israel and the world."[46] Nothing less than a "new state of affairs," the "long-awaited rule of Israel's God on earth as in heaven," was being "launched into the world."[47]

In his deeds and parables Jesus enacted the kingdom; he "cracked open" the expectations of his hearers and called them to come to grips with how God's reign was now breaking upon them. He, the Lord of the Sabbath, confronted and rejected Israel's kingdom dreams and visions. By doing so, he unleashed a storm that steadily built toward the cross.

There were *three main dimensions* in Jesus's understanding and teaching about the kingdom of God (Matthew uses the term "heaven," 3:2): (1) the end of exile,[48] (2) the call of a "renewed people," and (3) a warning of "disaster and vindication" to come.[49]

First, Jeremiah and other prophets linked establishing God's kingdom to the end of exile. After that, God would accomplish the great work of new creation. Whatever the promised Messiah might be expected to do, he would certainly bring an end to exile. With their land under the domination of pagan rulers, clearly exile (begun in 587/6 BC when Jerusalem and the temple were destroyed) had not ended.

Jesus's parables were rooted in the Jewish Scriptures. When unpackaged, they reveal how the prophetic language of returning from exile was setting the stage for the work of new creation that was being fulfilled in the words and deeds of Jesus. The parable of the sower in Mark 4:1-20, for instance, is a Jewish story about how the kingdom of God was arriving. Prophets such as Jeremiah had spoken of God again *sowing* his people in their own land (Jer. 4:3; 31:27; Ezek. 36:8-9). Isaiah used the image of sowing and reaping to speak of God's great work of new creation to be accomplished after the exile (Isa. 40:6-8; 44:4; 55:10). To explain the parable of the sower (Matt. 13:13-15; Mark 4:12; Luke 8:10), Jesus quoted Isaiah 6:9-10. Then verse 13 describes new shoots springing from a burnt tree stump. In judgment the tree had been cut down. But from its stump new shoots would spring. Jesus's parable of the sower is about what God was now doing in Jesus's ministry. He was fulfilling what the prophets promised—judging Israel for her idolatry while bringing into existence a new people, a renewed Israel, the returned-from-exile people of God.[50]

The story of the prodigal son (Luke 15:11-32) is another parable about exile and the kingdom of God. The account of a scoundrel son wasting his inheritance in a pagan country and then being welcomed home is a "sharp-edged, context-specific message about what was happening in Jesus' ministry. More specifically, it was about what was happening through Jesus' welcome of outcasts, his eating with sinners."[51] The long-awaited return from exile was actually happening, and it didn't look the way people, such as the Pharisees and lawyers, had expected. Like the elder brother, they thought Jesus's version of "return from exile" was scandalous. So they rejected the return. But there it was, "happening under the noses" of the blind, "self-appointed guardians" of Israel's expectations.[52]

The long-awaited end of exile had arrived! This was the "good news," the *euangelion*. In Jesus, Israel's God was becoming King. "Would Israel recognize what God was doing in their midst in the person of his Son?"[53]

Second, in Jesus's announcement of the end of exile and in his embodiment of the arriving kingdom, he was calling into existence a renewed people. His hearers had been waiting for the arrival of God's kingdom. Now, at this, the climactic turning point of history, they were being "invited to audition" for roles in it, "to become kingdom-people," the "true, renewed people of God."[54] Jesus called his hearers to "repent [Greek, *metanoia* (reconsider, turn around)] and believe."[55] He was telling them to give up their own agendas and trust his utterly risky way of being Israel.[56]

Repent. Embrace with your entire being Jesus's way of being Israel, his way of bringing in the kingdom—turning the other cheek, going the extra mile with a Roman soldier, losing your life to gain it (Matt. 5). Abandon your prized dreams of nationalist revolution, Jesus said. Instead, become the light of the world, the salt of the earth, the city set on a hill that cannot be hidden, where the one true God will reveal himself for all humankind (vv. 13-16). Only then will you be "converted."

Romano Guardini carefully considered Jesus's call for repentance and concluded that when one "repents" a "profound revolution begins."[57] One born anew by the Spirit into God's kingdom recognizes Jesus Christ and his kingdom as the "supreme measure of all possible reality."[58] All "world-anchored self-glorification" is surrendered "into the hands of the God of Revelation. . . . All that until now has seemed certain suddenly becomes questionable. The whole conception of reality, the whole idea of existence is turned upside-down."[59] Candidates for kingdom entry, Guardini insists, must resolutely confront and answer the question, "*Is* Christ really so great that he can be the norm of all that is?"[60]

Taking up the cross and following Jesus entailed shouldering his utterly risky agenda and abandoning all others.[61] His radical invitation was accompanied by a radical welcome. To the absolute scandal of many of Jesus's contemporaries, in repeated celebrations, and with joy, he welcomed into the kingdom, as the new people of God, persons completely lacking in credentials for such an honor. His free meals and free-for-all welcome were a central feature of his vision of the kingdom—joyous and radical acceptance and forgiveness. And he was doing all this while claiming to be one with his heavenly Father (see John 10:30). Asserting what would have been blasphemy had it not been true, Jesus declared, "Anyone who has seen me has seen the Father" (14:9, NIV). "The inbreaking kingdom Jesus was announcing created a new world, a new context, and he was challenging his hearers to become the new people that this new context demanded, the citizens of this new world."[62]

"This is the context" in "which we should" read the "Sermon on the Mount," the new way of being Israel, the kingdom way, the people of God (Matt. 5–7).[63] "This was to be the way of true love and justice through which Israel's God would be revealed to the watching world."[64] Jesus so subverted the kingdom agenda, cherished by his opponents, that either his agenda or theirs would have to be displaced. The same is true for us today (Matt. 16:24; Mark 8:34; Luke 9:23).

Third, Jesus and his contemporaries lived with a grand scriptural narrative told in terms of a new exodus when God would deliver Israel from the pharaohs who exalted themselves against God's people. He would bring them through their trials; vindication would come at last. The traditional story that formerly featured Egypt, Babylon, and Syria now featured Rome. But Jesus stood against the way this story was told and against its anticipated military and political outcome. "God's purpose would not after all be to vindicate Israel as a nation against the pagan hordes. . . . On the contrary, Jesus announced . . . that God's judgment would fall not on the surrounding nations but on Israel that had failed to be the light of the world."[65] Who then would be vindicated? "Back comes the answer with increasing force and clarity: Jesus himself and his followers. They were now the true, reconstituted Israel. They would suffer and suffer horribly, but God would vindicate them."[66]

Warnings about a great, coming judgment that occupy much of the first three Gospels (Matt. 24:1-51; Mark 13:1-37; Luke 21:5-36) were like those of the great prophets, warnings about impending judgment within history. Like Jeremiah who viewed Babylon as God's agent in punishing his rebellious people, Jesus prophesied the fall of Jerusalem. God would judge Israel for choosing the way of violence instead of the way of his Messiah. The eventual destruction of Jerusalem and the temple (AD 70) should not have come as a surprise. In Luke 13 Jesus warns that if Israel refuses to repent of her flight into national rebellion against Rome, Roman swords will become the instruments of God's judgment. The warnings reach their climax as Jesus rides into Jerusalem on Palm Sunday and weeps:

> If you, even you, had only known on this day what would bring you peace—but now it is hidden from your eyes. The days will come upon you when your enemies will build an embankment against you and encircle you and hem you in on every side. They will dash you to the ground, you and the children within your walls. They will not leave one stone on another, because you did not recognize the time of God's coming to you. (Luke 19:41-44, NIV)

What memories might have flooded Jesus's mind as he looked at the city of David, lying there across the brook of Kidron? Did he recall the words of Jeremiah, "Long ago you broke your yoke and burst your bonds" (Jer. 2:20, NRSV)? Did he remember the moment after his first public sermon in Nazareth when his listeners rose up and attempted to cast him over the brow of a hill (Luke 4:28-30)? Maybe he recalled when, after he had said "I and the Father are one," the people picked up stones to kill him (John 10:30-31, NIV). The generation that rejected the kingdom of God as proclaimed by and embodied in Jesus would also be the generation upon whom God's judgment would fall.[67]

The Grace of the Kingdom

No New Testament writer more faithfully or insightfully proclaimed the gospel of the kingdom than did the apostle Paul.[68] In recent groundbreaking work, New Testament scholar John Barclay has helped us comprehend how faithful Paul was to his Lord and what will be required of us to receive, understand, live, and proclaim the gospel of the kingdom. Barclay maps six ways human and divine "gifts" were understood in the Greco-Roman world, including Second Temple Judaism. The six delineations include, "but [are] not limited by, theological discourse on 'grace.'"[69] Normally, gifts were given generously but selectively "to suitable, worthy, or appropriate recipients."[70] Only when we comprehend the vast distance between Greco-Roman understandings of gifts (grace) and how Paul understood and proclaimed the radical grace of God manifest in Jesus Christ can we begin to grasp the enormous reconstruction of human life that receiving the grace of Christ entails—its "transformative dynamic."[71]

Paul is an apostle of the "grace of our Lord Jesus Christ" (Gal. 6:18, NIV),[72] God's completely unconditioned, unmerited gift in Christ. Barclay classifies Paul's understanding of grace as "incongruous," which means it is given indiscriminately "without regard to the worth of the recipient."[73] In Christ, through the gift of grace, God *revalued* human life. His grace annuls all other ways of establishing human worth, community, and vocation. It voids all human schemes of value. Human measures are "out"; God's measure is "in." There is nothing people have done or could do, have been or could be, to deserve the gift. This is "good news" intended in abundant richness for one and all, including publicans and sinners. Receiving it entails embracing all its implications.

Paul's understanding of grace is consistent with Jesus's ministry as seen in the Gospels. Jesus's kingdom agenda was radical, reorienting, and renewing. In his epistles, Paul joyously and faithfully extends the lines of grace to all dimensions of human life, just as we observed in Jesus's teaching about the kingdom. The epistle to the Galatians is a prime example. Here, Paul is interested not only in informing the Galatians about grace but also in placing them "within its transformative dynamic," beginning with the implications of Christ's self-giving, self-donation in death (Gal. 2:20).[74] Proceeding from the radical grace of God manifest in Jesus Christ—who is God's grace incarnate—Paul worked to form communities beholden not to the Torah (the Law) but solely to the "law of Christ" (6:2, NIV).[75] This new people, radically formed by the (incongruous) grace of Christ, is the "Israel of God" (v. 16, NIV).

Thus what Paul believed and taught about God's grace had primarily to do with the creation of a new community,[76] the new people of God, created by and in conformity with the (incongruous) grace of God in Christ Jesus. Though individuals are included, community, not isolated individuals, is primary. Consistent with what Jesus proclaimed about the kingdom of God, Paul believed the outcome of grace is the formation of innovative, countercultural communities impossible for Jews or Gentiles alone. This new people of God, called into existence by God's unmerited and indiscriminate grace, spans the boundary dividing Gentiles and Jews. In Galatians, Paul vehemently rejects anything—including the Jewish law—that would compromise this new community of grace, this new people of God called into existence by Jesus Christ (5:1-26).[77]

The "good news" of the kingdom as Paul understood and preached it, Barclay says, will "realign and recalibrate" all loyalties.[78] The "incongruous gift enacted in Christ" will place its recipients "at odds with the normative conventions that govern human systems of value."[79] This being "at odds" with governing norms "signals a relation of misfit, even contradiction, between the 'good news' and the typical structures of human thought and behavior. The good news stands askance to human norms because its origin lies outside the human sphere."[80]

Paul, who was taught by the risen Christ (Gal. 1:11-12), was faithful to his Lord's rejection of all value systems that made works, merit, or any other forms of cultural or religious capital the basis for forming God's people. Grace must be received just as it was received by the publican at prayer (Luke 18:9-14), Mary Magdalene (Mark 16:9), and Zacchaeus (Luke 19:2-10), *or it won't be received at all.* For those whose lives are reconstituted in Christ, the supreme definition of worth for everyone is the good news of the kingdom of God. The kingdom of God dispenses with all values that would subvert it.[81]

Because the concrete life of this new people of God cannot be conceived apart from a norm for conduct, Paul teaches that certain kinds of communal conduct, Christian behavior, proceed from God's gift in Christ (see Rom. 12:1–13:14). The new people of God are to be marked by particular disciplines and behavioral norms that socially and publicly express their obedient response to the gift (Rom. 12:1–13:14). They are called to live out a "gospel-driven holiness" because they now "live in the Spirit-driven 'age to come.'"[82]

The next chapter will extend these lines into other parts of the New Testament. Here we have seen enough to know that fidelity to the Scriptures rules out identifying as "Christian" any understanding of "gospel" not formed and governed by the kingdom of God as it came in the grace of Jesus Christ. In all four Gospels, N. T. Wright explains, the proclamation of the kingdom and that of the crucifixion are inseparable. "The kingdom comes through Jesus' entire work, which finds its intended fulfillment in his shameful death."[83] Too often we try to separate themes that "belong inextricably together."[84] There is always a danger that some part of the faith will break away and become the basis for a new and less comprehensive, less demanding quasi-religion.

Confessing that the reign of God in righteousness, justice, and new creation has begun upon this earth is "good news." However, when reading the morning news about the rape of helpless women by soldiers in South Sudan, for instance, the confession becomes daunting. Nevertheless, no less of a confession is required of an Easter faith (1 Cor. 15:20-28; Rev. 11:15).

Like all expressions of the Christian faith, evangelicalism stands ever in need of correction and instruction and of being called forward by the crucified, risen, and reigning Lord of the kingdom, who victoriously strides among the "lampstands" as the "Alpha and the Omega" (Rev. 1:7-16, NIV).

For Further Study

Barth, Karl. *Evangelical Theology: An Introduction*. Grand Rapids: Eerdmans, 1979.

Boyd, Gregory A., and Paul R. Eddy. *Across the Spectrum: Understanding Issues in Evangelical Theology*. Grand Rapids: Baker Academic, 2009.

Packer, J. I., and Thomas C. Oden. *One Faith: The Evangelical Consensus*. Downers Grove, IL: InterVarsity Press, 2004.

Wright, N. T. *The Day the Revolution Began: Reconsidering the Meaning of Jesus's Crucifixion*. New York: HarperOne, 2016.

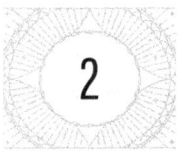

THE GOOD NEWS OF THE INAUGURATED KINGDOM OF GOD

SVETLANA KHOBNYA

IN THIS CHAPTER we turn to the Scriptures to understand the gospel of the kingdom of God. We will move from anticipation to fulfillment and then to a profile of life in God's kingdom.

THE GOOD NEWS OF THE KINGDOM OF GOD

The good news, the gospel, in the Bible is essentially presented through the actions and proclamation of God (Isa. 40:9; 52:7; 61:1; Mark 1:14-15; Rom. 1:1) and preeminently through God's work in Christ (Mark 1:1; Rom. 15:19; 1 Cor. 1:17). Historically the Greek term *euangelion*, translated "good news" or "gospel,"[1] was associated with messages and reports declaring the power and blessing of peace provided by Roman emperors. The biblical understanding of good news can be summed up as the proclamation of God boldly fulfilling the promises made to his people in Holy Scripture and what he achieved for us—their children—by raising Jesus from the dead (Acts 13:32-33). The content of the gospel is inseparable from the kingdom of God that has come near in Jesus (Matt. 4:23; Mark 1:14-15; Luke 4:18). Consequently, the gospel must be studied within this framework.

Graeme Goldsworthy's definition of the good news serves us well: "the event (or the proclamation of that event) of Jesus Christ . . . interpreted by God as his preordained programme for the salvation of the world" from sin, the devil, and death.[2] Goldsworthy adds that the goal of the good news is the "new creation where the people of God redeemed by Christ will enjoy the presence of God for eternity."[3]

Several important implications emerge. First, the foundation for understanding the revelation of the good news in the New Testament lies in the Old Testament. The whole Scripture progressively reveals God's purposes for humanity, how he achieves his purposes, and how he establishes his kingdom. Second, Jesus Christ is the key for interpreting the entire revelation. Evangelical Christians stand firmly on the conviction that they "know God through his Son, Jesus Christ, whom, in turn, we know only through Scripture."[4] Third, God acts in Christ *for* us prior to his action *in* us. This understanding points directly to God's grace as the source and measure of all things and to our complete dependence on his grace. "God puts us into a right relationship with himself as the prerequisite for the ongoing change in our lives."[5] Fourth, the kingdom promised for the future has come near; this is the heart of the good news.

Let's expand these points and then draw the conclusions they support.

A JEWISH PICTURE OF THE KINGDOM: PROMISE AND ANTICIPATION

Although the phrase "kingdom of God" does not occur in the Old Testament, and rarely in other Jewish writings,[6] the idea of God's kingdom is expressed in other ways. For example, the Old Testament describes God as "King of all the earth" who will reign forever (Pss. 47;

103, NIV) or presents him as mighty and invites God's people to give him appropriate glory (Ps. 99). The kingdom of God refers to the presence of God's ruling activity among humans. The function of God as King is expressed specifically as righteousness and care. He exercises his kingship on behalf of the weak and oppressed (Deut. 10:14-19). The Hebrews found themselves oppressed in Egypt, and in need of God's rescue and redemption. They kept falling short of God's glory, disobeying him and his commandments. Moses accused Israel of having forgotten that God is the faithful one who cares for his people (32:4-5). Later (922 BC), Solomon's kingdom was divided and eventually captured by Assyria and then Babylon. The return from Babylonian exile failed to produce the kingdom promised by prophets such as Isaiah, Jeremiah, and Ezekiel. People anticipated the reign of God as pictured by the prophets: justice would come for the oppressed, and the wicked would be overthrown. This good news was intended not only for the people of Israel but also for the nations, for "all the ends of the earth will see the salvation of our God" (Isa. 52:10, NIV; cf. Jer. 31:10). The closing sections of Zechariah picture the rise of a theocratic kingdom where God will reign over all the nations (14:1-21).

In various Jewish writings, which are not part of the canonical works, but which reflect a particular historical period (around 300 BC to AD 70),[7] we find references to the ultimate reign of God over his people. But the precise expectations for God's coming kingdom are quite diverse. Some texts describe the restoration of Israel as a whole or only of the faithful within Israel.[8] By this picture, Gentiles are seen as enemies of the Jews; there is little hope for them.[9] But other documents reiterate hope for God's reign over all the nations.[10] But even then, Gentiles will be subjugated to Israel's King.[11] Many historical scrolls found near the Dead Sea (perhaps dealing with the political uncertainty and dissatisfaction over Israel's leadership in centuries just before Christ's birth, prompted by Greek and Roman dominion) depict a righteous branch and prince from Davidic lineage, a messiah who will correct their situation.[12] He will be the agent of God's redemption and the instrument of universal divine blessing. One of the common themes in Jewish texts is God's faithfulness and an attending hope for God's intervention in the life of his people. However, how this new era of God's powerful reign will transpire, or what it will look like, is not clear.[13]

The story of fulfillment extends to the New Testament.

GOD'S KINGDOM IN THE PERSON OF JESUS

The Gospels

All four Gospels testify to the arrival of God's kingdom. They look back to the Old Testament to demonstrate that the long-awaited kingdom of God has come in Jesus. As the New Testament writers interpret the founding of God's reign in Christ the Messiah, the Old Testament promises make perfect sense for them (Matt. 26:56; Luke 24:28-33; John 5:39). New Testament scholar Richard B. Hays says the Evangelists reread Israel's Scriptures in light of the coming of Christ, showing how the Scriptures prefigure and illuminate Jesus.[14] In John 5:39 Jesus plainly urges his audience, "You search the scriptures because . . . they . . . testify on my behalf" (NRSV). Luke explains how Jesus, "beginning with Moses and all the prophets, . . . interpreted" to his companions on the road to Emmaus "the things about himself in all the scriptures" (Luke 24:27, NRSV).

The Gospel of Mark succinctly and abruptly announces "the beginning of the good news of Jesus Christ" (1:1, NRSV). His Gospel has the same opening as Genesis 1: "in the beginning" (NRSV). The phrase may signal that the story Mark is about to tell is a new beginning of God's good purposes, for it evokes the same anticipation as Genesis 1. "The same God who brought order out of chaos was doing a new thing in the face of Roman occupation."[15] According to Mark, the beginning of the good news corresponds to the pattern laid down in Isaiah 40:3 and Malachi 3:1 (Mark 1:2-3). Both Old Testament passages deal with the return of the divine glory to his people, and the messenger who will prepare for the return. By announcing the arrival of John the messenger (Mark 1:2-8) and the glory (9:2-13; 10:32-45) that comes through suffering (rooted in Isaiah's Suffering Servant motif, Isa. 52:1–53:12), Mark leaves no doubt that the good news about the kingdom's arrival has now happened in and through Jesus.

Matthew begins his Gospel by tracing Jesus's genealogy back to Abraham to show the forward movement of God's saving purpose now reaching its goal in Jesus.[16] Matthew cites Isaiah's promise of "Emmanuel," or "God with us," in 1:23 (NRSV) to show that the promised Messiah has now brought God's presence to his people. In the last chapter (28:18), alluding to Daniel 7:14, Matthew declares God has given to Jesus "all authority in heaven and on earth" (NRSV). This sets the theological framework for Matthew's Gospel: God's kingship and presence have been established *through* and *in* Jesus.

The Gospel of Luke places the scene for Jesus's life and ministry within the history and expectations of the Jewish people. Elizabeth, Zechariah, Mary, Simeon, and Anna are faithful Jews who anticipated great things for God's people. They listened to his call and welcomed Jesus as the good news and fulfillment of God's promises. He will turn God's people back to the Lord their God (Luke 1:16). "Today this scripture has been fulfilled," Jesus announced after reading from Isaiah (Luke 4:21, NRSV; see Isa. 58:6; 61:1-2). Later, upon his arrival in Jerusalem, and pointing to his own mission, Jesus pronounces judgment upon those who refused to recognize the time of God's visitation (Luke 19:41-44). In Luke's Gospel, Jesus demands acknowledgment of the arrival of God's reign. By this Luke demonstrates the significance of Jesus's coming as the redemptive intervention of God.

John's Gospel most obviously reveals Jesus's identity as the one who was eternal with God before becoming incarnate. God in Christ *tabernacled*, pitched his tent, among us; in him we have seen God's glory (1:14; 11:40; 17:5). John's language recalls the Old Testament imagery of the wilderness tabernacle—God's meeting place, or location of his hidden glory. John says that in Christ, God has now taken residency among his people; his glory is revealed in his Son.

Jesus as a healer and miracle worker is depicted throughout the Gospels as one who is active in daily lives. In all he says and does, Jesus reveals the presence and power of God's long-promised reign. He creates transformation in otherwise hopeless circumstances. For example, Jesus accepts marginalized and alienated people, eats with them, and welcomes them into community. He is the revelation of God on earth. Graeme Goldsworthy explains that first, "the gospel is a declaration of what God has done *for* us in Jesus Christ." Then, importantly, it is a declaration of "what God does *in* the believer" through Jesus Christ. The two, and their order, are inseparable.[17] Stated another way, first the good news refers to "the facts of Jesus coming in flesh." Then follows the God-given interpretation and application of those facts.[18]

In sum, the Gospels tell the story of Jesus as the story of Israel, and of Israel's God, reaching the anticipated climax. They thereby tell the good news of how Israel's God becomes King of the whole world.[19] In the ministry of Jesus, the kingdom of God is powerfully breaking through in the world (Luke 17:20-21). His kingdom in Christ is the good news; the Gospels are written to explain its significance.

The Apostle Paul

When Paul preaches the good news, he shoulders a task somewhat different from that of the Gospel writers. Paul articulates the meaning of the good news for the young churches that were wrestling with how to comprehend the breadth of Christ's supremacy and sufficiency for salvation in the Gentile polytheistic world. Just what are its practical implications? In their communities the new Christians had to learn how to embrace each other in Christ. So Paul explains the essence of the good news by referring to Christ's death on the cross for our sins, and his resurrection according to the Scriptures (1 Cor. 15:1-11). Paul tells how Jesus the Messiah became a "servant of the circumcised" people in order to demonstrate the truthfulness and faithfulness of God and how Jesus confirmed the "promises given to the patriarchs" and brought the nations to praise "God for his mercy" (Rom. 15:8-9, NRSV).

Old Testament Scriptures are essential for Paul. But they matter in a way that points to Christ. For example, Paul's interpretation of Old Testament passages (Pss. 18:49; 117:1; Deut. 32:43) in Romans 15:8-13 confirms he understands Christ to be the one who perfectly fulfills God's redemptive purposes. It is he who makes salvation and glorification of God's name possible for Israel and all nations. Paul is convinced that in Christ all the Gentiles and God's historical people now form a community (a new humanity, Eph. 2:14-16; Col. 1:15-23) that can together truly worship God. Both Jews and Gentiles can, through the Holy Spirit, place their hope in Christ. Paul concludes his Romans exposition with a prayer: "May the God of hope fill you with all joy and peace in believing, so that you may abound in hope by the power of the Holy Spirit" (15:13, NRSV). Cultural and ethnic differences in Paul's communities (chaps. 12–15) are marginalized by a common denominator: Christ who has brought hope and peace (cf. Eph. 1:18; 2:12; 4:4; Col. 1:5). In Christ community members can welcome one another, just as Christ has welcomed them, all for the glory of God (Rom. 15:7; 16:27; 2 Cor. 4:13-15; Phil. 1:9-11).

Paul assures his readers that God keeps his promises (Rom. 15:8; 2 Cor. 1:19-22).[20] God has sent his Son, the Messiah, to redeem the world; and he has already raised him from the dead. Christ is the Lord. This is the good news; and all people and nations can now glorify God.

The result of Jesus's ministry—his life, death, and resurrection—is not only to call Israel back to their God but also to create a new community composed of all nations that will respond to him and become incorporated in him as its head (Eph. 1:22; Col. 1:18; 2:10). People in the newly created kingdom of God are those who by trusting in the obedience of Christ belong to God through Christ, not by social or ethnic identity. Because of their new life in Christ, the new communities are "capable of disregarding distinctions between Jew and Greek, slave and free, male and female (Gal. 3:28)."[21] Social identities are not erased. But "they are declared insignificant as markers of worth in a community that is beholden to Christ."[22]

In very practical ways, Paul and the first followers of Christ crossed boundaries that separated Jews and Gentiles. Generated and sustained by the Holy Spirit, they proclaimed the good news about Jesus. The book of Acts, in particular, tells of the tremendous expansion among those who heard and received the good news about Jesus as Lord and Savior. Acts traces the spread of the gospel as it moves beyond the original group of Jewish believers to include Hellenized Jews, Samaritans, Greeks, and then people of many ethnic groups in Asia Minor and Rome itself.[23] The good news of Christ the Redeemer launched a movement aimed not only at restoring Israel but also "at the ingathering of the *nations* to the new messianic people of God."[24]

The good news is the "power of God for salvation" (Rom. 1:16, NRSV). This power is able to penetrate the entire person, the entire community, and the entire world (2 Cor. 5:17-21; Gal. 6:14-15). Paul urges his communities not to conform "to this world," but to "be transformed by the renewing" of their minds, so that they "may discern what is the will of God—what is good and acceptable and perfect" (Rom. 12:2, NRSV). He explains that for anyone who is "in Christ," there occurs a "new creation" (2 Cor. 5:17, NRSV). The Greek reading of this verse allows at least two nuances. *One* is that anyone who is committed to Christ is a new person; his or her new identity now comes from Christ. The *other* translation, referring to the new created order established in Christ, captures Paul's breathtakingly grand vision of the manifestation of the divine reign in Christ. The phrase "in Christ, there is a new creation" (NRSV) means that anyone in Christ belongs to Christ and is positioned in the sphere of Christ's dominion. Paul has thereby expanded our understanding of the scope of the good news in Christ.

The gospel is not only a message about the new kingdom that shapes Christians in every aspect of their lives, and not only a new way of life in the kingdom, *but also the new kingdom itself.* It is constituted by a new set of values put in place under Christ's rule. The values that mark Christ's kingdom entail a new way of living with each other and in the world.[25] If the world has come under God's new rule, as it has in Christ, then "the world has the monumental possibility of coming to participate in God's life."[26]

THE PRIORITY OF GOD'S GRACE

The Bible presents a very distinct picture of one God who is constantly and creatively at work in the universe and in human history. Christopher Wright describes this as the redemptive mission-driven work of God for his own glory and for the well-being of his creation.[27] Although the Bible contains numerous story lines, there is one clear overall direction, a unified flow in the whole of Scripture. It is the "biblical worldview" that "locates us in the midst of a narrative of the universe behind which stands the mission of the living God" (past, present, and future).[28] The Bible tells of a God who is intensely engaged with humans and who repeatedly takes the initiative to act for his creation's well-being. In other words, God acts graciously toward his creation. To speak of God's good news in Christ is to speak of God's grace as the source and measure of his care, and of our absolute dependence upon him. *The good news is God's way of acting before we hear it as such; he is the first evangel.*

God's grace is so richly textured that it must be spoken of from various angles. New Testament scholar John Barclay helps us by identifying some of them. First, we must speak of God's grace as being "pure," which means that God is entirely benevolent. Second, God's grace is not offered on the basis of what we can guarantee in return. Third, God's grace is not obstructed or constrained by prior circumstances or conditions. Fourth, his grace is offered without regard for our worth or merit. And fifth, God's grace is extended even when there is no promise it will yield human obedience.[29]

The good news revealed in Christ manifests all the dimensions Barclay identifies. Jesus is a vivid sign and exhibition of God's grace. The apostle Paul, in particular, explores the majesty of God's grace as being freely given without regard for our worth or merit. For Paul, Jesus

Christ is the definitive expression of God's love for the unlovely. This is the nerve center of his Gentile mission; God's gifts ignore ethnic differences of worth as well as definitions of value based upon the Torah (Law).[30] From the time Paul encountered Christ, his mission was that all people and nations would come to know and experience God's free grace embedded in his name, his glory, his salvation, and his mighty deeds in Christ. By grace, all people and nations would come to worship God.

Paul knew God alone is the source of salvation and that Jesus shared identity with God (John 10:30; 2 Cor. 4:4; Col. 1:15-20; 2:9; Heb. 1:2-3). That is why Christ could be the source of redemption for all people. The apostle Peter, filled with the Holy Spirit on the Day of Pentecost, announces that "there is salvation in no one else, for there is no other name under heaven . . . by which we must be saved" (Acts 4:12, NRSV). This is a consistent message in Acts; it receives its climactic expression at the first church council: "We believe that we will be saved through the grace of the Lord Jesus" (15:11, NRSV). The entire New Testament, building on the massive foundations of Israel's faith in God their Savior, proclaims that the climatic work of God's salvation happened in the person and work of Jesus Christ.[31] The very glory of God shines in and through him (John 1:14; Heb. 1:3).

So experiencing the glory of God is now possible through Jesus Christ (2 Cor. 4:6). By God's grace, through faith, we can see the glorious light of the gospel of Christ. And by God's grace, and through the Spirit, we can engage in the ministry of its proclamation (vv. 4-6; cf. Matt. 28:19; John 16:12-15; Acts 2:4; Rom. 15:18-21).

According to what Paul says in 2 Corinthians 4:4-6, five key elements are involved in proclaiming the good news. First, its proclamation must always be attributed to God, not to human merit. We proclaim Jesus as Lord, not ourselves. Authentic proclamation requires that "we *have embraced the gospel* and *continue to experience gospel mercy* in our own lives."[32] Second, authentic proclamation is inseparably joined to integrity. We must live righteously before God, and the message must live in us. Third, not everyone will accept the good news. We recognize the activity of opposing spiritual forces and human rebellion. Nevertheless, we preach the good news in full dependence upon God in the power of the Holy Spirit. Fourth, we must faithfully serve God as we preach the good news, for we are simply Christ's servants (v. 5). Fifth, we must preach Christ as Lord and as the manifestation of God's glory. Only here do we find the true gospel, the good news of God's design for the ages, the ultimate culmination of the grand story he has inscribed on the world.[33]

We see here a two-part mission: (1) the *mission of Jesus* as sent by God to inaugurate his kingdom and its blessings and (2) the *mission of Jesus's disciples* to continue Jesus's work by proclaiming him as Lord and Savior and by calling people to faith and obedience.[34]

Faith (Greek, *pistis*) is the distinguishing mark of those who respond to the good news. The Greek word for "faith" can also be translated as "trust," "faithfulness," "loyalty," and "obedience." Faith is a characteristic of Christ himself in the first place (Rom. 3:22; Gal. 3:22), namely, the faithful obedience of the Son to God the Father.[35] Our faith is a response to Christ's faithfulness and our participation in his obedience. The element of faithful obedience is expressed in a continuing relationship with Christ. A living faith characterizes newness of life in Christ and marks membership in God's renewed people. By grace, we have responded to the "message in repentance and faith, and [have] thereby come into the sphere of God's salvation and life."[36]

Christian hope is an essential result and corollary of faith. Living in the eschatological era of the Spirit, that is, anticipating the promised consummation of God's kingdom and our salvation, hope is a present and abiding reality (Rom. 5:5; 8:24; Gal. 5). For the Roman Christians, Paul succinctly captured the meaning of Christian hope: "May the God of hope fill you with all joy and peace as you trust in him, so that you may overflow with hope by the power of the Holy Spirit" (Rom. 15:13, NIV).

THE CROSS AND THE KINGDOM OF GOD

The people of God are gathered around the Messiah who died on the cross and who was raised on the third day. The crucifixion and resurrection of Jesus are affirmed to be "according to the Scriptures" (1 Cor. 15:4, NIV). The early church believed the cross of Christ to be the event in which "the rescuing purposes of Israel's God were finally enacted and fulfilled."[37] The cross became a visual symbol of the story of God in Christ; very early it began to shape the church's practice.

Two important implications of the cross need to be emphasized.

First, the cross was a "stumbling block to Jews and foolishness to Gentiles" (1 Cor. 1:23, NIV). The message of a crucified Messiah was very difficult for the Jews and was absolute nonsense for the Greeks. Crucifixion represented not only a shameful death in Greco-Roman society but also for Jews a curse on the one "hung on a tree" (Deut. 21:23, NRSV).

To the eyes of the world, the cross may appear weak, foolish, and shameful; yet it is paradoxically the expression of divine power (2 Cor. 13:4). The good news is about the crucified and risen Christ, the Messiah crucified in weakness but raised in power through the Holy Spirit (Rom. 8:11). The Savior was prepared to be humble. Jesus emptied himself and remained obedient to the Father, even to death on the cross (Phil. 2:6-8). In his greatest moment of weakness, he became strong by relying on the grace of God. He was exalted by God (vv. 9-11). The cross, then, becomes the expression of God's power and wisdom. Through the death and resurrection of the Messiah, God has brought us back into a right relationship with him. The implication of the cross for Christ's followers is that they must rely on the power of God, which transforms weakness into a strength. The strength is then the experience of God's grace that enables Christians to cope with difficult situations and hardships, to be filled with love and peace.

Second, the cross is an essential part of God's renewing work in the world. In the words of N. T. Wright, God chose the cross to do something "new . . . world-changing," "counter-cultural . . . counter-imperial," and "shocking."[38] It would become the "new way of being human" and a "paradoxical climax to the long story [of redemption], the 'covenant' narrative."[39] The cross radically transformed the narrative of God, "even as it fulfilled it."[40]

The cross tells the story of God's love for, and redemption of, humanity. The Bible is clear that universal sin and guilt separate humanity from God. God's gracious calling of Israel out of Egypt, his gift of the Law as their guide to living as holy people in the presence of a holy God, and his provision for atonement within the sacrificial system are all part of God's redeeming activity for his rebellious people and marred creation. But the possession of the Law did not preserve people from sinning. In fact, sin infected the Law, according to Paul. It was therefore only capable of making people aware of their sins (Rom. 7:7). God's ultimate solution to the alienation of his creation was through the redemption from sin that comes through Christ's death on the cross (6:22). Paul in Romans 3:25 reminds us that God put Jesus forward as a "sacrifice of atonement" (NIV; Greek, *hilastērion*). The idea of atoning sacrifice comes from Leviticus 16, which recounts that the blood of the sacrificed animals was sprinkled for the sins of the people. That ritual had to be repeated. But Paul explains that because of Christ, something different and new has happened in the relationship between God and humankind. Animal sacrifices were completely supplanted or completed "through the sacrifice of the body of Jesus Christ once for all" (Heb. 10:10, NIV). We are now justified (put into a right relationship with God and reconciled to God) by Christ whom God set forth as our atoning sacrifice. The precious blood of Christ delivers people from their sin and its consequences. This atonement is complete and does not need to be repeated. God's righteousness has been revealed through Christ's obedience. This is the act of perfect obedience through which "many will be made righteous" (Rom. 5:19, NIV).

The core of the gospel is the righteousness of God, God's promised redemption for both Jews and Gentiles that is finally revealed in Christ's faithful obedience on the cross for all who believe. Through participation in the faithful obedience of the Messiah, a right relationship with God becomes reality for individuals. What God has done in Christ transforms believers—those who, in him, become what he is, God's righteousness (2 Cor. 5:21). Through relationship with Christ believers are transformed as new-creation people in the world (2 Cor. 5:17; Col. 3:9-10; 2 Pet. 1:4) and become an expression of God's righteousness before the world (Rom. 6:18; Phil. 1:11).

THE RESURRECTION

The resurrection of the Messiah on the third day is a powerful and essential sign or confirmation of the inaugurated kingdom of God. The Scriptures describe Christ's resurrection as a concrete event that has signified "a fresh marker of *time*: the new age has dawned, 'now is the time of salvation' [2 Cor. 6:2]."[41]

Christians correctly and confidently believe in a bodily resurrection, like Christ's, of all deceased believers at the kingdom's consummation. "For as all die in Adam, so all will be made alive in Christ. But each in his own order: Christ the first fruits, then at his coming those who belong to Christ" (1 Cor. 15:22-23, NRSV; cf. Phil. 3:20-21).

But that is not the whole Christian story of resurrection. In an extremely important sense, the apostle Paul and other early Christians believed resurrection has already happened. Paul and other New Testament writers call us to die with Christ to sin and its old way of life and then to be raised with him to new resurrected life (Rom. 6:1-11). In other words, Christ's resurrection entails immediate consequences for Christians; they must be formed and directed by it (Col. 2:6-13).[42] Christians now live in the power of the resurrection (Rom. 8:11; Eph. 1:17-21; 1 Pet. 1:3) even as they await the final resurrection, the redemption of their bodies.

Resurrection signals the new way of living that conforms to the likeness of God's Son (Rom. 8:29). When Jesus returns in glory, our preparation must show that already we were being shaped by Jesus's life, death, and resurrection (6:12-14). Already we are "new creation[s]" in Christ Jesus (2 Cor. 5:17, ESV). Together we are a new order in Christ. "The old has passed away; . . . the new has come" (v. 17, ESV). Paul speaks of living in the sphere of Christ's rule, set free from sin's dominion by dying to the "old Adam that once defined our existence as humans," bringing to an end *our career as sinners*"[43] (see Rom. 6:6). This doesn't mean that one who dies to sin will never sin but that already we are "alive to God in Christ" (v. 11, NIV). Christians are, by the Spirit, commissioned "to live accordingly" in newness of life.[44] Although Christians still live in the world of the two realms of sin and grace (5:21), Paul is very clear on where Christians are supposed to be: in the realm of the resurrected Christ controlled by the Spirit of Christ, belonging to him and in him to God. Living in the resurrection of Christ is living in obedience with him and with the mind set on God, on Christ, and on the Spirit (8:4-14).

The conviction that God raised Christ from the dead and exalted him to unparalleled heavenly glory ignited the early church's faith and devotion to Christ (Phil. 2:9-11). It also fueled the church's confidence in the risen Christ's future return in glory (1 Cor. 6:14).[45]

Hope for Jesus's second coming (1 Thess. 4:13–5:11), the final resurrection, and future cosmic dimensions of salvation (Rom. 8:18-23) as consummating God's kingdom are all pivotal for the New Testament. But it is essential to recall that those born of the Spirit already inhabit the kingdom of God. Paul says in Colossians, "He has rescued us from the power of darkness and transferred us into the kingdom of his beloved Son" (Col. 1:13, NRSV). This implies that all future dimensions of the kingdom must be shaped by our already having been rescued from the power of darkness and transferred into the kingdom of God's beloved Son (v. 13). Already the people of God occupy his kingdom (the "first fruits" [Rom. 8:23, NRSV]) and must even now participate in God's unfolding plan for humanity and all creation.

THE KINGDOM OF GOD HAS COME NEAR: THE "ALREADY" AND THE "NOT YET"

The kingdom of God has in fact come near, because the Messiah (or King) has arrived with authority. God's kingdom is powerfully present in Jesus. But proclamation of the inaugurated kingdom may mistakenly suggest that its future and present are the same, that God's reign in the world is complete. In fact, the inaugurated kingdom has yet to be consummated. The future dimension does not dissolve into the present (Luke 9:11-17; 1 Cor. 15:20-28).

On the other hand, as N. T. Wright observes, today there is a widespread assumption that the kingdom of God denotes a realm altogether separated from this present life, namely the "'heaven' to which God's people . . . hope to go after their death."[46] To correct this misperception we must first locate the revelation of the good news of the kingdom within the historical context of the first century. When Jesus announced the arrival of God's kingdom, and "taught his followers to pray that it would arrive 'on earth as in heaven,' he was right in the middle of first-century Jewish" expectations about God's reign among his people.[47]

Furthermore, while the good news of the kingdom importantly includes personal forgiveness, assurance of salvation, hope of the resurrection, and future life with God, it also entails a this-worldly moral imperative to live with kingdom integrity in all the social, economic, and political dimensions of human life. Kingdom living entails an active commitment to seek justice for others, to practice compassion, and to evidence a loving concern for the physical, familial, social, and ecological needs of the world.[48] Kingdom life leaves no space for privatized pietism void of a prophetic voice and witness in the world (Matt. 5:14-16; 7:21; Luke 9:23; Eph. 5:8; Col. 1:9-11). According to Luke, the early church put kingdom life and principles into practice. "There was not a needy person among them" (Acts 4:34, NRSV).

Those who have heard and received the good news live in a creative tension between the *now* of living 'by faith' and the *not yet* of knowing the full reality of the kingdom 'by sight'" (see 1 Cor. 13:12; Phil. 3:12-16).[49] The "already" anchors Christian hope for God's final intervention, founded upon Christ's death, resurrection, and ascension (Rom. 15:13; Gal. 5:5; Titus 2:13). New Testament scholar Jörg Frey tells us that while fully expecting the *parousia* (Greek, "second coming"), the bodily resurrection, and the final transformation, the apostle Paul gives most of his attention to the "comforting hope" for our "final communion with Christ."[50]

We have examined essential and fertile biblical contours of the good news of God. We have seen how God progressively prepared the way and finally revealed his kingdom in Christ. We have noted a range of implications for Israel and all humankind. Bearing the "exact imprint of God's very being" (Heb. 1:3, NRSV), as God incarnate, Jesus Christ revealed God's kingdom. He fulfilled all the promises of God (2 Cor. 1:20) and inaugurated a sweeping new worldview that abolished the old divisions that alienated Jews from Gentiles. The good news of the kingdom reveals who Christ is and what he has accomplished to restore people to a right relationship with God. To his Father's glory, he gathers a new people—the people of God—to himself. By his life, death, and resurrection, Christ has founded a new order of redemption and a freedom and peace in which all forms of human captivity, whether by the guilt and bondage of sin or by injustice, are overcome now, and fully in the age to come.

According to the New Testament, Jesus Christ is the true and reliable Word of God, the very good news that gives birth to the church and its mission to "make disciples of all nations, baptizing them in the name of the Father and of the Son and of the Holy Spirit" (Matt. 28:19, NRSV).

As Christians mentored by the Scriptures, we affirm that our Lord Jesus Christ stands in continuity with the rich salvation history of Israel. We affirm that our hope for the consummation of God's kingdom rests on the promises found in the New Testament. In turn, the promises themselves affirm that Christ reveals God's perfect and finished work for the salvation of all who will obediently turn to him. We confess that we live in the fullness of time, under the reign of King Jesus, a reign that calls and equips us to love God and our neighbor as ourselves. By grace alone, through Christ, and in the power of the Holy Spirit, we are citizens of God's kingdom. And we await the return of the same Christ who once walked among us on the shores of Galilee.

In the following chapter we will see how, by the Spirit, the good news of the kingdom of God extended into and shaped the faith of the early post–New Testament church.

For Further Study

Bright, John. *The Kingdom of God.* Nashville: Abingdon Press, 1980.

Goldsworthy, Graeme. *The Goldsworthy Trilogy: Gospel and Kingdom, Gospel and Wisdom, Gospel in Revelation.* Milton Keynes, UK: Paternoster, 2002.

Ladd, George Eldon. *The Gospel of the Kingdom: Scriptural Studies in the Kingdom of God.* Grand Rapids: Eerdmans, 1990.

Treat, Jeremy R. *The Crucified King: Atonement and Kingdom in Biblical and Systematic Theology.* Grand Rapids: Zondervan, 2014.

Wright, N. T. *How God Became King: Getting to the Heart of the Gospels.* New York: HarperOne, 2012.

———. *Surprised by Hope: Rethinking Heaven, the Resurrection, and the Mission of the Church.* New York: HarperOne, 2008.

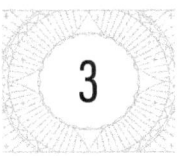

3

PROCLAIMING THE GOOD NEWS OF CHRIST THROUGH TRADITION

DAVID RAINEY

IN THIS CHAPTER we provide a necessary bridge between the New Testament and the eighteenth-century evangelical revival. We will explore the development of some essential doctrines upon which orthodox Christian faith and practice rest. Our approach will encompass several key areas. We will begin by surveying the thoughts of three pivotal early theologians: (1) Irenaeus of Lyons (ca. 120/140–ca. 200/203), (2) Athanasius of Alexandria (ca. 296–373), and (3) Cyril of Alexandria (ca. 376–444). Next we will consider decisions made by the first four ecumenical councils. Then we will take note of the content and importance of the Apostles' Creed and the Athanasian Creed.[1]

We will conclude by briefly considering how doctrinal foundations laid in the early church supported Protestant reformers Martin Luther (1483–1546) and John Calvin (1509-64).

As we focus on the development of doctrine in the early church, a question naturally arises about the importance of tradition in this development and in the proclamation of the gospel. New Testament theologian Richard B. Hays explains that tradition is "the church's time-honored practices of worship, service, and critical reflection."[2] It includes the ancient ecumenical creeds. It also includes the contributions of formative theologians such as Augustine, Thomas Aquinas, Martin Luther, John Calvin, and John Wesley.[3]

Church historian D. H. Williams proposes what amounts to an inadequate description of tradition in the church. He says, "Tradition should be understood as a set or network of enduring practices rather than a particular set of propositions."[4] But if we free the word "proposition" from its pejorative connotation as "objective facts," then tradition is indeed an enduring set of doctrines that, as we shall discover, should lead to a consistent set of practices.

But this requires us to ask, "Which tradition should we choose?" When different theological groups battle for correct doctrine, they appeal to different traditions. For example, when the apostle Paul defended his mission to the Gentiles, he appealed to the Old Testament. Most students of Paul agree with him, but not everyone. Even in the early church, as seen in the book of Acts and the epistle to the Galatians, not everyone agreed with him.

Tradition *always stands under the authority of Scripture*.[5] But it does provide an important aid for interpreting Scripture. Tradition shows how Scripture instructed the church in the past and how we, too, can read it obediently. In the Protestant tradition, the rule is that Scripture is the defining "norm" for tradition.[6] It aids in maintaining doctrinal integrity over time and helps us make sure we are being faithful to what the apostles taught (Acts 20:17-35; Col. 1:23; 2 Thess. 2:15; 2 Tim. 4:1-22; Titus 1:9).[7]

By understanding, valuing, and heeding essential Christian doctrine as it was formulated in the early church, we affirm that Jesus's promises about the Holy Spirit coming as "teacher" (see John 14:25-31) were fulfilled. Believing this, evangelicals are, or should be, irrevocably committed to apostolic faith and to Christ's church, which it supports.[8]

The evangelical tradition began in Scripture and continued onward from the second century. Evangelical theology *comes from* church tradition and *is* a tradition. Some historians place the origin of the evangelical tradition in the eighteenth century, with Jonathan Edwards in colonial America and with John Wesley and George Whitefield in the British Isles. However, these leaders would have found it impossible and undesirable to leap from their era back to the first century. They knew they were indebted to the witness of tradition for understanding the Christian faith and for helping them interpret Scripture.[9]

With this point in mind, we can turn to three key figures in the early church.

THREE CHURCH FATHERS

Irenaeus of Lyons (ca. 120/140–ca. 200/203)

Irenaeus was probably from the city of Smyrna in Asia Minor. As a youth, he may have learned the Christian faith from Polycarp, bishop of Smyrna, whom tradition says had been a student of the apostle John.[10] Around 170, Irenaeus traveled as a missionary to Gaul (present-day France), where persecution of Christians awaited. After the martyrdom of the bishop of Lyons, Irenaeus was elected to replace him (ca. 178). In Lyons Irenaeus wrote his theology while also shepherding the church during perilous times.

Irenaeus testified that the gospel spread throughout the Roman Empire as a universal, consistent message.[11] At no time, he said, had the gospel changed while reaching diverse cultures. However, his opponents, principally the Gnostics,[12] attempted to alter the gospel by forcing it to comply with their myths. Because the Gnostics believed everything material arose from an evil source, they resolutely denied the humanity of Christ; he only *seemed* to be human. To refute their errors, Irenaeus wrote the five-volume *Against Heresies* (*Adversus hae-*

reses). This great work is an extended exposé of Gnostic teachings and a detailed indictment of how they distorted Christian belief about Jesus. In the last three volumes, Irenaeus uses Scripture to refute the Gnostics. Later he wrote *Demonstration of the Apostolic Preaching*.[13] Its purpose was not so much to refute the Gnostics as to instruct those who "desire to walk in godliness."[14]

Because the Gnostics believed the material world to be inherently and irremediably evil, they taught that salvation is radically discontinuous with creation. The God who created the material world is evil and hence could never be the source of salvation for the spirit or soul, which is inherently good, though polluted by its contact with matter (the fall). Only the supreme God, who has nothing to do with the material world, could redeem spirit or soul.

But Irenaeus knew there is absolutely no disjunction in the Bible between the God of the Old Testament and the God of the New Testament; they are one and the same. Moreover, according to the New Testament, the creator God is the same God who became redemptively incarnate, fully human, in Jesus of Nazareth.[15]

God created humans in his own image.[16] The Son of God is the true image of God *in* and *by* whom humans were created. The Son, not Adam, was God's model for what humans should become.[17] So Christ, not Adam, came first; from eternity, Christ was the goal for all humankind (Eph. 3:10-11). British theologian Denis Minns puts it this way: "Adam's humanity bears the stamp of Christ; it is shaped and defined by the shape and definition of Christ's humanity. When God took up the mud to fashion Adam, the pattern according to which he fashioned him was Christ."[18] According to Irenaeus, God always intended to be revealed to humanity in the incarnation.

Thus the likeness of God seen in Jesus Christ is the direction in which we should grow, reaching toward the full stature of Christ (Eph. 4:11-13; 2 Pet. 1:3-11). The likeness of God in Christ is made possible by the Holy Spirit (Rom. 8:9-17; Gal. 5:16-24).[19] Christ, the Word of God, could become incarnate in human form, in the world, because he, not some corrupt being, is the Author and Redeemer of creation (Col. 1:9-20; Heb. 1:1-4).

God wills and provides that the whole creation, including humans, always be in process of becoming what God intends for it (Rom. 8:22-25). This confidence harmonizes with Irenaeus's teaching about salvation. Unlike the Gnostics who rejected the physical creation, Irenaeus said the whole creation—created by God out of nothing, and afterward called "very good" by him (Gen. 1:31, NIV)—is the object of redemption (Rom. 8:18-25; Eph. 1:9-10). Salvation entails being drawn ever closer to the God of love through Jesus Christ. By grace the triune God, who is holy and always in relationship with his creation, constantly draws persons to himself; his love is persuasive, not coercive.

In the virgin birth, the human flesh of Jesus Christ's humanity came from Mary. Clearly, through this Irenaeus exalted the physicality of the female. So Christ taking human flesh from Mary gave humanity the gift of victory *over* Satan by Christ's perpetual victory *in* human flesh (Col. 2:9-15).[20] Incarnate, he lived faithfully and victoriously among us (Heb. 2:10-18). Through his union with us, without sin, Christ "gather[ed] up all things" (Eph. 1:10, NRSV; the Greek word means "to sum up," "to gather together").[21] "Our Lord Jesus Christ, through his transcendent love, became what we are, that he might bring us to be what he is himself" (see 2 Pet. 1:3-4; 2 Cor. 3:18; 1 Thess. 5:23).[22] Christ partook of every stage of human life in order to save every aspect of human life.[23]

Our Lord became our representative in restoring humankind to God; through his obedience he *undid* Adam's disobedience.[24] Begun in the virgin birth, Christ's work of "gathering up" culminated in his resurrection.[25] His life, all parts of it, contributed to the saving activity of the Creator-Redeemer God. Only through Scripture inspired by the Holy Spirit can such heights for humankind be understood.[26]

British theologian Colin Gunton insightfully notes the Trinitarian dimension of Irenaeus's doctrine. All his teaching is "embraced within a Trinitarian framework, according to which the creating and redeeming work of God the Father is mediated by the Son and the Holy Spirit."[27] Another interpreter observed, "Irenaeus deserves his reputation as the first theologian to try and pull Christian teaching together as a cohesive whole."[28]

Irenaeus's influence is immense and enduring. The God who created this world became incarnate in Jesus of Nazareth. God is in the process of redeeming his creation through his eternal Son, through whom the world was created. For the gospel to be good news, our Redeemer must be fully God *and* fully human. He must be able fully to identify with us, fully to assume our humanity, without becoming alienated from God as we are (Phil. 2:5-11; Heb. 2:10-18). What it means to be human must be provided by Christ, our eternal Elder Brother (Heb. 2:11-15),[29] and made endlessly available through the Holy Spirit (John 16:12-15; Rom. 8:9-11). In Jesus Christ we encounter the comprehensive Victor and Author of *new* creation.

To be "evangelical" entails embracing a gospel of the magnitude proclaimed by this early church father.

Athanasius of Alexandria (ca. 296-373)

The city of Alexandria, Egypt, was recognized as a major cultural center in the Roman Empire. It became a major center of Christian leadership and education. Early in the fourth century a conflict erupted between Bishop Alexander of Alexandria and one of his presbyters (priests), Arius (ca. 256–336). Arius had great gifts as a leader. Athanasius was Alexander's theologically astute secretary. He and Alexander strongly disagreed with Arius. Athanasius would soon accompany his bishop to the Council of Nicaea (325).

The controversy revolved around the "essential identity" or "nature" (Greek, *physis*) of the Word or Logos of God. What is the relationship between the Son of God (the Logos, the Word, who became incarnate in Jesus) and God? Arius believed that Christ, called the Son of God in the New Testament, was God's first creation, a creature. "There was," Arius insisted, "a time when the Son was not."[30] Accordingly, the Son is "subordinate" to the Father, not just in obedience, but in essence, that is, a lesser being.[31]

According to Arius, God first created the Son; then the Son created everything else. God also appointed the Son to be the world's Redeemer (a created Redeemer). He is to be highly honored, even hymned, but never worshipped as the Father is worshipped. Arius's followers were known as Arians, and his teaching known as Arianism. For decades, Arianism threatened to take over large parts of the church, particularly in the (Greek) East.[32] Depending upon a given emperor's allegiance, sometimes Arianism was recognized as "orthodox."[33]

Standing resolutely against Arius and his followers, Bishop Alexander insisted Christ had a divine nature as well as a human nature. He was fully God and fully human in one person. All attempts to resolve the conflict proved unsuccessful. Major social unrest and struggle resulted, so much so that it threatened the peace of the Roman Empire that Emperor Constantine hoped a unified church would help deliver. Determined to achieve resolution, Constantine called for a council of the entire church. It would meet in 325 at Nicaea, a city of the Roman province of Bithynia (located in northwest Asia Minor). Constantine would preside and thereby guarantee a successful resolution.

After intense wrangling, the council concluded that Christ had a divine nature that was of the same essence or substance as that of the Father. The pivotal term provided by Athanasius and used by the council to declare Christ's full deity was the Greek word *homoousion*. It means "of the same substance." When confessing the Nicene Creed, Christians today say that Christ is "true God from true God, begotten, not made, of *one Being* with [the *same substance* as] the Father" (italics added; see appendix A).

Three years after the council's decision, Bishop Alexander died and Athanasius succeeded him as bishop of Alexandria. In spite of intense opposition from the Arians and their imperial supporters, and in spite of repeated exiles, Athanasius remained an unflinching champion of Nicene orthodoxy.[34] Two of his writings in defense of Christ's deity and against the Arians are *On the Incarnation of the Word* and *Four Discourses against the Arians*.[35]

Like Irenaeus, whose chief opponents were the Gnostics, Athanasius knew that apart from a correct understanding of who Christ is—fully divine and fully human—there can be no gospel, no adequate promise of salvation. The Arians were wrong to believe that salvation can be procured for humankind by anyone less than God himself.[36] Only the gracious God who created to begin with can be the gracious Author of a new creation. Athanasius spelled this out in *On the Incarnation of the Word*.[37]

God's mercy and grace, extended to humankind through Christ, are central. Grace is the gift granted to us through participation in God the Word. Being God, the Word *bestows* grace; he does not *receive* grace as creatures do. All created things *received* and continue to *receive* their existence from him (Col. 1:15-17).

The gospel is revealed in the Word of God by his condescension (incarnation) into human life. As God incarnate, Christ the Word of God "submitted to appear through a body, so that as a human he might bring humans to himself."[38] Through his works the Word incarnate sought to show humankind that he is not only man "but God and the Word and Wisdom of the true God."[39]

The divine Word's incarnation in Jesus of Nazareth stands not only against the Arian denial of Christ's deity but also against humanity's idolatrous creation of its own gods. The gospel is the good news of God's humble descent in human form to exalt humanity to Christ's own image. Incarnate, God himself, not some creature, is the Mediator between himself and humankind.

Cyril of Alexandria (ca. 376-444)

The period between the Council of Constantinople (381) and the Council of Chalcedon (451) was a doctrinally tumultuous time. One of the most influential figures was Cyril, patriarch of Alexandria.

During this time the church, guided by the Holy Spirit, sought to define more clearly the unity and diversity within the Godhead and to state the deity and humanity of Christ in a way that preserved both in the life of one undivided person. The integrity of the faith and the meaning of the gospel were at stake.

Prior to Cyril, in the latter part of the fourth century, the three Cappadocian Fathers (Basil [ca. 330-79], bishop of Caesarea; Gregory of Nyssa [ca. 332-ca. 395]; and Gregory of Nazianzus [ca. 329-ca. 389]) had successfully provided language for effectively articulating the doctrine of the Trinity. They clarified two ambiguous Greek terms often misleadingly used synonymously—"essence" (*ousia*) and "person" (*hypostasis*). The Cappadocians explained that "essence" is the general term for the definition of a subject while "person" refers to a particular expression of "essence." God is one essence, while Father, Son, and Holy Spirit are particular or distinct eternal expressions (persons) of that single, undivided divine essence. Hence, there is one God in three persons. Neither the unity of God is to be divided nor the persons confused.[40] It might help to understand the importance of using correct language if we think of the distinction in this way: each of us is human (our essence), but each of us is a particular human (our person).

Eventually, the Cappadocians' explanation became the norm. But their explanation left unanswered the question of the relationship between Christ's deity and his humanity. How could Christ, in one person, be both fully divine and fully human?

Two main antagonists in the Christological debates were Cyril, patriarch of Alexandria, and Nestorius (ca. 386–ca. 451), patriarch of Constantinople. The intrigue and conflict associated with this debate are too complex to trace here.[41] Both theologians supported the Nicene Creed (the full deity of Christ). Both supported the divinity and humanity of Christ. However, they used different language to do so. Consequently they became suspicious of each other's Christology, with neither side fully understanding the other.[42]

The problem was that Nestorius seemed to explain the relationship between the divine and human natures in Christ in a way that made it difficult to see Christ as one unified person. Communion between the two natures seemed to be minimal at best. Cyril, on the other hand, was determined to keep the human and divine natures united in one person so as to insure communion between the two. He emphasized the unity of the Savior. The divine and the human are united in one concrete existence, centered in the Word (Logos). While there is in Christ an interchange of qualities between the divine and the human, each nature is complete and joined in one person.

According to Cyril, it was God made flesh, who was born of the Virgin Mary, who died, and of whom we partake in the Lord's Supper (Eucharist). It is, Cyril said, "plain to all that . . . being God and by nature from God, the Only-begotten became man in order to condemn sin in the flesh, kill death by his own death and make us sons of God."[43] Cyril's position prevailed.

THE FIRST FOUR ECUMENICAL COUNCILS

Amid bitter struggle for control of the Roman Empire, and toward the end of the great persecution of Christians executed by Emperor Diocletian, in April 311 three competitors—Constantine, Galerius, and Licinius—issued an edict of toleration to Christians. The edict was issued "on condition that nothing be done by them contrary to discipline."[44] Persecution ceased, except in Asia and Egypt. In 313 Licinius, emperor of the East, and Constantine, emperor of the West, met in Milan, Italy, and granted full freedom to Christianity. This act gave Christians legal equality with other religions of the empire.

In 324, after defeating Licinius, who had reinstated persecution, Constantine became sole ruler of the Roman world. Along with Constantine's success came complete freedom from persecution (except for a brief time under the reign of Julian the Apostate, 361-63). Constantine, now himself a Christian, hoped Christianity would help secure unity and peace in the empire.

With the cessation of persecution, the church was free to address doctrinal conflicts openly as never before. No sooner had Constantine gained control of the empire than bitter controversy in the church jeopardized his hopes about the church's benefit for the empire. In North Africa the Donatist controversy erupted and led to schism (division). The Donatists rejected the legitimacy of bishops who had been ordained by bishops who had themselves surrendered the Christian Scriptures to Roman authorities during Diocletian's persecution.[45] Donatists took their name from Donatus the Great, who in 313 succeeded Majorinus, "bishop" of the schismatic (divisive) "church."

Donatists refused to submit to decisions reached during a church synod held at Arles (France) in 314. Constantine unsuccessfully tried force to make them comply. Donatism grew rapidly, claiming to be the only true and pure church.

The Council of Nicaea (325)

As we learned in our discussion of Athanasius, the Council of Nicaea dealt with questions about the deity of Christ. The council affirmed what all orthodox Christians today confess, namely, the full deity of the Son, who became incarnate in Jesus of Nazareth. He is of the same divine nature (substance) as the Father. He is "true God from true God." Although some of the language the council chose may seem strange to us, its meaning is nonnegotiable for apostolic faith (see appendix A).

Arianism, however, did not cease to exist after the Council of Nicaea. It continued to plague the church in the East for decades. The Arians sent missionaries into the Germanic lands. Alaric I, the Visigothic king who sacked Rome in 410, was an Arian "Christian." But the fundamental flaws of Arianism were exposed, and its fate sealed at Nicaea.

The Council of Constantinople (381)

In 381 Emperor Theodosius called a council that met in Constantinople (later called the second ecumenical council). Although no bishops from the Western part of the church were present, the Western church accepted its doctrinal decisions.

The language of the Cappadocian Fathers about the doctrine of the Trinity (one essence in three persons) prevailed. The bishops did not produce a new creed; instead, they reaffirmed the Nicene Creed and again condemned Arianism. The council also affirmed the deity of the Holy Spirit by condemning the Macedonian party,[46] which refused to accept the Holy Spirit as of the same substance or essence with the Father. Also condemned were the teachings of Apollinaris of Laodicea (d. 390). Apollinaris taught that Jesus could not have a human mind, since it would have been a sinful human mind (including emotions). So Apollinaris maintained that the Logos replaced the human mind. But if Jesus had not been fully human, there would have been no salvation for humanity, for salvation is based on the God-human in Jesus, not only the divine.

The creed that Christians now confess as the Nicene Creed is actually the Nicene-Constantinopolitan Creed. With the Council of Constantinople the doctrine of the Trinity was established as orthodox; Arianism ceased to be an important part of theological discussion.

The Council of Ephesus (431)

The conflict between Cyril, patriarch of Alexandria, and Nestorius, patriarch of Constantinople, over the person of Christ was still unresolved. So the Emperors Valentinian III (reigned in the West 425-55) and Theodosius II (reigned in the East 408-50) called a general council to meet in Ephesus on June 7, 431. The council (the third ecumenical council) actually met from June 22 through July 31. Nestorius's teachings were condemned. However, controversies surrounding the council and resulting confusion continued to flare, especially in the Eastern part of the church.

Regardless of the intrigue and personality conflicts that often surrounded these debates, the critical issue was that any Christology that jeopardized the integrity of Jesus Christ—the unity of his divine and human nature in one complete person—also jeopardized the doctrine of salvation. Although the process was often messy, the church knew that to safeguard the gospel it had to formulate its faith correctly.

In the Council of Ephesus and later in the Council of Chalcedon, the influence of the earlier Cappadocian Fathers was in play. In harmony with the New Testament, they had insisted correctly that what Christ in the incarnation did not assume (become), he could not heal or redeem. Because the whole of our personhood is infected by sin, the Redeemer must be joined to the whole of our personhood for salvation to be complete. In other words, omit any part of what it means to be fully human (e.g., mind) and you eliminate that element of human life from salvation. God became what we are in order that our whole selves might be transformed into Christ's image.

The Council of Chalcedon (451)

More controversy was yet to come. No matter how carefully Cyril worked to state his Christology, there was a lingering suspicion that Christ's divinity overwhelmed his human nature.

In the meantime, a new controversy had erupted in the person of Eutyches of Constantinople (ca. 380–ca. 456). He was charged with *confusing* the two natures. He said that before the incarnation there were two natures; but after the incarnation there was only one nature. A "confusion" of the two natures is what the term "Eutychianism" has come to mean.

The final resolution of the Christological controversies was achieved at the Council of Chalcedon in 451, where some six hundred bishops gathered. The Definition of Chalcedon (also known as the Formula of Chalcedon or the Creed of Chalcedon) is recognized by all orthodox Christians as the final and adequate statement of the relationship between the divine and human natures in Christ.[47] For orthodox Christianity, in the Definition of Chalcedon all prior Christological debates are terminated. Recognizing the mystery of the incarnation, the Definition does not attempt a rational explanation of how two complete natures—divine and human—can be united in one complete person. Instead, it clearly states what *must* be true for Christian faith to be whole and complete. Think of the Definition as a confession of faith that doesn't try to iron out the central mystery of the Christian faith—what Paul refers to as the "mystery of Christ" (Eph. 3:4, NIV).[48]

Chalcedon calls on Christians to confess that our Lord is "consubstantial [coessential] with the Father according to the Godhead, and consubstantial with us according to the Manhood; in all things like unto us, without sin." (See appendix A for the complete creed.)

The Definition of Chalcedon remained unchallenged through the Protestant Reformation and until the beginning of the eighteenth-century Enlightenment. Then many began to enthrone "reason" as the arbiter of Christian doctrine. But Chalcedon was bedrock doctrine for leaders of the eighteenth-century evangelical revival, such as Jonathan Edwards in America and George Whitefield, Charles Wesley, and John Wesley in England. It unquestionably retains its primacy among evangelicals today.

TWO CREEDS

The Apostles' Creed

The Apostles' Creed had an early history in the Eastern and Western Church. Its basis seems to be the Old Roman Creed (also known as the Old Roman Symbol). It is called the Apostles' Creed because early on, it was believed that the creed was formulated by the twelve apostles on the day of Pentecost. The creed has twelve articles or sections; hence there are supposedly twelve apostolic authors, with each composing one article. In its early role it served as a personal baptismal statement of faith. But it could also be recited in personal devotions and in worship services as a communal confession of faith. Along the pathway of its development, the creed changed in the way it was stated.

During the sixteenth-century Protestant Reformation, Martin Luther, John Calvin, and Huldrych Zwingli assigned it authoritative status. But Anabaptists have generally rejected it because they were and are wary of what they view as fixed statements of belief formulated by the church and not found in the New Testament.[49]

Although the Apostles' Creed doesn't state in detail all the Trinitarian and Christological elements found in the Nicene and Chalcedonian Creeds, it clearly confesses the divinity of the Father, Son, and Holy Spirit, while stating the role of each in salvation. Conception of Christ by the Holy Spirit in the womb of the Virgin Mary (the creed's third article) is pivotal. This affirmation countered the early *adoptionist* controversies that denied Christ's eternal deity.

The phrase "descended into hell" located in the fourth article became troublesome. What does the phrase mean? Whatever its meaning, it derives from a statement in 1 Peter 3:19: Christ "preached to the spirits in prison" (NKJV). The phrase first appeared in the creed midway the fourth century[50] but likely had an earlier history. One way of interpreting the phrase was as an affirmation of Christ's victory over Satan and death.

The phrase "communion of saints" (tenth article) appeared in the Western church by the late fourth century, and possibly earlier in the Eastern church. Eventually the phrase became a reference to all Jesus's disciples who comprise the church (Latin, *ecclēsia* [fellowship]) of which Christ is the Head.

In his magisterial work on the early Christian creeds, J. N. D. Kelly said that in the Apostles' Creed[51] the early church continues the scriptural tradition and hands on the "same venerable rule of faith which she herself had compiled in the second century as an epitome of the everlasting gospel."[52]

The Athanasian Creed

Although the Athanasian Creed bears the name of Athanasius, bishop of Alexandria (part of the Eastern church), it is clearly a Western statement of faith. The creed is not used by the Eastern church. A major reason is that the creed says the Holy Spirit proceeds from the Father *and* the Son. While Roman Catholics and Protestants affirm the double procession, the Eastern Orthodox Church teaches that the Holy Spirit proceeds *only* from the Father.[53] The Nicene Creed as restated at the Council of Constantinople in 381 does not contain a double procession.

The creed's authorship remains unknown. It was presumably formulated sometime after the middle of the fifth century. It is sometimes identified by its first two Latin words: *Quicunque vult* (Whosoever will).

The creed stresses the unity of the Father, Son, and Holy Spirit. While maintaining that unity, the creed assigns attributes to each person. Thus the creed avoids *subordinationism* (treating the Son and/or the Spirit as less than God) and *tritheism* (turning the Trinity into three deities). Both errors perpetually threaten the doctrine of the Trinity.

The Christological section of the creed shows the influence of the councils of Ephesus (431) and Chalcedon (451). It clearly states that all salvation is in Christ and that he will come again to judge humanity. In God's presence each person will account for his or her life. Unlike the other ecumenical creeds, the Athanasian Creed condemns anyone who rejects its content. Although the creed is not widely used, in many churches it is confessed on Trinity Sunday.

THE SIXTEENTH-CENTURY PROTESTANT REFORMATION: MARTIN LUTHER AND JOHN CALVIN

Two topics bear on the importance of tradition at the time of the Reformation: First is the significance of the Italian Renaissance and the revival of studying original documents and sources. Before Luther appeared on the scene, there was an emphasis on returning to the Bible by carefully studying the original texts. Second, there was an emphasis on returning to the church's patristic writers (early fathers). This included the early theologians in the East and West. British theologian Alister McGrath observes:

> There was general agreement that the fountain stream of tradition was purest at its head, and that patristic scholarship was the

means by which that purity might be tapped. In many respects, the humanist movement and the early Reformers were united in their common appeal to the fathers as witnesses to a form of scriptural exegesis and doctrine which avoided the distortions and accretions of the mediaeval period.[54]

But while the Reformers acknowledged the importance of tradition, they did not assign it the same importance as Scripture. Rather, they thought of the fathers as guides for interpreting Scripture. *Sola Scriptura* (Latin, "by Scripture alone") was a hallmark of the Reformation. Nevertheless, properly employed, tradition offered a lively engagement with Scripture as beneficial for the church.

Martin Luther (1483-1546)

Martin Luther was in intense spiritual conflict when he entered Augustinian orders as a monk and, later, when he became a lecturer at the new University of Wittenberg. No spiritual exercise could resolve his conflict and procure peace with God. Only after he began intensely to engage Scripture, to permit it to speak from its depths, did his evangelical faith come alive. The change happened as the Scriptures, through the Holy Spirit, offered a picture of Christ that Luther had never seen. Christ the Punisher became Christ the Redeemer, who completely identifies with the forsaken by being himself forsaken on the cross.

Luther gloriously discovered that God is made known in Christ, not as one bent on condemning sinners, but as a loving Redeemer. This was good news, the gospel, the word of God that radically altered Luther's life, direction, and proclamation. God, Luther discovered, is revealed in the incarnation. Luther's contemplation of the cross revolutionized his understanding of reconciliation with God—that is, his understanding of justification. Christ, he discovered, took our place; faith in him as Savior is a gift we receive through the Spirit, not an achievement gained by toilsome works.

Using Paul's language, Luther said, "Then I grasped that the justice of God is that righteousness by which through grace and sheer mercy

God justifies us through faith. Thereupon I felt myself to be reborn and to have gone through open doors into paradise."[55]

John Calvin (1509-64)

Like Luther, John Calvin, who had been educated as a humanist scholar, also encountered the gospel of God's redeeming grace as transforming.[56] As an eminent Christian teacher, he proclaimed that since Christ has been revealed to us with all his benefits, and all that belongs to him is made ours through the Spirit, by faith, through grace alone, we become members of Christ and one with him. Christ's righteousness covers our sins; his salvation extinguishes our condemnation. Christ "interposes with his worthiness, and so prevents our unworthiness from coming into the view of God."[57] Regeneration of the believer by the Holy Spirit is prominently taught in Calvin's writings.[58]

Permit Calvin to offer a fit conclusion for this chapter: "And this is the true proof of faith, when we never [permit] ourselves to be torn away from Christ, and from the promises which have been made to us in him. . . . Faith will never reach heaven unless it submit[s] to Christ, who appears to be a low and contemptible God, and will never be firm if it do[es] not seek a foundation in the weakness of Christ."[59]

Limited space has made it necessary to deal selectively with tradition. Consequently, we have skipped from the sixth to the sixteenth century. This can be misleading. In the church of Jesus Christ, evangelical faith has never been lost; it was perpetually present in the testimony of Scripture and the witness of tradition.[60]

For Further Study

D'Ambrosio, Marcellino. *When the Church Was Young: Voices of the Early Fathers*. Cincinnati: Servant Books, 2014.

Johnson, Luke Timothy. *The Creed: What Christians Believe and Why It Matters*. New York: Image Books, 2004.

Kelly, J. N. D. *Early Christian Creeds*. 3rd ed. London: Longman, 1972.

Oden, Thomas C. *The Rebirth of Orthodoxy: Signs of New Life in Christianity*. San Francisco: HarperSanFrancisco, 2003.

Trueman, Carl R. *The Creedal Imperative*. Wheaton, IL: Crossway, 2012.

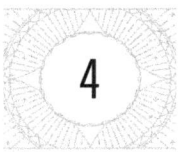

4

THE EVANGELICAL REVIVALS OF THE EIGHTEENTH CENTURY

TIMOTHY J. CRUTCHER

TO UNDERSTAND evangelicalism—especially as it appears today in North America—we must understand its roots in the religious awakenings of the early-to-middle eighteenth century. These revivals—particularly those in Germany, Britain, and Britain's American colonies—would profoundly shape the lives of those who experienced them, along with the broader religious culture. In this chapter we will trace those revivals. We will begin by examining the awakenings from the end of the Protestant Reformation up to eighteenth century. Next we will study the eighteenth-century religious awakenings. And finally, we will consider the lasting influence of the evangelical awakenings upon America and American religion.

FROM THE PROTESTANT REFORMATION TO THE EIGHTEENTH-CENTURY AWAKENINGS

Evangelicalism may be seen as a reweaving of some of the more significant threads or convictions of the Protestant Reformation to suit a new set of circumstances. The three interconnected convictions or emphases most important for our story are (1) the priority given to God's activity over human effort in salvation, (2) the importance of personal or individual faith over (and sometimes against) communal or "institutional" faith, and (3) the articulation of faith as an experience more than as a set of doctrinal affirmations. Protestants prioritized God, the individual, and the experience of faith. But doing so does not necessarily devalue the larger human standing or condition before God, the role of the church and community, and the importance of theology or doctrine. However, for Protestants the latter are given a distinctly secondary role. The three "evangelical" convictions generally distinguished the Reformers from the Roman-based church.

Three "Evangelical" Convictions

The first conviction that motivated the Protestant Reformation was the idea that God's work in salvation overshadows anything humans do. By proclaiming "grace alone" through "faith alone," the Reformers presented salvation as completely the work or gracious gift of God. The traditional medieval understanding of the human role in salvation was radically reduced or eliminated altogether. For the Reformers, this was the "good news," the *evangel*. For this reason they identified themselves as "evangelical." Human effort and ecclesiastical structures took a back seat to the overriding grace of God. God alone determined who would be saved and how. Legitimate moral effort (Christian ethics) was understood as a faithful response to God's gift of salvation, not a precondition for receiving it. Moral living was important, but it was seen as human life empowered by the Holy Spirit in response to faith. One could not earn salvation by good works, as the Reformers accused the Roman Catholic Church of teaching. This also meant that divine authority—and for the Reformers, this meant Scripture—superseded any human-based authority such as the traditions of the church or the pope. Hence the affirmation "Scripture alone" was also foundational for the Reformers.

The second conviction that motivated much of the Reformation was that individuals, rather than communities or institutions, are God's primary point of contact in the process of salvation. So long as the church adheres to proper doctrine and governance, it is an important ally in God's saving activity. But the communal dimension was decidedly secondary to God's work in individual believers. Bibles and liturgies were translated into the common language so that individual believers could have access to Scripture and understand its exposition in services of worship. The Reformers accused the Roman Catholic Church of teaching that mere participation in church was redemptive. They insisted that personal and individual faith is required.

A third conviction was woven in: the priority given to faith as an inward experience. This was set against faith viewed as an affirmation or apprehension of external divine truth. The mystical tradition in the medieval church emphasized this. But it blazed to the fore with the Reformers. For them, the process of salvation was not merely a new understanding of truth but a complete "conversion" of one's way of life, a "new birth." Faith was less a belief in doctrine than a trust and confidence in God that arose from an experience of God's grace.[1] Only on the foundation of this inward reality could the outward manifestations of correct doctrine and Christian life be constructed.

The Convictions Fade

In the 1500s, these three convictions—the priority of God's gracious activity, of individuals, and of personal experience—gave the Reformation a common theological cast. However, by the middle of the 1600s, the force of these convictions had waned. Following the Thirty Years' War (1618-48) in Europe and the Puritan conflicts in England (1642-60), many people became apprehensive about an emotive religion that could use God as a justification for violence. Churches and people in Protestant areas began to acquire patterns of thought that restored the role of human effort and intellect. Christianity became more a matter of church attendance and agreement with doctrine than of personal piety.

After the initial theological creativity of the Reformation, a period of consolidation set in. The churches that followed Luther and Calvin focused on creating stable orthodoxies. And by the use of reason, defenders fought off those who challenged them. Ironically, defenders of the various orthodoxies usually appealed to the Scriptures. Strict Lutherans, for instance, objected to the "innovations" introduced by Philipp Melanchthon (1497–1560)—Luther's successor. They also condemned the broadly tolerant ideas of Georg Calixtus (1586–1656) in the so-called syncretistic controversy of the middle 1600s. Strict Calvinists, on the other hand, waged intellectual battles against followers of the Dutch theologian Jacob Arminius (1560–1609), culminating in the Synod of Dort (1618-19). The synod defined Calvinism according to five points.[2] Thus the Reformation revolt against the priority of human tradition and effort was reversed; the Reformation itself largely became a set of human traditions and doctrines.

Outside the church, things were also changing. Among the learned and elite in Europe, the Enlightenment (eighteenth century) began to take hold. This, too, affected the inheritors of the Reformation. The individualism of the Enlightenment paralleled Protestant sensibilities. But Enlightenment thinkers focused much more on human reason than on divinely revealed religion and individual religious experience. An intellectual belief in a God who created a clockwork universe that ran by its own rules[3] was preferred over faith in a miracle-working deity that intervened in human lives to give them a "new birth."

Thus the human, the institutional, and the intellectual components of the Christian faith began to reassert themselves, and the evangelical convictions of the Reformation began to fade. However, while such a religion might have satisfied many, particularly among the upper classes or the educated elite, it was not at all satisfactory for many "ordinary folk." Many people, particularly those lower on the social ladder, hungered for something beyond what this world offers.[4] Thus the revivals of the eighteenth century may be seen in part as a reassertion of the primary Protestant convictions against a religious culture that had come to be dominated by orthodoxy, and a secular culture dominated by Enlightenment standards.

THE RELIGIOUS AWAKENINGS OF THE EIGHTEENTH CENTURY

Although the power of the three evangelical convictions had waned, many worked to keep them alive. This resulted in an evangelical resurgence in the eighteenth century. While this was true in many places, we will focus on three interconnected stories in Germany, Britain, and America. They are particularly important because of the impact on the Protestant churches in those places. From there, Protestantism eventually expanded around the world.

In Germany, leaders of the religious awakening included Johann Arndt (1555–1621), who stated its meaning in *True Christianity* (1605-10), and Philipp Jakob Spener (1635–1705), whose 1675 book *Pia Desideria* sparked the Pietist movement in German Lutheranism.

In England and America, Puritans and their devotional writers such as William Ames (1576–1633) and John Owen (1616–83) kept the evangelical convictions of the Reformation before people. They continued to call for a personal faith in and complete conversion to God, who is the sole actor in salvation.

Still, more was needed to move devotional ideals from an individual level to that of a large-scale movement with long-term social consequences. Adherents of the subsequent revivals attribute their impetus to the Holy Spirit. Secular historians, on the other hand, offer material and sociological explanations. In either case, the evangelical convictions of the Reformation burst into new life with renewed power. Largely because of these events we have what is today labeled "evangelical."

The Moravians in Germany

In 1722, a group of Protestant refugees fled Catholic persecution in Moravia (southeast Czech Republic) and asked permission to settle on the lands of Count Nikolaus Ludwig von Zinzendorf (1700–1760). He was a young minor German noble with an estate in far eastern Saxony, near the Polish border. Members of the United Brotherhood, these Moravians traced their religious heritage to the pre-Reformer Jan Hus (ca. 1369–1415). Zinzendorf eventually granted the Moravians a permanent settlement at a place they called Herrnhut, "The Lord's Watch."

Zinzendorf had been raised by his grandmother in a family so closely connected to the Pietist movement that Philipp Spener was Nikolaus's godfather. Spiritually sensitive from an early age, Zinzendorf soon became intrigued by the religious community developing on his estates. Though living in Dresden, he made regular visits to Herrnhut (a distance of seventy miles) and began to participate in the Moravian community. Always uneasy with the court life of the Holy Roman Empire, Zinzendorf desired to devote his life to God. Finally, a combination of growing theological divisions in the Moravian community and the death of Zinzendorf's grandmother—out of loyalty to whom he had maintained his duties as a noble—led him to resign his political position and move permanently to Herrnhut. He became a pastor there in the late spring of 1727.

Zinzendorf used his influence to help the Moravians heal their dissension. Throughout the summer of 1727, the Herrnhut community, which numbered about three hundred, gathered for prayer, mutual confession, and services designed to promote unity. On August 13, 1727, during a Communion service, the community witnessed God's presence in an extraordinary manner that left its mark for generations.

Twenty-seven years later, Zinzendorf described to an English audience the event's impact:

> On this day twenty-seven years ago the Congregation of Herrnhut . . . were all dissatisfied with themselves. They had quit judging each other because they had become convinced, each one, of his

lack of worth in the sight of God and each felt himself at this Communion to be in view of the noble countenance of the Savior. . . . [T]heir hearts told them that He would be their patron and their priest who was at once changing their tears into oil of gladness and their misery into happiness. This firm confidence changed them in a single moment into a happy people which they are to this day, and into their happiness they have since led many thousands of others through the memory and the help which the heavenly grace once given to themselves, so many thousand times confirmed to them since then.[5]

Zinzendorf spoke of the event as "a sense of the nearness of Christ bestowed in a single moment upon all the members that were present."[6] Though the occurrence was communal, each member experienced an individual encounter with God. A rejection of emphasis upon individual effort and worth was coupled with a profound reliance upon the work of God, which Zinzendorf described as "confidence." In Zinzendorf's brief account we observe a reaffirmation of Protestantism's foundational evangelical convictions.

Of course, an emotional religious occurrence does not in itself constitute a revival. Only when there are enduring consequences can we conclude that large-scale revival or renewal has happened. Among the Moravians at Herrnhut, two long-term consequences are notable.

First, a group of twenty-four male and twenty-four female Herrnhut Moravians formed a twenty-four-hour prayer circle. They agreed to pray around the clock for the work of the church. That round-the-clock prayer meeting lasted more than one hundred years. That commitment not only outlasted the initial religious experience but also the lives of the original members.

Second, the revival renewed the Moravians' commitment to missionary activity. The evangelical renewal quickly became evangelistic. As Zinzendorf noted, the Moravians "led many thousands of others" into the joy they themselves had found. Within five years, the Moravians sent their first missionaries to the West Indies. The next year, they sent missionaries to Greenland, and soon to Native Americans in the New World. The Moravians in England would eventually publish *Periodical Accounts,* a magazine that told of Moravian missionary efforts. This publication would eventually inspire William Carey (1761–1834)—often called the father of the modern missionary movement—to launch his missionary enterprise. Moravian missionaries also played a significant role in the conversion of John Wesley—a central figure in the evangelical revivals of Great Britain.

While the measurable consequences of the Moravian revival might not seem large, the connection they forged between their trust in God and their desire to share that trust with others—the evangelical/evangelistic connection—would become a central feature of the evangelical movement in general. Their indirect impact on William Carey and John Wesley also bore fruit in striking ways.

The Evangelical Revival in Britain

As the Moravians were experiencing their revival, George Whitefield (1714-70) was a twelve-year-old boy and a new student at St. Mary de Crypt's school in Gloucester. John Wesley (1703-91) had just finished his master's degree at Oxford. Their lives would soon intertwine. The results (in spite of their doctrinal disagreements) would lay the groundwork for the movement known as evangelicalism in the English-speaking world.

John Wesley was born to Samuel and Susanna Wesley, both of whom were "dissenting dissenters." That is, they were children of Nonconformist[7] pastors who had independently returned to the Anglican Church before Samuel and Susanna married. This made the Wesley household loyal to the Church of England. But it was also influenced by the Nonconforming Puritan tradition. John was raised in a disciplined environment serious about all things religious, a discipline that would characterize his life. He went to Christ Church College, Oxford, in 1720, earned a master's degree, and was eventually elected a fellow of Lincoln College in 1726. After a short stint of pastoral service under his father, Wesley returned to Oxford and helped revive a small group his brother Charles had initiated in John's absence. The small group was soon derisively known as the Holy Club because its members were very serious about holy living. They met to read Scripture and other devotional works. They held each other accountable and performed charitable works such as visiting the sick and those in prison and caring for the poor.

In 1734, at Charles Wesley's invitation, a poor young Oxford student named George Whitefield joined the Holy Club. Whitefield was the son of the innkeeper of the Bell Inn in Gloucester. His father died when George was two. George grew up surrounded by his mother and siblings in the environment of an English public house (a pub). After finishing grammar school, Whitefield temporarily worked at his family's inn before at age eighteen entering Pembroke College, Oxford, in 1732 as a "servitor." Servitors were poor students whose fees were paid by serving upper-class students. After a couple of years at Oxford, he fell in with John and Charles Wesley, as well as members of the Holy Club.

On the one hand, we can observe some of the Protestant convictions at work in the Holy Club, particularly its attention to Scripture and its focus on supporting each member's faith. On the other hand, the club's quasi-legalistic attention to Christian practice was at odds with a more evangelical, grace-based cast that eventually came to characterize its most prominent members. Nevertheless, the Holy Club's religious seriousness laid the groundwork for what would follow.

George Whitefield's evangelical conversion occurred while a student. His journal reveals a drawn-out experience of temptation and wrestling that lasted nearly a year. His struggle culminated in a striking experience of relief and communion with God. It was an experience of faith that happened in a moment,[8] much as had happened among the Moravians nearly a decade earlier. Also like the Moravians, Whitefield's individual encounter with God turned him outward rather than inward. As soon as he was ordained a deacon in the Church of England (1736), he began to preach in ways that challenged the comfortable institutional religion he saw around him. He called people to their own "saving encounters" with God.

John Wesley's evangelical conversion was a bit longer in coming and was more the result of his encounters with others than of a sustained period of spiritual wrestling. In 1735, upon the death of their father, John and Charles accepted an invitation from James Oglethorpe, founder of the colony of Georgia in America, to become chaplains in the new colony. Leaving the Holy Club in Whitefield's care, the Wesleys headed to America.

They shared their voyage with a group of Moravian missionaries whose witness to personal faith profoundly impacted John. Once a storm arose that threatened to sink the ship. John was stricken with the fear of death. The Moravians, however, in the face of death were calm and assured in their faith.

The Wesleys' sojourn in Georgia was short and unproductive. Six months after arriving, Charles headed home. John lasted less than two years. He left Georgia under threat of legal prosecution and returned to England at the end of 1737 a disillusioned man. In London, he immediately sought out the Moravians living there. Peter Böhler, their leader, became instrumental in helping John deal with his acknowledged deficient faith. Through Moravian influence, he entered the personal dimension and assurance of faith that had eluded him. May 24, 1738, turned out to be the fateful day. Here is Wesley's account.

> I continued thus to seek it [i.e., the experience of faith] (though with strange indifference, dulness, and coldness, and unusually frequent relapses into sin) till Wednesday, May 24. . . .
>
> In the evening I went very unwillingly to a society in Aldersgate-Street, where one was reading Luther's preface to the Epistle to the Romans. About a quarter before nine, while he was describing the change which God works in the heart through faith in Christ, I felt my heart strangely warmed. I felt I did trust in Christ, Christ alone, for salvation: And an assurance was given me, that he had taken away *my* sins, even *mine*, and saved *me* from the law of sin and death.[9]

With their personal evangelical conversions in place, Whitefield and Wesley fully embraced the three grounding Protestant convictions or principles. Their preaching launched a sustained period of renewal in both Britain and the American colonies. Whitefield's approach, being a convinced Calvinist who believed in predestination, was insistent about the exclusive priority of God's work in salvation over any human activity or involvement. On this point he clashed with Wesley, whose Arminian convictions placed a greater weight on the individual's active response to God's gift of faith, which Wesley believed God empowers. For Wesley, the offer of faith extends to everyone, not just to those predestined for salvation. Despite these differences and the tensions they produced, people still responded in significant numbers, particularly when the preachers took their message outside church walls.

In early 1739, shortly after his ordination to the priesthood and after his first of seven voyages across the Atlantic to evangelize in the American colonies, Whitefield began experimenting with preaching in the open air; churches could not contain the people who wanted to hear him. At the end of March, he convinced John Wesley to engage in field preaching. Wesley's words tell the story:

> I could scarce reconcile myself at first to this strange way of preaching in the fields. . . . [I had] been all my life (till very lately) so tenacious of every point relating to decency and order, that I should have thought the saving of souls almost a sin if it had not been done in a church. . . .
>
> Mon[day,] [April] 2 [1739].—At four in the afternoon, I submitted to be more vile, and proclaimed in the highways the glad tidings of salvation, speaking from a little eminence in a ground adjoining to the city, to about three thousand people.[10]

Whitefield and Wesley spent the rest of their lives traveling about, preaching their evangelical message. While much of Britain's "polite society" denied Wesley and Whitefield access to their church's pulpits, thousands of ordinary folk flocked to hear them. Their message that salvation is a gift one need only accept from God, that it is God's work in a person's life that generates faith, spoke to people in ways the doctrinal and institutional religion that typified the Anglicanism of the day could not.

One important and lasting difference between Whitefield and Wesley—related to, but more significant than their theological disagreements—was their attention to organizing and preserving the fruit of their labors. Wesley consciously tempered his Protestant focus on the individual with a much more Catholic/Anglican appreciation for the importance of structured community. While Whitefield preached, called for decisions of faith, and then moved on, Wesley gathered his people into organized groups, visited them regularly, and cultivated their growth in Christian discipleship. Early on, these groups were given the name Methodists possibly because of the methodical way they approached their faith.

Organization of the Methodists assured that Wesley's work would endure much longer than that of Whitefield. When old, Whitefield acknowledged this. He told a friend, "My Brother Wesley acted wisely. The souls that were awakened under his ministry he joined in class, and thus preserved the fruits of his labor. This I neglected, and my people are a rope of sand."[11]

Methodists never composed a large part of the British population. But their growth is noteworthy. In 1770, the year of Whitefield's death, Methodists in Britain numbered twenty-nine thousand. When Wesley died in 1791, the number had more than doubled to seventy-two thousand. Methodists such as William Wilberforce were principal advocates for the abolition of slavery in Britain. By the early part of the 1800s Methodists were vigorously advocating additional social reforms.[12]

The focus on the individual and a personal experience of salvation that Wesley and Whitefield preached harmonized to some extent with romanticism in British culture.[13] However, neither Whitefield nor Wesley would have endorsed the secular turn romantic ideals eventually took. In spite of Wesley's reservation, soon after his death Methodists were advocating cross-cultural evangelism and missions as practiced by the Moravians. One hundred years after Wesley's death, Methodist missionaries had spread Methodism around the globe.

As important as the evangelical revival was in Anglican Christianity, it never became the norm. Historically, Anglicans have tended to favor the Catholic side of its via media[14] tradition. There was, however, a place where the evangelical revival would become a dominant religious force: the American British colonies, soon to become the United States of America.

The "Great Awakening" in America

After Wesley's fateful foray in Georgia, he never again ventured to America. George Whitefield, on the other hand, made seven trips to the New World, dying during his last trip there in 1770.[15] His first preaching tour began in the fall of 1739 and lasted for more than a year. That tour helped set off a revival known to history as the (First) Great Awakening in America. Before we take up that story, however, we must first see how the seeds had been carefully planted by the Puritan and Pietist preachers who preceded Whitefield.

Once the first generation of Puritans who settled in New England passed on, it was common for their descendants to decry the loss of piety and morality in the community. Religion had become a social rather than a personal reality. But many Puritan preachers kept exhorting their people to personal faith and an absolute reliance on an absolutely sovereign God. These Puritan ideals aligned well with the Pietist ideals of personal and heartfelt religion that informed the Moravian revival in Germany and would be brought to America by Dutch and German immigrants.

Here and there, small groups and communities would respond to these calls for repentance, and there would temporarily be an uptick in religious seriousness and morality. In the decades leading up to 1740, Puritan preachers such as Samuel Danforth and Solomon Stoddard in Massachusetts and Theodorus Frelinghuysen in the Middle Colonies promoted regional revivals. The most significant of these early, regional revivals were those promoted by Jonathan Edwards, Stoddard's grandson and successor in Northampton. Edwards was already known as a staunch supporter of the Calvinist approach to the priority of God's work in salvation, particularly in contrast to the "rationalist Arminianism" he detected in some of New England's schools and pulpits. Soon he would be known as an advocate of the personal and experiential religion that became a hallmark of the American evangelical tradition.

The revivals Edwards and others witnessed and encouraged occurred periodically from 1731 to 1742. The awakening first burst into flame in the tiny hamlet of Pascommuck, about three miles from Northampton, part of Edwards's congregation.[16] In his *Faithful Narrative of the Surprising Work of God* (1737), Edwards lists thirty-three communities up and down the Connecticut River that experienced a vital surge in piety. The revivals resulted in a reformation of public life. Although these periods of revival fervor would eventually fade, Edwards's account of them would be translated and reprinted. They became seed for many more awakenings in America and beyond. The Great Awakening birthed a "revival culture" that has persisted in American evangelicalism to the present day.

Against this backdrop, and contributing to it, George Whitefield made his stirring American public appearances. He was the "grand itinerant." Historian George Marsden says Whitefield's tour of the colonies "was a truly international phenomenon. It was also the first intercolonial cultural event, the beginning of a common American cultural identity."[17] Whitefield's preaching and the vast publishing enterprise of books and newspaper reports that surrounded it turned the more-or-less regional revivals into an event that united all the colonies in a common religious experience.

Whitefield arrived in Philadelphia in early November 1739. He preached his way over the Middle Colonies and developed contacts with other revivalists such as Frelinghuysen and Gilbert Tennent. His personal, experiential, and often anti-institutional approach to the faith inspired many and scandalized others. Nevertheless, everyone knew about it. Ever the staunch but evangelistic Calvinist—like Edwards and the Puritans who preceded him—Whitefield also emphasized God's initiative in the call for repentance and a "new birth." Human efforts toward salvation were rigorously excluded. As Whitefield's sermons and journals bear witness, he embodied and proclaimed the three Protestant convictions we have been tracking. However, although Whitefield's effectiveness as a preacher cannot be denied, not everyone liked what they heard. One observer, Stephen Bordley, summed up Whitefield by saying, "In short, he has the best delivery with the Worst Divinity that I ever met with."[18]

After nearly a year in the Middle and Southern Colonies, Whitefield arrived in New England in September 1740. There he met with Jonathan Edwards and saw the fruit of the 1735 awakening. As he traveled north from Newport through Boston to Maine and back, his preaching continued to spark revival and controversy. His sermons had notable effects. Though not everyone liked them, few could ignore them. Even Benjamin Franklin, no friend to experiential religion, became good friends with Whitefield. He recorded the impact of Whitefield's first visit to Philadelphia in his *Autobiography*: "It was wonderful to see the change soon made in the manners of our inhabitants. From being thoughtless or indifferent about religion, it seem'd as if all the world were growing religious, so that one could not walk thro' the town in an evening without hearing psalms sung in different families of every street."[19]

Whitefield would finish his first tour of America by late 1740. After a final check on his orphanage in Georgia, he returned to England in early 1741. After his departure, other dramatic and controversial preachers such as Gilbert Tennent and James Davenport continued Whitefield's pattern of itinerant preaching and stirring up controversy. Over the next thirty years, Whitefield would return to America five more times. His many publications and strategic use of the press made each visit a newsworthy occasion. Whitefield may have been America's first genuine celebrity; even his opponents recognized his preaching tours as a public phenomenon that was more than a series of religious services. One opponent exclaimed, "He is the Wonder of the Age, and no one Man more employs the Press, and fills up the Conversation of people, than he does at this Day. None more admir'd and applauded by some, contemn'd and reproach'd by others."[20]

THE LASTING INFLUENCE OF THE AWAKENINGS UPON AMERICA AND AMERICAN RELIGION

The move from small and private religious services to a public phenomenon contributed to making the awakening "great." It instilled the basic features of American evangelicalism into American public culture in a way that would be reinforced in the coming centuries and that continues to shape the American experience, religious and otherwise.

The Great Awakening has had a lasting impact upon American Christianity, particularly upon evangelicals. Three important dimensions of its impact should be noted.

First, although England and Germany had established churches that encouraged institutional stability often at odds with personal and experiential faith, America had none of that. The type of people who settled in the New World tended to prefer adventure. The type of religion preached by Whitefield certainly seemed more vibrant to many than the staid religion of Anglican or Lutheran churches in the Old World. America's native individualism made its inhabitants open to calls for personal and experiential faith. Such appeals matter as much today as they did nearly three hundred years ago.[21] The focus on personal faith also accented a need for missions and evangelism. This emphasis helped America become the largest missionary sending country in the world.

Second, although the primary exponent of the British revival, John Wesley, was an Arminian who believed salvation is intended for all persons, the deep roots of American evangelicalism are largely in Calvinist soil. From the Puritans to Edwards to Whitefield and beyond, an emphasis on the absolute sovereignty of God, including predestination and limited atonement, and a suspicion of any active human participation in salvation continues to mark many evangelicals. Even the typical evangelical insistence on the authority of the Bible over (and often against) human experience as a source for understanding the Christian faith is anchored here. By contrast, for John Wesley, Scripture *and* experience—with Scripture having primacy—are sources.[22]

Third, the Great Awakening was the first truly "American" experience, and it was a religious one. The sense of shared-but-individual experience the revival spawned contributed to an American identity that transcended the identities of the individual colonies. This identity was distinct from the colonies' identity as British. As one set of writers states, "What was awakened in 1740 was the spirit of American democracy."[23] Moreover, from the beginning, the Puritans had a sense that their New World community was a new Israel and that their religious and political life were really one and the same. The Great Awakening gave many outside of New England a similar lens. This may be a key reason why religion in America remains a vital public force, unlike the rest of the Western world, where it is not.

In the early-middle 1700s, the religious convictions that propelled the Reformation two hundred years earlier blazed to new life in a collection of revivals and awakenings that solidified an idea we can now label "evangelicalism." With both Pietism and Puritanism in its religious DNA, the movement focused on a personal and experiential faith in a God who alone can save individual human beings from their plight, a faith that was deeper and more powerful than any of its institutional expressions. Whether or not one shares these evangelical convictions or believes them to be sufficient by themselves to guide a coherent religious life, it is difficult to deny their power in the lives of those who experienced them and who shaped their world in light of them. Protestants today, especially those living in America or who are influenced by American religion, continue to find themselves affected by these events. That is not likely to change anytime soon.

For Further Study

Bushman, Richard L., ed. *The Great Awakening: Documents on the Revival of Religion, 1740-1745*. Chapel Hill, NC: University of North Carolina Press, 1969.

Gaustad, Edwin Scott. *The Great Awakening in New England*. Gloucester, MA: Peter Smith, 1965.

Kidd, Thomas S. *The Great Awakening: The Roots of Evangelical Christianity in Colonial America*. New Haven, CT: Yale University Press, 2007.

Lambert, Frank. *"Pedlar in Divinity": George Whitefield and the Transatlantic Revivals, 1737-1770*. Princeton, NJ: Princeton University Press, 1994.

Marsden, George M. *Jonathan Edwards: A Life*. New Haven, CT: Yale University Press, 2003.

Miller, Perry. *Jonathan Edwards*. New York: World, 1959.

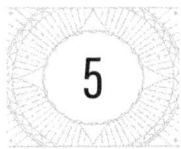

5

THE MODERN EVANGELICAL MOVEMENT IN NORTH AMERICA

MICHAEL K. TURNER

ACCORDING to the 2008 American Religious Inventory Survey (ARIS), "34 percent of all American adults and 45 percent of American Christians self-identify as 'born-again or evangelical Christians.'"[1] In contemporary usage, the term "evangelical" often refers to a wide variety of conservative Christians, ranging from Pentecostals to Baptists and Presbyterians. But while there is considerable diversity, most evangelicals share certain core theological positions, such as the importance of personal conversion, the primacy of Scripture, the deity of Jesus Christ, and the doctrine of the Trinity. Historically, modern American evangelicalism is mostly an outgrowth of portions of eighteenth- and nineteenth-century revivalism. It has been further shaped in the twentieth century by its encounter with modernity and liberalism.[2]

In this chapter we will (1) explore the role nineteenth-century Protestant revivals played in shaping modern evangelicalism, (2) examine how evangelicalism was transformed by its encounter with modernity during the late nineteenth and early twentieth centuries, and (3) seek to understand the neoevangelical movement that emerged in the late twentieth century.

FORMATION OF EVANGELICALISM: 1776-1869

In the years immediately following the American War of Independence, numerous forms of Protestant Christianity that emerged during the First Great Awakening (1730s and 1740s) flourished in the young country. These groups were popularly referred to as evangelical because of their strong emphasis on religious conversion and the primacy of Scripture. Their success was made possible partly by new federal policies that separated church and state. The First Amendment of the Bill of Rights, ratified in 1791, prohibited the federal government from making laws regarding the "establishment of religion" or "prohibiting the free exercise" of any faith.[3] The amendment prevented the United States from following the example of many European countries that had state-sponsored churches. The First Amendment was strongly supported by political leaders (such as Thomas Jefferson and James Madison) and by leading Baptists (such as Isaac Backus and John Leland) who called for a free marketplace of competition among religious groups.[4]

The emerging evangelical groups—especially Methodists, Baptists, and Presbyterians—greatly benefited from the geographic expansion of the newly formed nation. With the organization of the Northwest Territory in 1787, and the Louisiana Purchase in 1803, the United States more than doubled in size from what it had been during the colonial era. Baptist and Methodist leaders and preachers were particularly effective in following the population as it expanded into the South and West. The flexibility of Baptist polity (form of government) allowed congregations to form easily in the territories being newly settled by Euro-Americans. Because ordinations were performed at the congregational level, a capable Baptist lay leader could be set aside for ministry without having to navigate a complex denominational hierarchy.

The Methodists were even more effective than the Baptists in reaching the expanding populations. The Methodist Episcopal Church (MEC), officially formed in Baltimore in 1784, operated according to a connectional polity; its bishops took the lead in establishing preaching circuits and appointing preachers to serve in areas experiencing population expansion. The primary architect of Methodism's growth was Bishop Francis Asbury (1745–1816), who retained sole power of appointment during his lifetime. He possessed remarkable organizational ability and an almost prophetic ability to predict population growth. Asbury orchestrated the establishment of circuits in the Western Conference and made the critical decision to roll back efforts in New England because of the strong presence of Congregationalists. As a Methodist society or mission gained success and stabilized, Asbury and his lieutenants oversaw the establishment of additional circuits in distant regions. Even after Asbury's death in 1816, Methodists continued to succeed in planting churches and societies where population migration was expected. Methodists established societies in Dakota, months before the Dakota Territory was created, and in California shortly after the gold rush began.[5]

Evangelical groups also refined the revival techniques used during the First Great Awakening. In particular, the camp meeting revival was an important tool for helping evangelicals gain popularity and widespread acceptance. These large outdoor revivals normally lasted multiple days and served as important religious and social events. They brought together disparate parts of the population. Camp meetings were carefully planned. They usually occurred after the harvest season when people could be away from their homes and farms. Camp meetings were widely advertised by flyers and through congregations. The primary goal of camp meetings was to make converts. Preachers implored their listeners to turn from their sinfulness and embrace Christ as Redeemer. Lay exhorters shared their personal testimonies of redemption. Potential converts were encouraged to sit on "mourners' benches," where they would receive special instruction. Singing occurred throughout the meetings, ranging from popular hymns written by figures such as Isaac Watts and Charles Wesley to pieces worship leaders composed extemporaneously.[6]

The first camp meetings in America were conducted in Kentucky under the leadership of Presbyterian preacher James McGready. After arriving in Kentucky in 1796, McGready began holding protracted worship services for his three Logan County congregations that concluded with Communion; these meetings were inspired by the outdoor Communion services conducted among Presbyterians in Scotland. During the summer of 1800, McGready invited local Methodist and Presbyterian preachers to assist him at one service. They included Methodist John McGee and his Presbyterian brother William McGee. The preaching of the McGee brothers inspired widespread weeping, fainting, and emotional ecstasy throughout the congregation. John McGee later recalled that "screams for mercy pierced the heaven, and mercy came down."[7] In the following months, thousands of people began attending the joint services, many of whom decided to camp at the meeting site. In the following years, similar revivals spread throughout much of the nation.

The most popular evangelical revivalist of the nineteenth century was Charles Finney. Shortly after being ordained as a Presbyterian minister in 1824, Finney began conducting his own revival meetings in western New York and the surrounding region. Finney was a skilled orator, a talented musician, and remarkably effective at working a crowd into religious frenzy. His most famous revival was held in Rochester in 1830-31. Between September 10 and March 6, most of the city's residents attended Finney's revivals. Businesses closed so customers and employees could hear Finney preach.[8]

Finney was also an avid student of revivalist methods. He adapted many of the revival techniques used by Methodists on the western frontier. After joining the faculty of Oberlin College in 1835, Finney began writing and teaching about the proper methodology for conducting revivals. He insisted that revivals were not just spontaneous works of God but that they could be generated by using distinct techniques with predictable results. These "new measures," as he called them, included conducting revivals over multiple days, using everyday language in prayer, employing powerful gestures and colorful language while preaching, allowing women publicly to pray and exhort at revivals, praying for sinners by name, and making use of the mourners' bench.[9] Clearly influenced by Methodism, Finney opposed teachings of Calvinism he believed inconsistent with biblical principles. Most importantly, he believed human volition played a role in the salvation process. He rejected the claim that God's grace is irresistible in the process of salvation.

Finney's popularization of techniques used in revivals on the western frontier contributed to the further growth of evangelical Protestantism throughout the country.

Due to evangelical success in making converts, by the middle of the nineteenth century evangelical denominations emerged as the largest religious groups in the United States. Methodists enjoyed the greatest success. By 1850, 34 percent of all persons claiming church affiliation identified as some form of Methodist. Roughly one out of every fifteen Americans belonged to a Methodist church. Baptists were close behind, claiming as many as 967,000 adherents. Presbyterians, who divided over the use of revival techniques, also grew dramatically in the nineteenth century.[10]

The nineteenth-century revivals irrevocably changed evangelicalism. No longer on the periphery of American society, Methodists, Baptists, and Presbyterians emerged as the nation's quintessential religious bodies. As wealth and industry increased during the first half of the nineteenth century, evangelical denominations became more established and middle class. Evangelical churches directly contributed to helping their members become more socially and economically mobile. Churches contributed to the education of their members. In some areas, such as

Rochester, New York, wealthy members established savings banks and provided small business loans for less affluent church members.[11] By the time of the American Civil War, the robust revivalism that had spurred the growth of the evangelical denominations had declined and was generally viewed by many as a relic of the previous era.

As evangelical denominations grew in size, so, too, did their focus on addressing social problems. Many converts from early nineteenth-century evangelical revivals embraced the idea of volunteerism. Laity as well as clergy played strategic roles in spreading Christian principles throughout the nation. Volunteer associations or benevolent societies, whether associated with a denomination or independent, were largely comprised of clergy and laity from evangelical groups. They were formed to promote the distribution of religious tracts, and home and foreign missions. In addition, many of these voluntary associations were committed to efforts at social betterment. In the nineteenth century, societies committed to causes such as temperance, Sabbatarianism (enforcing rules governing Sabbath activity), abolition, and antipoverty proliferated. Participation rates were incredibly high. For example, in New York City alone, by 1860 nearly half of all males were involved in one of these societies.[12]

Women played a vital role in the voluntary associations, as well as in almost every aspect of leadership in evangelical denominations. During the early nineteenth-century evangelical revival, women had frequently served as lay exhorters, class leaders, and even preachers. But in the mid-nineteenth century, as the evangelical bodies grew wealthier and more established, women in major denominations were increasingly barred from serving in preaching and other visible leadership roles. Voluntary associations were one of the few places where women could exercise public leadership. They took advantage of their opportunity by using voluntary associations to launch crusades against many social injustices and to fight for women's suffrage. Many of the nation's most formidable female leaders, including Sojourner Truth,

Anna Howard Shaw, Harriet Beecher Stowe, and Frances Willard, first gained prominence in evangelical denominations.[13]

Evangelical leaders and denominations also worked at improving education. They started Sunday schools in the 1790s to provide children with basic religious instruction and to teach literacy. Prior to introduction of mandatory state education after the Civil War, Sunday schools were incredibly popular and important for educating American children. During the mid-nineteenth century, American evangelicals also built numerous colleges to promote education, including schools now known as Emory University, Duke University, Brown University, Vanderbilt University, Northwestern University, Temple University, and Wake Forest University. Evangelicals also founded many of the most important hospitals in the United States.

RESPONSES TO MODERNITY: 1870-1945

Urbanization, immigration, and advances in the natural sciences challenged the theological outlook and popularity of the major evangelical denominations after the American Civil War. By the early twentieth century, evangelical bodies that had held cultural power during the previous century became deeply divided over how best to respond to the new developments.

During the first half of the nineteenth century, the majority of the US population was agrarian, living in small villages and towns. Most people in small, close-knit communities attended or at least had family ties to one of the evangelical Protestant congregations. These churches were integral parts of towns and villages. They provided religious sustenance and core rituals important for community cohesion, including conducting weddings and funerals.

After the Civil War, the population began to shift to large urban areas. Between 1860 and 1900, Americans living in cities increased from approximately 17 percent to 40 percent of the population. Philadelphia and Chicago grew to over a million people each, with New York City exceeding two million. Expansion of transportation networks, especially railroads and steamboats, contributed to creating large nationwide markets that connected previously isolated communities. Factories appeared in large cities to capitalize on increased market demands. Americans migrated to cities in order to take advantage of expanding employment opportunities.

The demographic transformation proved detrimental to the growth and cultural dominance of evangelical Protestantism. It was less successful in large urban areas than it had been in small towns and rural communities. Cities lacked the intimacy of villages and towns. The major Protestant denominations were also overwhelmingly middle class during this period, whereas the jobs propelling urban growth paid very little. Factories filled their employment needs with immigrant workers from countries such as Ireland and Italy, whose wages were minimal. These predominantly Roman Catholic immigrants provoked dramatic religious diversification in major urban areas. Between 1860 and 1900 the country's Roman Catholic population grew from three million to twelve million, dramatically outpacing the growth of Protestant bodies. Roman Catholic immigrants represented moral and theological sensibilities not common to evangelical Protestants. For instance, Roman Catholics had fewer scruples about dancing, alcohol, and working on Sunday. Most Protestant denominations lacked an infrastructure equipped to reach the diverse working-class population—immigrant laborers and African-Americans migrating from southern states.[14]

In addition to the challenges posed by shifting demographics in American culture, evangelical Protestants also saw much of their theological worldview challenged by advances in modern science and increased secularization in higher education. Divisions about how to react to these challenges irrevocably splintered the early nineteenth-century evangelical Protestant consensus. At midcentury, there was much agreement between what was taught in school classrooms and in local congregations. This made sense because most of the faculty and administration at major American colleges were church members or clergy from prominent evangelical denominations. However, by the end of the century, American colleges began to imitate German research universities, which emphasized academic freedom, rational inquiry, and the natural sciences.

Evangelical Protestants found their worldviews directly challenged by ideas infiltrating American intellectual circles. One such challenge was Sigmund Freud's theory of the unconscious; he taught that human beings are motivated by primal instincts as opposed to personal volition. Another challenge was posed by Charles Lyell's popularization of uniformitarianism, which is the idea that features of the earth's surface had been altered by uniform natural processes occurring over billions of years. Many Protestants were troubled that little effort was made by academics to reconcile such new theories with Scripture.

The theory that most deeply troubled many evangelical Protestants was biological evolution. In his 1859 book *On the Origin of Species*, Charles Darwin asserted that all organisms change over time by inheriting variations that allow them to survive through the process of natural selection. Protestants were divided over how best to react to Darwinism. Most liberals believed the essence of Christianity was compatible with Darwin's theory, while conservatives mostly insisted that Darwin's claims were in conflict with the biblical account of creation and historic Christian faith. Arguments about how to react to Darwinism and other theories in the natural sciences played a critical role in dividing evangelical Protestants into conservative and liberal camps.

Liberal Protestants accepted evolution and other scientific theories as being part of God's design. Henry Ward Beecher, probably the best-known evangelical Protestant preacher of the mid-nineteenth century, epitomized liberal accommodation to modern science. He called for study of the natural sciences in higher education and warned against Christians allowing the "intelligent part of society" to go past them.[15] He even suggested that God ordained advances in the sciences and insisted the "providence of God is rolling forward a spirit of investigation that Christian ministers must meet and join."[16] Beecher and many other liberal Christians believed the Christian faith, like nature, evolved over time.

Rather than focusing on a literal understanding of Scripture, liberals emphasized the ethical teachings of Christ. They downplayed the miraculous and placed special emphasis upon religious feeling, or the notion that the heart can *intuit* certain religious truths.

Most conservative Christians rejected Darwinism and other theories that contradicted literal readings of Scripture. Charles Hodge (1797–1878), a Presbyterian theologian on the faculty of Princeton Theological Seminary, typified the conservative response. He answered the question posed by his book *What Is Darwinism?* by saying, "It is Atheism."[17] The basic position held by Hodge and others was that the Bible is the supreme source of authority and, as originally inspired by the Holy Spirit, is completely free of any kind of error. Any scientific theory that contradicts Scripture must, therefore, be erroneous.

Insistence on biblical inerrancy, along with criticism of how liberal Protestants had accommodated Christian faith to modernity, created controversy in most major denominations during the early twentieth century. Heresy trials of seminary professors and contests for control of theological schools were fairly common.[18]

By 1918, many conservative Protestants mobilized to combat liberal theology and modern science if it conflicted with Christian doctrine. Support for biblical inerrancy, the substitutionary theory of Christ's atonement, Jesus's virgin birth, and an outright rejection of modernity when it was at odds with historic Christian doctrine galvanized Bible conferences. This was particularly true of the Niagara Bible Conferences held between 1876 and 1897 and in the ministry of revivalists such as Dwight L. Moody and Billy Sunday. Conservative teachings were also promoted through widespread distribution of *The Fundamentals: A Testimony to the Truth*, a collection of ninety essays published in twelve volumes by the Bible Institute of Los Angeles. The essays focused on core doctrines defended by conservative Christians. They condemned liberal theological emphases and attacked many other ideas believed to be heretical. Approximately three million volumes of *The Fundamentals* were distributed free of charge to Christian leaders throughout the world.[19]

Postmillennial dispensationalism (belief that Jesus will return *after* a thousand years of God's righteous reign upon the earth) was popular among American Protestants until the early twentieth century. It was based on a belief that society and humans are constantly improving and would eventually become Christian. But as conservative Christians became convinced that civilization was regressing and not showing signs of moral improvement, premillennialism (Christ will return *before* the thousand years) emerged as the more compelling position. Premillennialism was also promoted by teachings on "biblical prophecy" developed by English Pietist John Nelson Darby (1800–1882). Darby taught that history is composed of seven dispensations or eras. During each one, God has provided a different plan of salvation. In each instance, humans have failed to comply with God's plan. We are now living in the sixth dispensation—the age of grace—which will end with Christ's second coming and the great tribulation. The seventh age will be a millennial reign of Christ upon the earth.[20] Darby's teachings were widely promoted in Bible conferences and churches, and through the influential *Scofield Reference Bible*, first published in 1909.[21]

Popularly labeled "fundamentalists," in the 1920s these conservative Protestants fought the growth of liberalism in many major northern denominations, including the Northern Baptist Convention, the Presbyterian Church in the United States of America, and the Disciples of Christ. Princeton Theological Seminary professor J. Gresham Machen's 1923 book *Christianity and Liberalism* typified the fundamentalist critique of modernists. He argued that any understanding of Christianity that does not include belief that Christ died on the cross for humanity's sins is not Christian at all. Liberals and many Christian moderates criticized fundamentalists for their intolerance and militancy.[22]

Fundamentalism suffered a major setback following the infamous 1925 Scopes "Monkey" Trial in Dayton, Tennessee. Fundamentalists had been successful in passing legislation in almost half of the country's state legislatures. It outlawed teaching Darwinian evolution in public schools. The American Civil Liberties Union (ACLU) convinced John Scopes, a new teacher in Dayton, to challenge the Tennessee law. After Scopes was charged with a misdemeanor for teaching evolution, the ACLU secured the services of Clarence Darrow, perhaps the most famous trial lawyer in the country, to defend him. William Jennings Bryan, a former US secretary of state and candidate for the US presidency, assembled a team of lawyers to act as the prosecution. Bryan was famous for his antievolutionist views; his opposition grew partly from a deep fear of what would happen if the principle of natural selection were to be socially applied.

The high-profile trial was covered by most major American and international news outlets. The atmosphere outside the courthouse was almost circus-like. There were monkey-themed souvenirs, and refreshments were sold. Bryan made a critical misstep and allowed the shrewd Darrow to cross-examine him for nearly two hours. At a critical point Bryan conceded that the words of the Bible should not always be taken literally (e.g., Joshua making the sun stand still [Josh. 10:13]).[23] While Bryan successfully argued that Scopes had violated Tennessee law, the press portrayed fundamentalists as foolish. Fundamentalists subsequently lost considerable national standing.

Fundamentalism never captivated all conservative evangelicals. At least initially, it failed to gain very much ground in the South, partly because most types of Southern Christianity were already fairly conservative. Despite attempts made by Harold P. Sloan and his Methodist League for Faith and Life during the General Conferences of the 1920s, fundamentalism was never particularly popular in the Methodist Episcopal Church.[24] This didn't mean Methodists were unified on how best to respond to modernity.

The late nineteenth-century holiness movement, which began in part as a conservative critique of Methodism, represents a second and distinct strand of modern evangelicalism. It reacted against the accommodation to secular culture by Methodists and other major Protestant groups. Most of its early leaders were Methodists who believed Methodism, in pursuit of social respectability, had strayed too far from its founding principles. B. T. Roberts (1823-93), who founded the Free Methodist Church in 1860, insisted that the MEC was dominated by "a class of preachers whose teachings are very different from that of the fathers of Methodism."[25] Roberts charged that they had embraced "liberalism" and reduced Christianity to charitable work. Methodist leaders had exchanged the revivalism for which Methodists were once famous for the "patronage of the worldly."[26]

Holiness leaders also were critical of moral decline in the church. They condemned dancing and alcohol, advocated a return to plain dress, and emphasized strict standards of personal conduct. Theologically, the heart of holiness theology was the doctrine of entire sanctification, or the belief that after a believer's conversion there remained a second "work of grace" that cleanses from original sin and gives victory over sin. Phoebe Palmer (1807-74) popularized this doctrine and experience during her famous Tuesday Meetings for the Promotion of Holiness. The meetings were conducted weekly in New York City during the decades prior to the Civil War. They attracted hundreds of male and female participants from many denominations.[27] Palmer promoted holiness theology through her preaching and written work, which included her popular magazine, *The Guide to Christian Perfection* (later renamed *The Guide to Holiness*).

The National Camp Meeting Association for the Promotion of Christian Holiness (later called National Holiness Association) was organized in 1867 by disaffected Methodist ministers. Its purpose was to advance the doctrine and experience of entire sanctification and to revitalize the practice of camp meeting revivalism. During the 1870s and 1880s the association gained considerable influence in Methodist circles. In the North Georgia Conference alone, two hundred of the three hundred ministers claimed to have experienced the "second blessing."

However, by the end of the nineteenth century, prominent Methodist leaders were routinely criticizing core beliefs of the holiness movement. To limit its influence, holiness preachers were being relegated to small and rural circuits. Reacting to such disenfranchisement, dozens of independent denominations were formed.[28] The holiness movement eventually included a large number of conservative Methodists as well as new denominations. Holiness denominations were distinctive for aiding the poor and allowing women to serve as ordained ministers. The Church of the Nazarene was likely the most important of the new holiness denominations. It originated in Los Angeles in 1895 under the ministry of Phineas F. Bresee (1838–1915), a former prominent Methodist minister.[29]

The holiness movement played a crucial role in shaping the largest evangelical movement of the twentieth century, Pentecostalism. Significant holiness leaders started calling for a "new Pentecost" in the 1890s. Under the leadership of figures such as A. J. Tomlinson, John Alexander Dowie, and Joseph Smale, divine healing and increased religious enthusiasm began to appear in radical segments of the holiness revivals. In the British holiness revivals, glossolalia (spontaneously speaking in languages not known by the speaker) became a regular occurrence.[30]

Pentecostalism first achieved national prominence during the 1906 Azusa Street revival in Los Angeles. William Joseph Seymour (1870–1922) was the leader. He was an African-American holiness preacher from Louisiana who believed the gift of speaking in tongues was consistent with biblical teaching. It was a sign of receiving the Holy Spirit. In April 1906, Seymour's small black holiness congregation moved from a worshipper's home on Bonnie Brae Street to a dilapidated former African Methodist Episcopal Church building located at 312 Azusa Street. This was an impoverished part of downtown Los Angeles. For the next three years, a revival that attracted people of many nationalities and social classes raged on in the church. Speaking and singing in tongues, falling into trances, weeping, and dancing were all regular parts of the revival. Seymour taught that believers could receive a

Pentecostal baptism (a "third blessing") following entire sanctification. Believers were to evidence the Pentecostal baptism by exhibiting gifts of the Spirit such as speaking in tongues and divine healing. Reports published in local newspapers and the church's newsletter, *The Apostolic Faith*, lauded the revival as a second Pentecost in the "American Jerusalem."[31] Many pilgrims who traveled to Azusa Street to experience revival helped spread Pentecostalism throughout the nation.

Charles Fox Parham (1873–1929), Seymour's teacher, helped popularize the practice of speaking in tongues. During a New Year's Eve watch-night service at Parham's Topeka, Kansas, Bethel Bible College (founded 1900), Agnes Ozman, a student, began "speaking in the Chinese language." In the following days, the other students and Parham himself experienced the gift of speaking in tongues. Parham spent much of the next several years traveling, teaching, and preaching about this experience. Eventually Parham became quite critical of the Azusa Street revival. Many early holiness leaders shared his criticism. They found Pentecostals too extreme in their religious enthusiasm. Alma White (1862–1946), founder of the Pillar of Fire Church in Denver, referred to Pentecostalism as an "invention of Satan."[32] Such opposition did little to quell the Azusa Street revival. Many Christians viewed Azusa Street as the hoped for "day of Pentecost." Several of the Southern holiness denominations, including the Church of God in Christ, the Church of God in Cleveland, Tennessee, and the Pentecostal Holiness Church, aligned with the new Pentecostal movement.[33]

Fundamentalism and the holiness-Pentecostal tradition represented complementary critiques of modernism in the late nineteenth and early twentieth centuries. Fundamentalism was largely a theological attack levied by conservative intellectuals in the Reformed traditions against liberals thought to be sacrificing the power and authority of Scripture. Their charge was that liberals were bowing to accommodate modern science. While not substantially disagreeing with the fundamentalists on these matters, the holiness and Pentecostal movements lodged a populist critique against the growing elitism, moral lapses, and formalism of Protestantism, especially as found in Methodism.

These groups reasserted the supernatural power of God in the world. They reclaimed the enthusiasm of the camp meeting revival traditions and stressed the importance of moral purity.

EMERGENCE OF NEOEVANGELICALISM: 1942 FORWARD

By the mid-twentieth century, evangelicals had fully integrated into most aspects of American society and, in fact, were vital parts of most major Christian denominations. Fearing a decline in morality and growing secularization, Americans flocked to evangelical churches and leaders. Evangelicals evidenced their prominence by participating in and influencing the nation's political processes.

In the 1940s, conservative Christians who were dissatisfied with the militancy and separatism of fundamentalism made overtures to create a neoevangelical movement that would maintain an emphasis on the "fundamentals" of Christian faith, while reengaging society more creatively. In 1942 the National Association of Evangelicals was established to promote this vision and bring together conservative Christians from many denominations. The publication of Carl F. H. Henry's *The Uneasy Conscience of Modern Fundamentalism*, which cautioned against separatism, and the founding of Fuller Theological Seminary in 1947 were also significant steps in forming a neoevangelical community.[34]

The most important spokesperson for this neoevangelicalism was evangelist Billy Graham (1918–). The son of a North Carolina dairy farmer, Graham early rejected some parts of his fundamentalist upbringing. In its place, he maintained that evangelicals should engage all Christians. A gifted orator, Graham became the most popular revivalist of the twentieth century. Between 1947 and 2010 he and his Billy Graham Evangelistic Team, an arm of the Billy Graham Evangelistic Association (BGEA), launched more than four hundred "crusades" in 185 countries. The BGEA estimates that 3.2 million people were converted through these initiatives. Graham's decision to cooperate with

New York's ministerial alliance during his 1957 revival in Madison Square Garden led to his final break with fundamentalists.[35]

Graham was more than a well-known revivalist; he was also one of the biggest celebrities in the United States during much of his life. He and his team were remarkably innovative in their use of new media such as radio, television, and film. He reached millions through his *Hour of Decision* radio program, wrote My Answer—a daily syndicated newspaper column—and even opened a motion picture division of the Billy Graham Evangelistic Association. Graham's celebrity status helped earn him the audience of leading politicians, including each president from Harry Truman to Barack Obama. Graham had close relationships with Richard Nixon and Lyndon Johnson.

Partially because of Graham's influence, by the middle of the twentieth century, neoevangelicalism had prominently entered the social mainstream. Parachurch organizations such as Young Life and Inter-Varsity Christian Fellowship met with wide success in their efforts to reach high school and university students. Evangelical seminaries such as Gordon-Conwell Theological Seminary, Trinity Evangelical Divinity School, Fuller Theological Seminary, and Asbury Theological Seminary attracted many students training for ministry in mainline and evangelical denominations. Evangelical journals such as *Christianity Today*, *Christian Life*, and *Eternity* were widely consumed in America and beyond. In the United Methodist Church, Charles Keysor launched the magazine *Good News* to strike back against liberalism in his denomination.[36] Similar efforts were made in other mainline denominations.

In the 1950s, Pentecostalism significantly entered the mainstream. The post-World War II economic boom helped Pentecostals become more middle class, which in turn gave them greater social respectability and financial resources to build large congregations. During this period many Christians in mainline denominations such as the Episcopal Church experienced speaking in tongues and other gifts of the Spirit. These Christians were referred to as charismatics (from the Greek word *charisma* [gift]).

Although many figures in the charismatic movement such as Jim Bakker, Oral Roberts, Pat Robertson, and Jimmy Swaggart were disgraced by personal and financial scandals, they played a vital role in popularizing Pentecostalism in the United States and elsewhere.[37]

By the last quarter of the twentieth century, evangelicalism in North America was thriving. *Newsweek* even proclaimed 1976 "The Year of the Evangelical." Nevertheless, in spite of evangelical numeric and financial success, there was little unity among evangelicals. Pentecostal denominations, which differed greatly among themselves, embraced a level of religious enthusiasm and an emphasis on the supernatural that made most other evangelicals uncomfortable. While holiness and Pentecostal bodies continued to emphasize charitable action, they moved toward the evangelical mainstream on modern science and secularization. They remained more strongly opposed to tobacco, social dancing, and popular entertainment than some other evangelicals. Fundamentalist bodies continued their militancy against the theory of evolution. Even in the Southern Baptist Convention, beginning in the 1970s, fundamentalists succeeded in removing more moderate Baptists from positions of leadership in convention-owned universities, seminaries, and missionary efforts.

Then, beginning in the late 1970s, substantial segments of the evangelical community put aside their differences to rally around national social issues. By then, fundamentalists, neoevangelicals, Pentecostals, and holiness believers shared increasing concerns about growing secularization and moral decline in the nation. In the 1960s they organized against sex education in the public schools. But it was the 1980 presidential election that thrust them into national politics and made them a core constituency of the Republican Party. While many evangelicals had supported the self-professed born-again Christian Jimmy Carter in 1976, the new religious right actively mobilized to support former California governor Ronald Reagan. Reagan voiced admiration for literal readings of the Bible and supported key evangelical interests such as opposition to abortion and the Equal Rights Amendment.[38]

At first, the most important segment of the new religious right was the Moral Majority, led by Rev. Jerry Falwell, a Baptist minister well known in evangelical circles for his nationally syndicated radio program, *Old Time Gospel Hour* (first aired 1956). In 1971, Falwell founded Lynchburg Baptist College (now Liberty University) in Lynchburg, Virginia. The Moral Majority was enormously successful during the Reagan era. It raised hundreds of millions of dollars and exercised significant political power, particularly in the South.

Pat Robertson has probably had a more lasting impact on American politics than Jerry Falwell. Robertson grew popular through his work in television. In 1960 he founded the Christian Broadcasting Network (CBN) and became famous for hosting *The 700 Club*, which has remained in production since 1966. Today CBN is viewed in more than 180 countries. It has given Robertson a platform for promoting charismatic Christianity and socially conservative politics. After a failed bid in 1988 to win the Republican presidential nomination, Robertson founded the Christian Coalition (now called the Christian Coalition of America), which continues to be the most important evangelical political activist group in the country.[39]

Combined conservative political efforts by American evangelicals are now better known as the Christian right instead of the new religious right.[40] Although the Christian right remains controversial among evangelicals, it has successfully injected certain social issues into American political discourse. And it has mobilized the evangelical community as active participants in American politics.

As influential as the Christian right has become, it has never been embraced by all American evangelicals. Some influential members of the evangelical community who identify with some socially progressive political goals have harshly attacked the movement. One of the best known evangelical critics is Jim Wallis, who first began identifying with socially progressive political efforts during the late 1960s civil rights and antiwar movements.[41] His *Sojourners* magazine (originally the *Post-American*) has since 1971 been an important outlet for the evangelical left. Many religious leaders in minority communities are reluctant to identify as "evangelical" because of how the term has often been politicized.

Today, in North America the term "evangelical" is largely used to refer to a loose coalition of conservative Protestant Christians, spread among various denominations. They emphasize the authority of Scripture, the saving work of Jesus Christ, the importance of personal conversion, and the doctrine of the Trinity. They generally agree, though by no means uniformly, on social issues such as abortion, protection of religious freedom against state interference, prayer in public schools, and same-gender marriage.

Despite a decline in cultural prominence, evangelicalism remains vibrant and influential in the United States. Questions remain, however, about how evangelicals will respond to changing demographics in American culture. The most important challenge currently facing American evangelicals is how faithfully and creatively they will proclaim and live out the good news of the inaugurated kingdom of God.

For Further Study

Dayton, Donald W., and Robert K. Johnston, eds. *The Variety of American Evangelicalism*. Eugene, OR: Wipf and Stock, 1997.

Dayton, Donald W., with Douglas M. Strong. *Rediscovering an Evangelical Heritage: A Tradition and Trajectory of Integrating Piety and Justice*. 2nd ed. Grand Rapids: Baker Academic, 2014.

Marsden, George M. *Understanding Fundamentalism and Evangelicalism*. Grand Rapids: Eerdmans, 1991.

Miller, Steven P. *The Age of Evangelicalism: America's Born-Again Years*. New York: Oxford University Press, 2014.

Smith, Gordon T. *Evangelical, Sacramental, and Pentecostal: Why the Church Should Be All Three*. Downers Grove, IL: IVP Academic, 2017.

Sweeney, Douglas A. *The American Evangelical Story: A History of the Movement*. Grand Rapids: Baker Academic, 2005.

Synan, Vinson. *The Holiness-Pentecostal Tradition: Charismatic Movements in the Twentieth Century*. Grand Rapids: Eerdmans, 1997.

Wacker, Grant. *America's Pastor: Billy Graham and the Shaping of a Nation*. Cambridge, MA: Belknap Press, 2014.

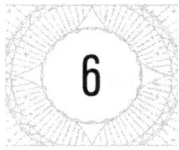

6

EVANGELICALS AND CONTEMPORARY SCIENCE

J. B. (JIM) STUMP

EVANGELICALS have a curious relationship with science. On the one hand, they seem to value science as much as the general population. Among white evangelicals surveyed by the Pew Research Center in 2009, 83 percent said science has had a mostly positive effect on society.[1] This compares similarly to the general US population, 84 percent of whom gave the same answer. Furthermore, in 2015 Pew found white evangelicals are far less likely to believe that science and religion conflict than do nonreligious Americans (45 percent to 76 percent).[2]

On the other hand, evangelicals do not seem to trust the conclusions reached by the overwhelming majority of scientists in the fields of cosmology and biology. When asked whether they accept the big bang as a scientific explanation for the origin of the universe, 99.9 percent of scientists said yes; only 27 percent of white evangelicals said yes. When asked whether humans have evolved, 99 percent of scientists working in the fields of biology and medicine said yes; only 23 percent of white evangelicals said yes.[3]

How are we supposed to interpret these statistics? Perhaps evangelicals report a low level of conflict between science and religion because they have their own version of science. It is easier to believe that the entire scientific establishment is wrong than that some elements of what we believe about the Christian faith are incorrect. So a parallel universe of "true" science opposed to a supposed false and biased scientific mainstream emerges. That strategy allows many evangelicals to say they love science while rejecting scientists' overwhelming conclusions about cosmology and biology.

In this chapter we will explore why evangelicals are often at odds with contemporary science. We will next offer evangelicals a model that not only permits respect for mainstream science but also holds fast to evangelical faith.

SOLA SCRIPTURA (BY SCRIPTURE ALONE)

It might seem strange that many evangelicals would not accept important parts of what the experts in mainstream science claim. That attitude partly derives from the sixteenth-century Protestant Reformation and from political revolutions of subsequent centuries. Concerning the latter, revolutions favoring democracy held that each citizen gets a vote and that each vote counts the same—no matter how informed or misinformed a voter might be. Buttressing that, the Reformation was founded on the principles of the priesthood of all believers and *sola Scriptura*.[4] Popularly understood, this means we don't need a professional class of priests to intercede or interpret the Bible for us; believers can do that for themselves.

The doctrine of *sola Scriptura* counteracted corruptions in the church and its claims to be as authoritative as Scripture itself. The Reformers thought that placing the ultimate authority in one source—unchanging Scripture—was the antidote to the shifting personalities of those who held power in the church. But for Scripture to have this authority, its meaning must be reasonably clear to its readers.

From the time of the church fathers there had been a multifaceted approach to interpreting Scripture. In addition to the literal meaning, allegorical, spiritual, and moral senses were employed. The last three proved to be more ambiguous and subject to individual interpretation. So the literal sense was emphasized by the Reformers. Even so, Scripture is not always clear, as is evident in continued disagreements about the meaning of the Lord's Supper and the proper mode of baptism. What began as a clear principle for uniting Protestants quickly became divisive when applied. Martin Luther's understanding of the Eucharist was challenged by Huldrych Zwingli and John Calvin. In turn, their interpretations were challenged by the Anabaptists, and so on. At last count, the number of Christian denominations worldwide exceeds thirty-three thousand.[5]

The democratized approach to Scripture seems to have conditioned evangelicals to adopt the same attitude toward science: Accept only those conclusions of science that are consistent with your other beliefs. If you don't like how the professionals interpret evidence for biological evolution or the big bang (or climate change or vaccines), then launch a version that explains things to your satisfaction.

In one sense, the democratized disposition toward science initially boosted scientific inquiry. Where names of plant and animal species appear in Scripture, translators wanted to know exactly what they referred to. Translators in the Middle Ages had been content to transliterate the names. But with the increased emphasis upon a text's precise meaning, Renaissance translators paid attention to biblical descriptions and turned to the natural world to identify plant and animal species.[6]

However, this engagement with the natural order came at a price. Were the descriptions of natural processes in the Bible at odds with emerging scientific descriptions? That set the stage not only for potential conflict but also for harmonizing Scripture with what we find in the natural order.

TWO BOOKS: A STEP IN THE RIGHT DIRECTION?

When we are confronted with fellow believers who in the name of Christian doctrine deny the clear findings of science, scientists who are evangelicals customarily remind us that the Bible is not a scientific textbook. They point to careful scholarly work on the languages and contexts in which Scripture was written. For example, they show why the creation accounts in Genesis 1–3 were not meant to provide scientific information about the material origins of the world.[7] Then they note that God has given another source of information for knowing the process by which he created the world. We should look to the created world itself when seeking answers for scientific questions.[8] This distinction is the source of the "two books" metaphor. That is, God has provided information or revelation through two different but coordinated sources—what God has said in Scripture and what he has said and done in nature—and we must carefully pay attention to these two sources or "books."

Many evangelicals, rooted in the Protestant doctrine of *sola Scriptura*, have adopted the "two books" metaphor for reconciling their faith with the claims of contemporary science. But often they have not adequately reflected on the tension between affirming "Scripture alone" and accepting the idea that God has revealed himself in "two books." Careful examination of the metaphor should promote some caution and perhaps even qualification of its acceptance.

First, the "two books" metaphor is not new. It extends back to the times of Justin Martyr (ca. 100–ca. 165), Irenaeus of Lyons (ca. 130–ca. 202), Tertullian (ca. 160–ca. 220), and Origen (ca. 185–ca. 254). In addition to revelation in Scripture, they acknowledged God's revelation in nature. The first clear use of the metaphor seems to be in the work of John Chrysostom (ca. 347–407):

> If God had given instruction by means of books, and of letters, he who knew letters would have learned what was written; but the illiterate man would have gone away without receiving any benefit. ... This however cannot be said with respect to the heavens; but the

Scythian, and Barbarian, and Indian, and Egyptian, and every man that walks upon the earth, shall hear this voice; for not by means of the ears, but through the sight, it reaches our understanding. . . . Upon this volume the unlearned, as well as the wise man, shall be alike able to look . . . and wherever any one may chance to come, there looking upwards towards the heavens, he will receive a sufficient lesson from the view of them.[9]

This seems entirely consistent with Paul's words in Romans 1:19-20, where he argues that God has made himself known through the created order. Those who were not privy to God's revelation through Scripture were still without excuse for not knowing about God. But notice that Paul's book of nature seems to have nothing to do with what we call modern scientific knowledge. Instead, he is talking about *knowledge of God*. Psalm 19 says "the heavens declare the glory of God" (NIV), not some specific scientific claim such as the big bang theory or how stars are formed.

Then at some point the metaphor took on a different meaning. Originally, access to Scripture was limited to the educated, but the book of nature was open to everyone. As literacy rates increased in Western Europe, and as the Bible was translated into the vernacular (one consequence of the Reformation), access to divine revelation in Scripture expanded. Ironically, at the same time, knowledge of the natural world was becoming more specialized; scientific knowledge became more and more the domain of a select class of "priests."

By the time of Francis Bacon (1561–1626) at the dawn of the scientific revolution, we find a changed account of the two books:

To conclude, therefore, let no man upon a weak conceit of sobriety or an ill-applied moderation think or maintain that a man can search too far, or be too well studied in the book of God's word, or in the book of God's works, divinity or philosophy [which includes natural philosophy, or what we call science]; but rather let men endeavor an endless progress or proficienc[y] in both; only let men beware that they apply both to charity, and not to swelling; to use, and not to ostentation; and again, that they do not unwisely mingle or confound these learnings together.[10]

The warning not to "unwisely mingle or confound" the information from these two sources suggests there is some danger of doing just that. The "two books" metaphor, which asserts one Author of both books, does not explain how the two are related. Among evangelicals who accept the findings of science, many recognize that the plain words of Scripture lead to the conclusion that the earth is only six thousand years old. These evangelicals reason that because God is the Author of both books, their messages must be consistent with each other. So when there appear to be conflicts, it must be an error in our interpretation of either nature or Scripture.

Perhaps we can appreciate a desire for the "two books" to agree with each other in all details. But forcing such an agreement errs in two ways.

First, saying that an author wrote two books doesn't require that she accomplish her purpose in the same way in both.[11] In the Chronicles of Narnia, C. S. Lewis fulfills his purpose the same way in each book. But when Frederick Buechner wrote his dictionary, *Wishful Thinking*, he fulfilled his purpose differently than in his fictional *Godric*. Similarly, it is a mistake to require that in the book of nature God must tell his story as Creator just as he does in Scripture, even though both books bear faithful witness to him. When the book of Genesis speaks of God creating the world, God's purpose is not to give a scientific account of how he accomplished this. To gain that knowledge, we must attentively turn to the book of nature.

But, someone might say, the book of Genesis also talks about God creating. Indeed it does. But rather than providing a book of nature, the purpose of Genesis is for God to tell us where the world fits into his loving covenant purposes, about what it means for humans to be given the important vocation of priestly stewardship in God's cosmic temple.

Old Testament scholar John H. Walton says that instead of primarily offering an explanation of origins, Genesis 1 is "offering a statement of how everything will work according to God's purposes."[12] In that sense Genesis looks to the future, and to our involvement in that future, rather than to the past.[13] New Testament theologian N. T. Wright agrees. The book of Genesis, and all sections of the Bible that deal with God as Creator, tell us how humans are supposed to "celebrate, worship, procreate, and take responsibility within the rich, vivid developing life of creation. According to Genesis, that is what humans were made for."[14] Walton notes that Genesis 1 actually describes how God was creating a temple in which he took up residence[15] and in which we are to engage in the work of worship by the quality of our stewardship.[16]

Both books—nature and Scripture—may be integrated into one overall story, but they are not the same. The uniqueness of each must be respected. As rich as the book of nature may be, it cannot successfully relay the covenant relationship God establishes with us and the rest of creation. On the other hand, Scripture does not explain—was not meant to explain—the scientific details of cosmic and human generation. Failing to recognize this critical distinction does a disservice to both books and to their single Author. Carefully respecting the distinction facilitates our worship of and service to God.

Second, the "two books" metaphor has conditioned us to view nature and Scripture as repositories of propositional revelation—rationally accessible information, written in books—that requires investigative work to uncover. It seems strange to think God intended to tell us about the Trinity and photosynthesis but did so in a way that took us hundreds or thousands of years to decipher those messages. Here is where the metaphor breaks down (as all metaphors eventually do). As Christians we believe God communicates to us through both nature and Scripture, but in neither case do we simply "read" propositions that came directly from God's "pen." The development of theories—both scientific and theological—is a longer and more complex process.

When both nature and Scripture are treated as sources of information, two dangers arise: *conflict* and *concordism*. A tempting response to these dangers is to completely separate science and theology—a view sometimes called *non-overlapping magisteria*. I'll discuss each of these briefly and then develop a more productive proposal for how science and theology should be related: *dialogue*.[17]

Conflict

The danger of conflict was thrust into the public consciousness by two books published toward the end of the nineteenth century: John William Draper's *History of the Conflict between Religion and Science* (1874) and Andrew Dickson White's *A History of the Warfare of Science with Theology in Christendom* (1896). These books set the tone for how the relationship between science and Christianity was treated in the first half of the twentieth century. That period was dominated by a philosophy known as positivism—that is, for an assertion to be rationally justified or potentially justifiable, it must be scientifically verified or capable of logical or mathematical verification. Conflict between science and religion became so deeply rooted in Western culture that even after the demise of positivism, it is still common to hear science and religion pitted against each other in warlike tones.

Draper's and White's historical analyses have been severely criticized by contemporary historians of science. They say Draper and White badly misrepresented the actual historical relationship between science and religion. But the rhetoric of warfare and sensationalized stories continue to play well in the broader culture. Popular media knows that controversy and conflict "sell." So when topics about science and religion come up, popular media dredges up historical episodes, such as Galileo's run-in with the church.

We almost inevitably perpetuate this conflict narrative when we treat the "two books" as equal sources of information about the material world. Treating the Bible as a source of information about nature— a source that can be interrogated in the same way scientists interrogate nature—assures conflict between science and the Bible. There are statements in the Bible that if taken as "revealed information" will conflict with mainstream science. For example, science has clearly established that the Earth is a sphere and is much older than the six thousand years some believe the Bible supports.[18] Our gastrointestinal organs are not the seat of emotions as the ancient Hebrews believed. And the mustard seed is not the smallest of all seeds as seemingly reported in the Gospels of Matthew and Mark. When these passages are taken as information about the natural world revealed by God, there is conflict with the sciences.

Many Christians, on the one hand, don't worry too much about the examples we've listed, since the theological implications are relatively minor. On the other hand, polling data shows that often when evangelicals find themselves in situations where science and Christian faith seem to offer conflicting answers to important questions, most will prefer their understanding of the Bible over the conclusions of the overwhelming majority of scientists. This unnecessary conflict is not healthy for Christian faith and not helpful for establishing the correct relationship between science and Christian faith.

Concordism

When attempting to resolve apparent conflicts between faith and science, an opposite danger is to force an integration of the two. Evangelicals take the Bible seriously and cannot just dismiss what it says. But when it is treated as the source of information about the natural order, some evangelicals believe it must be correlated with scientific findings. This is accomplished by identifying a passage of Scripture with a scientific theory. The effort is known as concordism. The term derives from "concord" and means a state of harmony.

Concordism seems to have originated with the old-earth creationist and Baptist theologian Bernard Ramm (1916-92). Ramm called his theory concordism because "it seeks a harmony of the geological record and the days of Genesis [by treating them] as long periods of time briefly summarizing geological history."[19] As an example of a concordist strategy today, consider Isaiah 40:22: "It is He who sits above the circle of the earth . . . who stretches out the heavens like a curtain"

(NKJV). Concordists say "circle of the earth" means the earth is a sphere. "Stretches out the heavens" means the universe is expanding. So according to concordists, the Bible is in harmony with modern cosmological science.

The problem with concordism is that to make the Bible agree with science, texts must be forced beyond their contextual meaning. Concordism's supposed "success" comes at considerable expense to the integrity of Scripture and to what evangelicals claim about its transparency.

Furthermore, the history of the relationship between science and the Christian faith reveals a serious danger in trying to align Christian doctrine with scientific theory. What happens when science changes its model because of new information and leaves the supposed concord behind? Then the Bible seems to have been invalidated.

A similar thing has happened in the "God of the gaps" approach to science. God as Creator was employed to "fill gaps" science supposedly could not fill, only to see him subsequently excluded as science closed one "gap" after another. Claiming that science has no possible explanation for the big bang again sets the stage for repeating the same error.

Non-Overlapping Magisteria

When we treat both Scripture and nature as sources of information about the natural order we inevitably end up with the errors associated with either conflict or concordism. One way to avoid this is to divide science and religion into two independent domains.

This approach was urged by evolutionary biologist Stephen Jay Gould (1941–2002). He coined the phrase "non-overlapping magisteria" or NOMA. The word "magisteria" comes from the Latin *magister*, meaning "teacher." Gould used the word as meaning "areas of teaching." He claimed the magisterium of science should be restricted to the empirical realm of facts, and the magisterium of religion should be restricted to matters of ultimate meaning and values. By observing this model, science and religion will not conflict, nor will we be tempted to combine them into a concordist whole, for the two domains or magisteria are different.

Gould's theory is sometimes presented simplistically, as though science and theology should have nothing to do with each other. But Gould recognized contact between the two magisteria while safeguarding their independence.[20] He cited two twentieth-century popes to show how the two magisteria should and should not relate to each other.

The first is the negative model: in 1950 Pope Pius XII issued the encyclical *Humani Generis*. In it he admitted that it may be permitted for scientists to investigate the origins of the human body along the lines suggested by evolution. But the Catholic faith obliges us to regard the human soul as an immediate creation by God. Furthermore, science cannot override the teaching of Scripture that all human beings are descended from a historical Adam. Pius allowed some room for scientific inquiry but made clear the church determines the space science is permitted.[21]

The second is the positive model for Gould. Pope John Paul II seemed to reverse the position of Pius XII. In his 1996 "Message to the Pontifical Academy of Sciences on Evolution" he acknowledged that since Pius's 1950 encyclical, the data for evolution had become impossible to ignore. He conceded that in some instances science can set the bounds for acceptable biblical interpretation by showing when some interpretations are incorrect. Gould interpreted John Paul's mandate as setting proper limits on biblical interpretation and theology and as carving out an independent sphere for science.

There is something to be said for NOMA. Most scientific research is done in isolation from Christian doctrine. Theology doesn't have much influence on how a scientist in the laboratory interprets his or her results on cancer research or superconductors. But when we come to topics such as the origin of the universe or of humans, evangelicals correctly believe Scripture and theology are important. But does this force a choice between conflict and concordism? No. There is a better option faithful to accepted standards of science and Christian doctrine. It avoids the errors associated with conflict and concordism.

TWO DIFFERENT WAYS FOR SEEING OR UNDERSTANDING

We've all seen the image that looks either like an old woman or like a young lady.[22] What the image "really is" is ambiguous. Depending on how one views the image, it can appear to be a young lady or an old woman. When the image appears to be an old woman, she has a pronounced nose and her left eye is open; when the image appears to be a young lady, the lines of the old woman's nose become the young lady's jawline and her eye becomes an ear.

Something similar to this is true of science and theology. They are best seen as different ways of looking at the world. Admittedly the old woman / young woman image is an imperfect model because both ways of seeing the picture yield a woman; a common vocabulary is in play (e.g., "ear" and "eye"). This is not true of science and theology because they do not use the same vocabulary. As such, they appeal to different realms of discourse. Still, the model can be helpful. For example, from the perspective of science, an event can be explained as the result of physical actions, which in turn resulted from prior actions. For example, saying yes to a proposal of marriage may have an explanation in physical terms, such as neuronal activity and brain chemistry. On the other hand, from the perspective of Christian doctrine we would explain the engagement differently. We would say two persons who love each other chose to begin a process (engagement) that would result in a Christian wedding having deep theological meaning. In this example, science provides the lenses for understanding the engagement from a physical perspective. But theology provides the lenses for understanding it as a choice made from deep Christian meaning. Neither of these tells the whole story; both are necessary. They are simply two different ways of understanding.

Philosopher Mary Midgley provides an illustration. She compares my two ways of understanding to our senses. An electrical discharge in the atmosphere might be explained as *vision* "seeing" a bolt of lightning and as *hearing* "listening to" a clap of thunder.[23] Vision and hearing are not observing two different events. They are deciphering an electrical charge in two different ways. We can't reduce or translate one of these to the other without losing something important about each.[24]

Bethany Sollereder also provides a helpful metaphor for science and theology. Both are "maps to reality."[25] A topographical map abstracts certain features from reality and represents them in a particular form. A heat map of the same space would do this very differently. Our knowledge is enriched by consulting both maps. Similarly, scientific theories are "maps" that abstract and represent certain features of reality; theology is a different kind of map. Their differences are complementary. They do not conflict with each other, nor can they be reduced to each other.

Or we can think of science and theology as styles of painting. Picasso's *Old Guitar Player* in his blue period of expressionism and *The Guitar Player* in the style of cubism are representations of the same thing (someone playing a guitar). But they look very different and could not be fused into one coherent image without breeching artistic integrity.

Analogously, a scientific description of the origin of human beings and a theological account of the same thing may look very different. But the differences don't count against the legitimacy of either. What matters is that the models faithfully represent the "style" for which each is intended.

Whether we use the metaphors of styles of art, maps, or different senses, the point is that science and theology are different and legitimate ways of conceptualizing reality. Sometimes philosophers use the phrase "carve up reality differently" to describe this. We don't merely absorb experience passively; our minds are active in shaping experience.

Whether we are considering how one enters the life of Christian faith or we are reflecting on what is required to comprehend theoretical systems, for each there is a distinct process for knowing, along with limiting conditions applicable to each: one through God's gift of faith and through obedient living, the other by employing reason and using established standards for research.

Consider two illustrations from sensory perception. When someone who has been deaf her whole life is given a cochlear implant, there is usually an extended transition period when she can't make sense of the chaotic mix of sounds she now hears. A transition is required for her to conceptualize and properly understand those sounds.

More dramatic is the story from the New Testament in which Jesus heals a blind man. He touches the man's eyes and asks him whether he can see. The man looks up and answers, "I can see people, but they look like trees, walking" (Mark 8:24, NRSV). Jesus touches the man's eyes again and performs a second healing so that the man can see everything clearly. These two examples show the difference between our sensory equipment working properly and the conceptual ability to interpret what we see and hear. That conceptual ability becomes even more important as we move away from the immediate experience of the senses and consider the more abstract beliefs in Christian theology or scientific theories.

So my appeal is that science and theology are two complementary ways of conceptualizing and organizing experience. They have developed into established and successful realms of discourse. Their accounts are not in competition, the way they are understood in the conflict model. They should not be forced together, as in the concordist model. And they are not restricted to separate corners of reality, like the NOMA model. Science and theology give different perspectives on the same reality.

A CALL FOR DIALOGUE

So what is the takeaway for a more productive engagement of evangelicals with science? When we understand that science and theology are different God-given perspectives or ways for understanding experience, we should create space for each and for productive dialogue. More precisely, dialogue happens between people who are willing to be instructed by the best in Christian doctrine and biblical interpretation and by the best in science.

For example, science might teach us that we humans have evolved from other life-forms. But while that "natural history" of *Homo sapiens* might be correct, it does not tell the whole story of the history of human beings. There are other aspects to our story that science leaves out. Sin and salvation are theological concepts, and these are just as true (or perhaps more true) of us as are the scientific concepts of DNA and natural selection. So we must also tell the theological history of human beings, which is made clear to us through the life, death, and resurrection of Jesus Christ.

It is not always clear how these two histories—the natural and the theological—are to be understood in relation to each other. That is why we need dialogue between people who are committed to taking science seriously and to taking seriously the revelation of God in Jesus Christ. As evangelicals, we celebrate God's creative work from two complementary angles and consequently have a better, richer view of the whole.[26]

For Further Study

Falk, Darrel R. *Coming to Peace with Science: Bridging the Worlds between Faith and Biology.* Downers Grove, IL: IVP Academic, 2004.

Haarsma, Deborah B., and Loren D. Haarsma. *Origins: Christian Perspectives on Creation, Evolution, and Intelligent Design.* Grand Rapids: Faith Alive Christian Resources, 2011.

McGrath, Alister E. *The Big Question: Why We Can't Stop Talking about Science, Faith, and God.* New York: St. Martin's Press, 2015.

———. *Enriching Our Vision of Reality: Theology and the Natural Sciences in Dialogue.* London: SPCK, 2016.

———. *A Fine-Tuned Universe: The Quest for God in Science and Theology.* Louisville, KY: Westminster John Knox Press, 2009.

Stump, J. B. *Science and Christianity: An Introduction to the Issues.* Chichester, UK: Wiley-Blackwell, 2017.

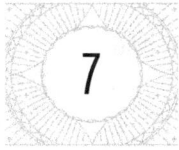

7

EVANGELICALS AND THE NEXT CHRISTENDOM

FLOYD CUNNINGHAM

HISTORIAN Kenneth S. Latourette analyzed the repeated cycles of the Christian faith's history of expansion and retrenchment. Sometimes it seemed Christianity was doomed. But while retracting in one place, it was expanding in another. He concluded that "in each major advance [Christianity] becomes more widely potent in human life than in the one before it, and each recession is marked by less dwindling of the impact of Christianity than the one which immediately preceded it."[1] Globally we are witnessing that phenomenon being repeated in astonishing ways. While the Christian faith is losing its historically strong voice in Europe and North America, it is rapidly and astonishingly becoming stronger in other world areas. The growth of the Christian faith in the Majority World (also called the Global South) is now commonly referred to as the "next Christendom." It is complex and challenging to describe. In this chapter, we will seek to do just that.

To be successful, we must be careful not to apply Western categories to the next Christendom without qualification. This is particularly true with reference to the term "evangelical." Even in the West the term has gone through several transitions. As we shall see, the term must be used guardedly when speaking of Christians and churches in the Majority World. Historian Timothy L. Smith used the term "evangelicalism" to denote "those historic American religious communities that are united by a commitment to biblical authority, a belief in the necessity of conversion or new birth, and an emphasis upon worldwide evangelization."[2] But as we shall see, even if Smith's definition is generally adequate for North America, it cannot be transferred neatly to the Majority World.

An essential difference between Christianity in Europe and North America and the next Christendom is that modernity influenced denominations in the West more than it did the younger churches. Most Christians in the Majority World have a worldview much closer to that of the Bible than that of the Western missionaries who brought the gospel to them. And whereas under the influence of modern criticism the Bible was being questioned in the West, it was accepted literally in the Majority World.[3]

To achieve our goal for this chapter we will examine (1) the changing face of Christianity, (2) the two periods of colonialism, (3) postcolonial churches, (4) the independent churches, (5) new religious movements, and (6) markers of Majority-World Christians.

THE CHANGING FACE OF CHRISTIANITY

Not until the twentieth century did Christianity truly become a global faith. The late twentieth and early twenty-first centuries witnessed one of the most epochal events in Christian history: the repositioning of the church from being predominantly a European and American church to becoming predominantly an African and Asian church. The change is comparable to similar shifts in the fourth and sixteenth centuries. As late as the 1920s Hilaire Belloc, an English

Roman Catholic, could claim, "*The Faith* is Europe and Europe is *the Faith*."[4] Fifty years later this was no longer true. In Europe, where the church once was strongest, Christianity was becoming a cultural memory. Church historian Martin Marty remarked, "It seemed as if the faith had become anything but Europe and Europe was anything but faithful."[5] Although the West continued to send missionaries (Europe in 2010 sent 132,800 missionaries; North America, 135,000),[6] by 1980 the vitality of the church resided largely in the Global South (meaning not only churches of the Southern Hemisphere but also those in India, China, Korea, and the Philippines). Churches in these areas have an identity distinct from those in the West. In 2002, in his highly influential book *The Next Christendom*, historian Philip Jenkins noted there were more Presbyterians in South Korea than in either Scotland or the United States, many times more members of the Assemblies of God in Brazil than in the United States, and more Anglican/Episcopalians in Nigeria and Uganda than in either the United States or England. Indeed, by 2009 the archbishop of York, John Sentamu, was born and raised in Uganda.[7]

Such trends signaled dramatic changes. In 1900, 54 percent of the world's population was not yet evangelized. By 2017 the percentage had declined to 28 percent. In 1900 the percentage of non-Christians who knew a Christian was 6 percent. By 2017 the percentage had risen to 18 percent. In 1917 the percentage of the world population identified as Christian was 33 percent, the same as in 1900. The church declined in Europe and shifted southward. Sometime between 1970 and 2000 the number of Christians in Africa surpassed the number of Christians in North America. In 2010 African churches sent more than 20,000 missionaries throughout the continent and the world. If such gains continue, Christians in Africa will number 1.25 billion by 2050. At the same time, the number of Christians in Latin America will increase from 591 million in 2017 to 705 million in 2050. Although Islam is growing faster than Christianity, demographers project that in 2050 Christians will total 3.44 billion adherents compared to Islam's 2.77 billion.[8]

Where do evangelicals fit into this emerging Christian pattern? In a somewhat circular fashion, demographers David Barrett and Todd Johnson define the term "evangelicals" as "church members of evangelical conviction, involved in Christ's mission on earth; synonymous with Great Commission Christians."[9] Evangelicals are "believers in Jesus Christ who are aware of the implications of [Christ's] Great Commission, have accepted its personal challenge in their lives and ministries, and are seeking to influence the Body of Christ to implement it."[10] Barrett and Johnson identify eight types of evangelicals: conservative, neo-, Protestant, Anglican, independent, Catholic, Orthodox, and liberal.[11] By their broad definition, in 2010 evangelical presence in Africa was twice as large—104 million—as any other part of the world. In Latin America the number was 48 million, in North America 44 million, in Asia 40 million, and in Europe 22 million. By 2017, evangelicals worldwide numbered 342 million. At the current growth rate, the number will rise to 581 million by 2050.[12]

Churches in the Majority World occupy a spectrum of relationships to historic denominations. They range from those who have retained ties to churches in the West to those who are autonomous. The spectrum ranges from churches doctrinally indebted to the West to independent churches that have either intentionally separated from Western traditions or that began indigenously. The expanse also includes new religious movements unaligned with traditional Christianity. Churches that retain identity with biblical faith and historic creeds and are evangelizing others can be identified as evangelical.

In many parts of the next Christendom, Pentecostalism is the proverbial elephant in the room. Sorting out the relationship between Pentecostals and evangelicals challenges demographers of Majority-World Christianity. They normally distinguish between Pentecostal and evangelical but recognize them as overlapping categories. They generally define a Pentecostal as "a person or group or movement stressing direct divine inspiration by the Holy Spirit and exhibiting glossolalia, faith healing, and parallel phenomena."[13] Though not all Pentecostals are classified as evangelicals, worldwide they compose the largest block of evangelicals. Allan Heaton Anderson, professor of mission and Pentecostal studies at the University of Birmingham (UK), observes that "Pentecostalism can transpose itself into local cultures and religions so effortlessly because of its primary emphases on the experience of the Spirit and the spiritual calling of leaders who do not have to be formally educated in church belief and practice."[14] Anderson adds that the "ministry of healing and the claims of the miraculous have assisted Pentecostalism in its appeal to a world where such supernatural events are taken for granted."[15] Whether Pentecostals remained in or departed from older faith traditions, they are united by a sense of the power and immediate presence of the Holy Spirit.[16]

Currently the term "renewalist" is used to identify three "waves" of Pentecostals.[17] The first wave was the traditional Pentecostal churches. The second wave included charismatics, or neo-Pentecostals—those "baptized" or renewed in the Spirit within non-Pentecostal denominations, such as Anglicans and Roman Catholics. Although they affirm the same creeds as evangelicals, they were not identified with the evangelical movement. In the Philippines, for instance—where in 2010, 78 percent of the population was Roman Catholic and only 3 percent evangelical—29 percent of the population was classified as renewalist. Third *wave* Pentecostals have no institutional ties to Western denominations. They emphasize divine healing, economic prosperity, and miracles. They pay strong attention to the Holy Spirit's confrontation with and conquest of malevolent spirits.[18] Preoccupation with the supernatural is attractive to persons living in "spirit-filled universes." Majority-World non-Pentecostal evangelicals also emphasize the deity and importance of the Holy Spirit. But they normally reject belief in the intrusion of evil or ancestral spirits in one's daily life.

THE TWO PERIODS OF COLONIALISM

Precolonial Evangelism

The next Christendom did not begin with the work of Western missionaries. Often evangelists and missionaries who planted churches were indigenous persons. Long-standing non-Western churches included the Mar Thoma Church in India, the Abyssinian Church in Ethiopia, and the Coptic Orthodox Church in Egypt. During the nineteenth-century missionary movement, Protestants thought of members of those ancient churches as candidates for evangelization. Greek Orthodox in Turkey were "evangelized" by American Congregationalists and Presbyterians, as were the Coptic Orthodox by the Church Missionary Society. The Russian Orthodox were the targets of Baptists and Pentecostals. Even though some from the churches joined with the Protestants, most of them remained in their traditional churches.[19]

From the beginning, indigenous people have been at the forefront of cross-cultural evangelism: Africans evangelized Africans, Indians other Indians, Pacific Islanders other Pacific Islanders, and Karens in Burma (Myanmar) other Karens. Francis Wayland (1796–1865), president of Brown University, wisely observed that in Burma God had preceded the missionaries. The Karens, who reside primarily in southern and southeastern Myanmar and who number approximately five million, told of two brothers who separated. One of them had been given a book. When he left, he promised to return. When missionaries told the message of the gospel to a Karen by using the Bible, he connected the announcement to the ancient story and ran to tell his tribe the legend was true; the book had returned. The Karen who first heard the gospel retold the message to the people. Because of the Karen story's power, the Karens who heard him did not need a missionary. Nevertheless, as Baptist missionaries came into contact with the Karens, they took credit for the tribe's conversion.[20]

Colonial Evangelism

Historian David Bebbington's definition of evangelicalism as including conversion, activism, Bible-centeredness, and cross-centeredness accurately identifies the primary interests of the Western missionary movement.[21] Missionaries were passionate about reaching the "lost." They planted churches loyal to their Western origins and translated the Bible, whose authority they valued even more than that of their own denominations. And while preaching the gospel, missionaries lived "crucified-with-Christ" lives.[22]

From the early nineteenth century, missionaries worked to establish self-supporting, self-governing, and self-propagating churches. These principles were formulated by Rufus Anderson, the corresponding secretary of the influential American Board of Commissioners for Foreign Missions, and by Henry Venn, his counterpart in the (Anglican) Church Missionary Society. Anderson, a Congregationalist, and Venn, who thought Anglicans should be freed from Canterbury, stressed local and national church autonomy. They saw no value in maintaining governmental and monetary ties between newly birthed and "mother" churches. Missionaries, they thought, should, like the apostle Paul, be itinerant. They must not settle down and dominate local Christians. Let missionaries engage in evangelism.

However, in spite of Anderson and Venn's philosophy, missionaries largely became localized. They learned languages, built loyalties to home denominations, and directed schools and hospitals. Missionaries taught men and women to read and write their own languages. By doing so, they preserved local languages. In many other ways, "settled" missionaries improved the well-being of the people among whom they ministered. In India they lobbied the British government to outlaw the practice of suttee—that is, forcing widows to throw themselves on the crematory fires of their deceased husbands. They convinced the Indian British colonial government to provide them finances for village education. In China, missionaries worked to change the practice of binding females' feet. They built schools for girls and boys. Missionaries dug wells and irrigation ditches, built dams, and taught Western agricultural techniques. They taught people how to build houses, instructed them in different modes of dress, and provided sewing machines and accordions. In many ways they introduced remote peoples to Western customs.

But in their efforts, missionaries imposed their Western perception of progress and measured others by those criteria. Ironically, the education provided by missionaries eventually empowered people to revolt against the colonial powers.[23]

Today it is popular to charge missionaries with intentionally or unintentionally serving as mere tools of Western foreign policy. But given the resources of Western churches, how could Christians have justifiably stood aside? The desire of missionaries to preach the gospel and improve the lives of the people among whom they ministered derived from a deeply felt love for the people, not from a desire to become agents of colonial oppression.[24]

Before missionaries could grant self-governance to developing Majority-World churches, the churches had to achieve financial self-support. The churches struggled to shoulder financial responsibility for schools, hospitals, and other institutions. This hurdle delayed self-governance. Moreover, the transfer of leadership to national leaders was agonizingly slow. Even though local leaders demonstrated their desire to evangelize, missionaries maintained leadership control. Missionaries were articulate and could write books. And they could write letters appealing for support from Western contacts.

Sometimes missionaries failed to recognize the extent to which they stood on the sidelines as indigenous evangelists led the way. During the 1910 Edinburgh Missionary Conference, Indian Anglican leader V. S. Azariah observed, "The relationship between the European missionaries and the Indian workers is far from what it ought to be, and . . . a certain aloofness, a lack of mutual understanding and openness, a great lack of frank intercourse and friendliness exists throughout the country."[25] His words revealed that when judged by local Christians, missionaries mostly worked *for* rather than *with* them. Too often the missionaries preferred their own ideas of what was best over local preachers' better knowledge of the language and local thought forms. Historian Edward Andrews observed that local evangelists could "tap into existing networks of kinship, trade, and friendship" and that because they could live simply, they were more cost-effective than Western missionaries.[26] In fact, in many ways "native peoples not only encouraged Christian missions, but actually led them. They drew from Christianity to frame new identities, amass spiritual power, preserve their cultures, and protect their peoples during a period of unprecedented change."[27]

POSTCOLONIAL CHURCHES

Since the rise of denominations after the sixteenth-century Protestant Reformation, a denomination's success was largely judged by how successfully its doctrines were received abroad. Members of global denominations envisioned a community of like-minded believers transcending national boundaries. Leaders of the missionary churches were often educated in the West and respected the traditions that had nurtured them. But they were also loyal to their own people. This was the situation in China, for example, both before and after the Communist revolution. In spite of antiforeign outbursts, mission churches sent Chinese leaders to be educated in the West. Timothy Lew, for instance, who in 1922 helped organize the National Christian Council of China, had earned a PhD at Columbia University. In 1925, C. Y. Cheng, the secretary of the National Christian Council, described the stages of church development in China. They began with the cultivation of individual conversions and extended to the discovery and application of the societal implications of the Christian faith. As early as 1925, Cheng anticipated the Chinese church becoming self-reliant, unified, and independent. He asked, "(1) 'How can Christ be so presented as to ensure meeting the real needs of the East?' and (2) 'How can the Church be so developed in China as to place direct responsibility for its development on the Chinese themselves?'"[28]

On the other hand, Christians caught up in an East Africa revival in the 1930s neither denounced the missionary-sending churches nor broke away from their influence.[29]

Concerns considered urgent in Western churches usually held little significance for churches in the Majority World. African theologian John Mbiti told of an African who, after over nine years of study, earned a PhD from Oxford in theology. He had written a dissertation on some obscure theologian. Carrying his books in overweight baggage, he arrived in his home village.

> His neighbors honored him with dancers, musicians, drums, and a roasted calf. Small children who had only heard his name gathered around in awe. They did not mind that he could barely speak his own language any more as he extended his greetings to them. Amid the singing and dancing, a young girl shrieked and fell to the ground. Naturally the villagers turned to their hero. Surely he would cast the demon out of the girl! He cried that they needed to get her to the hospital! (Had he forgotten that the nearest hospital was fifty miles away and there were few buses?) Besides, the villagers knew that the young girl had been possessed by a demon. But the young theologian had brought nothing in his mind or heart about casting out demons. The great books that he had brought back had all "demythologized" demons. He had no spiritual power. So what was the use of his PhD in theology, the villagers thought as they sadly left the celebration, if he could not even cast a demon out of a young girl![30]

Although missionaries had promoted indigeneity, the churches they planted still tended to resemble Western churches. Historian Sarah Ruble observes that discussions about missionaries in post-World War II America reinforced a paradox. Many Christians believed people abroad deserved freedom while also believing that "Americans knew what was best for the rest of the world."[31] Christians began to think more seriously about "contextualization," a term coined by Taiwan Presbyterian theologian Shoki Coe. He moved away from Anderson and Venn's "three selfs" (self-supporting, self-governing, etc.), which focused on institutions, to emphasize relationships and processes. He believed the gospel must be relevant to the context in which it is proclaimed. Accomplishing this would require joining cultural elements (e.g., music and dancing) with the gospel message. It would also require creatively addressing sickness and poverty. Local leaders must confront the spirit world that enslaved their people; they must concentrate on immediate cultural manifestations of good and evil—whether spiritual or political.

Once evangelicals had embraced contextualization, they were able to appreciate local efforts to express the gospel in indigenous cultural forms. Todd Vanden Berg, for instance, has suggested that African theology assumes that because God had already spoken through old African religions, claiming some harmony between the gospel and African culture was natural. Often contextualization helps explain why many Africans find Pentecostalism, with its message of healing and power, appealing.[32]

THE INDEPENDENT CHURCHES

In 2017, among the world's Christians, 1.23 billion were Roman Catholic, 559 million were Protestant (including Anglican), 437 million were independent, and 285 million were Orthodox. Among these, independents were growing fastest. Independent movements intentionally reject Western ways of being Christian. Feeding off of dissatisfactions, some independent churches broke away from mission churches. Others arose spontaneously. The Philippine Independent Church, for instance, separated from the Roman Catholic Church during the Philippine War for Independence (1896–1902) and attracted 25 percent of the Philippine population. In Africa, independent churches incorporated traditional religious practices. They associated divine healing with exorcism.[33] In Ghana, independent churches usually depicted Christianity as the religion of economic success. However, more recently popularity of the "prosperity gospel" has waned in Ghana and West Africa. In its place, a "holiness ethic" is emerging.[34]

Independent churches arose, members believe, by direct instruction from the Holy Spirit. Some independent churches began during the days of colonialism, and others after the Second World War, when European powers were giving up their African and Asian colonies. Like denominations elsewhere, independent churches give birth to offshoots and schisms. They are showing that Christianity is not just a Western religion. In a postcolonial world, one chooses to be part of a traditional denomination or an independent church; choosing the Christian faith is done so freely, not because of political or social manipulation.[35]

In 1965, in order to provide theological education and enhance their respectability, independent African churches formed their own association. As an affirmation of their identity with historic Christianity, many of the independent churches became part of the World Council of Churches.[36]

The Harris movement is paradigmatic of the African Independent Churches. Though born of African-American parents and influenced by Methodism and the Episcopal Church, William Wadé Harris (ca. 1865–1929), a native of Liberia, rejected the West. In 1913 and 1914, as the colonial powers began their fratricidal Great War in Europe, Harris went barefoot from village to village in the French Ivory Coast, wearing a simple white robe and destroying fetishes and cult objects. While he stressed that Christians must observe the Sabbath, he tolerated polygamy. Women were his closest associates. They summoned the Holy Spirit by using gourd rattles. Harris accepted the reality of evil spirits and the malevolent power of witchcraft. To counteract them, Harris carried a cane cross with supposedly inherent spiritual power. He defied the evil spirits and, through Christian baptism, offered his converts spiritual protection as well as purification. Baptism offered power over the French colonialists as well. Through diligence and hard work, conversion promised economic prosperity equal to the colonizers. Rather than Africans using their spiritual power to destroy themselves, as they had done under the reign of witchcraft, by using their spiritual power constructively as Europeans do, Africans would prosper in all ways.[37]

Where missionaries had failed, Harris succeeded, converting about one hundred thousand during his short ministry in the Ivory Coast. Entire villages became Christian when their leaders converted. Sociologist Sheila Walker observed that because Harris "was an African from a traditional background who could also interact effectively in the western milieu, [he] was culturally appropriate to the task of bringing to the Ivorians a new religious orientation and a gospel of liberation that was a synthesis of old and new."[38] Harris viewed the Roman Catholic and Protestant practices of the Lord's Supper as holdovers from African witchcraft. Nevertheless, Walker concludes, "Harris provided both a prototype for a Christianity that could be adapted to an African life-style and also a way in which an African religious system could be modified to fit the Christian framework with little injustice to either."[39] The Harrist Church confesses Jesus Christ as God and Savior and baptizes in the name of the Father, Son, and Holy Spirit.[40] It joined the World Council of Churches in 1998.

In another part of the Majority World, independent Chinese churches have a long history. Overall, independent churches have been more successful than Protestant missions.

The Taiping Rebellion (or Taiping Civil War, 1850-64), a massive civil war, was led by Hong Xiuquan. He compared himself to Jesus and called himself "God's Chinese son." Hong had been influenced by Christian missionaries who disowned him when his movement became messianic and millenarian.[41] During the turbulent twentieth century, Christian leaders longed to evangelize their own people. They gravitated toward New Testament teachings rather than denominational identity. For instance, Yu Cidu (1873–1931), known as Dora Yu, was trained as a medical doctor and served as a missionary to Korea (1897–1903). She was influenced by Methodism and the holiness movement. Returning to China, Dora Yu began itinerant preaching, translated hymns, and opened a summer Bible School in Shanghai.

Dora Yu became mentor to Ni Tuosheng, better known in the West as Watchman Nee (1903-72). Ni had attended the Church of England's Trinity College and was converted under the ministry of a Methodist evangelist. He became acquainted with the English Keswick or "higher life" movement, which emphasized Christian holiness. He blended this emphasis with Plymouth Brethren dispensationalism. Ni left the Methodist Church to found an independent congregation in Shanghai. Many of his followers came from the China Inland Mission (founded in Britain by Hudson Taylor in 1865, now OMF International). Though interested in Pentecostal phenomena, he discouraged glossolalia (speaking in tongues). Ni's churches, called the Little Flock, rejected formal organization and emphasized the local church. His independent churches spread throughout the Chinese-speaking world. Ni stressed that the church must be self-supporting, self-governing, Bible loving, and spiritual. After World War II, Ni's work expanded quickly; he personally assumed responsibility for commissioning workers to evangelize unreached areas. When the Communists came to power in 1949 there were seven hundred Little Flock congregations and seventy thousand members. During the 1950s some of Ni's congregations registered with the government; most went underground.[42]

Other independent Chinese movements of the same era included the Jesus Family, centered in Shandong Province and led by Jing Dianying. Like Ni, Jing broke with Methodism. The Jesus Family lived communally, spoke of being possessed by the Spirit, and spoke in tongues.[43] Another independent leader, Wei Enbo, once affiliated with the London Missionary Society, established the True Jesus Church. During the 1922 National Christian Conference, Wei Enbo explicitly denounced mission churches.[44]

Meanwhile, bands of holiness evangelists were spreading across China. One of these, Wang Mingdao, distanced himself from missionaries and Pentecostals. The church, he declared, is neither Western nor Chinese. He wanted to restore a primitive, New Testament church.[45] Another independent holiness emphasis was the Bethel Mission in

Shanghai, begun in 1920 by Shi Meiyu (Mary Stone, 1873–1954) and Kang Cheng (Ida Kahn). Medical doctors trained at the University of Michigan, they were sent to China by the Methodist Episcopal Church's Woman's Foreign Missionary Society. The Bethel Mission recruited and sent out teams of evangelists. Among them were Song Shangjie (John Sung, 1901-44), the brilliant son of a Methodist pastor. Having had an opportunity to study abroad, Song earned a PhD in chemistry at Ohio State University. Then, believing himself called to ministry, Song studied at Union Theological Seminary in New York City. He returned to China in 1927. From 1931 to 1933 Song traveled throughout China with the Bethel Mission. But in 1934 he was expelled because of differences stemming from Bethel's teaching on Christian holiness. Sung began an independent ministry. Between 1935 and 1939, in addition to China, Song conducted revival campaigns among Chinese in Indonesia, Malaysia, the Philippines, Taiwan, Thailand, and Singapore. Divine healing was a prominent part of the revivals. The revivals in China were largely provoked by the political crises of the 1930s. Though Song was ordained in the Methodist Church, he worked independently.[46]

After the Communists came to power in 1949, Christian churches in China became increasingly controlled. Foreign missionaries left. Churches had a choice. They could either register with the government, which formed the Three-Self Patriotic Movement,[47] or go underground. By 1958 only about one hundred government-controlled churches remained open. But thousands of independent churches refused to register. During the Cultural Revolution (1966-76) all churches were closed. In their absence, from one generation to the next, Christian faith was nurtured over kitchen tables, in farmhouses, and by word of mouth.

Astonishingly, when one is speaking of the government-recognized Three-Self Church or the unlicensed, underground church, Chinese Christians have established an impressive fabric of faith independent of the West. Demographers project that by 2050 China will have the second-largest number of Christians in the world with 225 million. The growth of the Christian church in China will eventually yield an important missionary-sending movement.[48]

In India, traditional denominational churches founded fifty or more years ago are declining; by contrast, independent churches are growing. Many independent churches have Baptist or Pentecostal backgrounds. They are led by women and men who lack formal theological education. Members reflect caste diversity; the different castes eat together during church fellowships. Villagers who join independent churches often do so because of religious experiences encountered in dreams, visions, and divine healing. Worship services emphasize praise and testimonies (many of them related to divine healing) and strong lay participation. Converts believe in "Jesus as the God who does what Hindu deities had failed to do for them: answer prayers for healing and for material blessings."[49] Ministers stress that Christ has power to heal and disperse malevolent magical spells. Even the few new Church of South India congregations are results of miraculous healing.[50]

In the Philippines, miracles play a major role in indigenous Pentecostal movements. This is true of the Jesus Is Lord Church, led by Eddie Villanueva, and the Roman Catholic group El Shaddai, led by Mike Velarde. Both movements promise that Christian faith produces miracles and yields material prosperity.

In 1978, Villanueva, once a Communist activist, founded the Jesus Is Lord Fellowship (JIL) as a Bible study. In 1980 JIL moved to a high school building. Attendance climbed to fifteen thousand. A popular television ministry, *Jesus the Healer*, began in 1982. Villanueva incorporated divine healing in his ministry; followers testified to miracles. He openly preached against Roman Catholicism's "idolatry" and veneration of Mary. He led campaigns against gambling and prostitution. In 1983, Villanueva organized a network of indigenous Pentecostal and charismatic denominations and organizations called the Philippines for Jesus Movement. Jesus Is Lord maintains a strong base among students and young people. It has its own discipleship and leadership training program. Villanueva believes that Jesus offers social, economic, and political solutions for the Philippine people. Although for a time, JIL was affiliated with the Philippine Council of Evangelical Churches (PCEC, the umbrella organization for Philippine Pentecostal and evangelical denominations), when in 2010 PCEC failed to endorse Villanueva for president of the Philippines, JIL withdrew from PCEC.[51]

With millions of followers, El Shaddai could have posed a threat to the Catholic establishment. But Mike Velarde, a layperson, remained within the Roman Catholic Church and invited high-ranking prelates to his open-air crusades. His crusades attracted hundreds of thousands in the center of Manila.

Globally, independent churches are proving that churches in the Majority World can find their own way toward Christian faith and practice.[52] They are conservative in their understanding of the Bible's authority and uncompromisingly preach Christ as the only Savior. They rely on the Holy Spirit to bring renewal.[53] Local leaders possess powers for blessing and healing that missionaries do not have. But at one central point the independent churches largely depart from traditional evangelicalism. The fourth part of historian David Bebbington's famous evangelical quadrilateral is cross-centeredness. That part of evangelicalism—that Christians must suffer with and for Christ—is unappealing in the Majority World. Most of the people are already suffering. They don't need a God who is merely with them in their suffering or who can comfort and strengthen them in their darkest hours. Rather, they need a powerful Deliverer, a God who provides healing and escape from poverty through material blessings.[54]

NEW RELIGIOUS MOVEMENTS

Normally, the independent churches value the ecumenical creeds and do not question the norms of apostolic faith. That is not true of a host of new religious movements that reject the doctrine of the Trinity and the deity of Christ.[55] One may then wonder why discussion of new religious movements is included in this chapter. The reason is that apart from them, the picture of the next Christendom is incomplete.

The Iglesia ni Cristo (Church of Christ) in the Philippines can represent the new religious movements. Felix Y. Manalo (1886–1963) founded Iglesia ni Cristo. After leaving the Roman Catholic Church, Manalo first joined, in succession, the Philippine Independent Church, the Methodists, the Presbyterians, the Disciples of Christ, and the Seventh-day Adventists. Finally, Manalo began preaching independently, launching a church that grew rapidly. In July 1914, he incorporated the Iglesia ni Cristo, with himself as its supreme head. Like the Disciples of Christ and Seventh-day Adventists, Manalo viewed the early ecumenical councils as having abandoned biblical teachings. In particular, he believed the councils' affirmations of the incarnation and Trinity to be contradictions of the New Testament. Instead of affirming Christ to be the eternal second person of the Trinity, Manalo was an adoptionist—that is, he adhered to the early Christian heresy that God adopted the human Jesus to be his Son.

Members of Iglesia ni Cristo believe in one God, the Father. They reject the preincarnational existence of Christ. Jesus was only human. Still, he is Mediator between God and humankind, the only "name" under heaven by which people can be redeemed. His being the Redeemer doesn't rely on his being the eternal only begotten Son of the Father but on his commission from God. Manalo disliked the free-wheeling style of evangelical preaching and loose forms of worship. Manalo trained his preachers in a closely reasoned style of debate. By using biblical proof texts, preachers learned to defend every Iglesia position. The church instructed members on how to understand the Bible. Iglesia ni Cristo ministers received their sermons from higher church officials. Manalo believed that his church alone maintained the truth and that only through the Iglesia ni Cristo could persons be saved. Only faithful members of the Iglesia were included in the atonement. Followers saw Manalo himself as the "angel from the East," or the "last Messenger." The Iglesia ni Cristo spread wherever Filipinos migrated.[56]

Let's briefly mention three additional new movements. First, after the Second World War, several new Japanese religious movements developed. Western missionaries actually contributed to the notion that Christianity is a foreign religion. Not surprisingly, many Japanese developed a synthesis of Christianity, Shinto, Buddhism, and traditional Chinese teaching. Second, in the Shandong Province of China, a new religious movement known as the Eastern Lightning emerged from the Shouters sect. Later its name became the Church of Almighty God. It emphasized the impending end of the world. Third, in 1954 Sun Myung Moon (d. 2012) founded the Unification Church in South Korea. It was founded as the Holy Spirit Association for the Unification of World Christianity. It is also known as the Family Federation for World Peace and Unification. With a controversial history to its credit, Unification teaches that God is the Creator, that he is the heavenly Parent, and that God possesses a masculine and feminine nature.[57] In 1982, in a highly publicized trial, Rev. Moon was convicted in the United Sates for filing false income tax returns.

MARKERS OF MAJORITY-WORLD CHRISTIANS

Five defining markers of Majority-World Christianity can be identified: (1) Bible-centered, (2) indigeneity, (3) physical healing and material prosperity, (4) belief in the spirit world, and (5) postdenominational.

Bible-Centered

Most Christians in the Majority World are Bible-centered. They have a literal and plain understanding of Scripture. Influenced by the Enlightenment, many Western Christians have wrestled with how to interpret biblical accounts of miracles, healings, evil spirits, and demonic possession. Christians of the Majority World believe that Western Christians too easily allowed their culture to supplant the biblical worldview and undermine biblical moral norms.[58]

Biblical texts that appeal most to Christians in the West are not the ones that appeal most to Majority-World Christians. For instance, the book of Hebrews appeals to Africans because it depicts, as theologian Kwame Bediako points out, "sacrifice, priestly mediation and ancestral function."[59] The books of Proverbs and Ecclesiastes tell global Christians how to live. So does the book of James, which is a regular for sermons in African Independent Churches. Similarly, Japanese missionary Kosuke Koyama found that in Thailand the book of James mirrors a "distinctively Asian manifestation of Christianity."[60]

People suffering under colonial powers identified the Jewish authorities in the New Testament with their own oppressors, and themselves with Jesus. They identified with the Bible's poor in ways Westerners could not. They recovered texts lost to the West. What did it mean, for instance, to "sow in tears" (Ps. 126:5, KJV), except that the sower has had to decide to eat the seeds for next year's harvest? The sower and his family were starving. Overall, Majority-World Christians discovered in the Bible a message that elevates those who are neglected and marginalized.[61]

Indigeneity

Increasingly, Majority-World Christians have reembraced many once-discarded traditions of their own cultures that Western missionaries had suppressed. These include dancing and the use of drums. They often assign spiritual authority to women who, after all, outnumber men in churches. In some places the prominence of women goes back to pre-Christian roles of women as healers, prophets, and shamans (someone with influence in the spirit world).[62]

Elements of shamanism have persisted among Korean Christians in their forms of worship and styles of leadership. Christianity grew rapidly in Korea from the 1960s through the 1980s. Presbyterianism mixed with Pentecostalism to find a thoroughly indigenized place within a Confucian hierarchical worldview. Korean Christians believe that God has blessed their country economically because they turned to Christ and because they obeyed his command to reach the world (as missionaries) with the gospel. They give generously to missions. Successes by their missionaries are based on Korean generosity and on their ability to identify with non-Western peoples who, like themselves, believe in a spirit-laden world. Korean missionaries normally emphasize miracles and divine healing.[63]

Physical Healing and Material Prosperity

As a result of their belief in the power of the spirit world, and because of insufficient medical resources, Majority-World Christians emphasize divine healing. Illness, many believe, is caused by demons, the spirits of disturbed ancestors, or malevolent spells cast by witches or demons. Women are involved either as inflicters of evil or as healers. For many, Western explanations for illness make no sense. If viruses cause illness, how do they land on a people?[64]

Attention to physical well-being extends to prosperity and material well-being. Majority-World Christians believe that God rewards faithfulness with health, wealth, and prosperity. Although Western evangelicals joined evangelism with social concerns, they did not, and perhaps could not, appreciate the importance poor Majority-World Christians assigned to divine healing, miracles, and material well-being. True, Western evangelicals urged a more equitable distribution of the world's goods, but that interest seemed abstract and distant to those daily facing poverty.[65]

Belief in the Spirit World

A very important difference between evangelicals in the West and Majority-World Christians is the importance the latter attaches to the power and influence of spirits.[66] While Western scholars were stripping away the Bible's "myths," including miracles and demonic spirits, Christians elsewhere were still living in a first-century world. While evangelical missionaries from the West looked with skepticism on witches and spirits, Pentecostal missionaries did not. This equipped them sensitively and effectively to enter Majority-World cultures. Sociologist David Martin observed, "As a self-generated vehicle of the aspiring poor [Pentecostalism] picks up contents within the universal shamanistic layer of spiritism overlaid by colonialism and integrates them into the frame of Holy Spirit Christianity."[67] Similarly, Paul Freston reasoned that Pentecostalism is "close to popular Latin American religiosity in many respects" and is "tuned in to an inspired world."[68] Peruvian theologian Samuel Escobar noted the irony that while Roman Catholic priests were most active in championing the "preferential option" for the poor, and protesting against the ruling classes, the poor in Latin America were making their way out of Catholicism and into evangelical Protestantism—especially Pentecostal—which offered healing and material prosperity.[69]

Postdenominational

During the 1910 Edinburgh Missionary Conference, Chinese Christian leader Cheng Jingyi told the Europeans and Americans, "Your denominationalism does not interest Chinese Christians."[70] That remains true of most Christians in the Majority World. They seek a Christianity that best suits their immediate needs, regardless of denominational labels and traditions. Few of them are looking for prepackaged religious doctrines or experiences. Even in the West, the importance of denominations is diminishing.

Revitalization of Christianity may rest with Majority-World Christians immigrating and sending missionaries to the homelands of missionaries that originally reached their people. Majority-World churches are sending thousands of missionaries throughout the world. For example, Hispanic evangelicals have learned French and are evangelizing in Quebec and France.[71]

What sort of Christianity is arriving from the Majority World? These Christians bring pre-Enlightenment ways of understanding the Bible and Christian faith. They are more aware of the threat posed by spiritual powers than they are of Enlightenment rationalism. Secularism and postmodern ways of thinking do not interest them. They are settling in urban centers abandoned by older populations and establishing thriving churches. "Ministries of revitalization have manifested themselves through the response of faithful witnesses to the mission of God for these people groups," says J. Steven O'Malley.[72] Based upon his case studies, O'Malley concludes, "These ministries have often arisen apart from and even without the involvement of official church bodies. Nevertheless, the resulting revival that has occurred has in many respects become transformative for those living in these developing transnational communities."[73] Majority-World Christianity is not beholden to Western cultures and does not conform to Western forms of worship.

As sociologists noted a generation ago, the fastest growing churches were conservative churches that required the most from their members. This norm is now being played out in conservative parts of Anglicanism that protest liberal trends in Anglican ranks. For seven days in June 2008, the Global Anglican Future Conference (GAFCON) was conducted in Jerusalem. Attending were 291 bishops from twenty-nine countries, including the Anglican primates of several African countries, and more than 1,100 lay and clergy delegates. Follow-up organizations include the Fellowship of Confessing Anglicans. Not only do they censure the liberal theology and social positions embraced by many Anglicans loyal to the archbishop of Canterbury, but they also encourage the rise of independent Anglican Churches such as the Anglican Church in North America (ACNA), formed in 2009.[74] In October 2013 GAFCON held a conference whose theme was titled "Re-evangelising the West."[75]

Having considered the impact on Western Christians by arriving Majority-World Christians, let's examine an alternative question. What impact will the West have on the Christianity of Majority-World immigrants? Will they or their children continue to emphasize divine healing once they have access to advanced health-care systems? Will they continue to make material blessings an essential part of their faith once they have jobs that pay living wages? Will the children and grandchildren of Christians first evangelized in Asia or Africa embrace the suffering Christ (cross-centeredness), or will they cling to a gospel of prosperity? Will Majority-World forms of worship be maintained, or will their encounter with the West yield significantly modified alternatives? Once receiving an education that relies heavily on Enlightenment reason, will the children of Majority-World Christians retain their parents' belief in the power of evil spirits? In response to such questions, Yale professor Lamin Sanneh predicts for Majority-World Christians a "collision" between the two worlds.[76]

Implicitly, our study has raised questions about the currency and adequacy of the term "evangelical." Is "evangelical" broad and pliable enough to incorporate the millions of Christians in the Majority World who may be only tenuously related to evangelicalism in the West? Is the term so historically and culturally constricted and politically compromised that, at best, its use should be confined to Western churches? Are Western evangelical scholars justified when claiming as fellow evangelicals Majority-World Christians who have very different histories and identities? If Majority-World Christians embrace the term "evangelical," are Western evangelicals prepared to expand the term's meaning so as to include the four markers of Majority-World Christians we have examined?[77]

We are now watching answers to these questions unfold.

For Further Study

"Christianity in Its Global Context, 1970–2020: Society, Religion, and Mission." Center for the Study of Global Christianity, Gordon-Conwell Theological Seminary, South Hamilton, MA, June 2013. http://www.gordon conwell.edu/ockenga/research/documents/christianityinitsglobalcon text.pdf.

Hastings, Adrian, ed. *A World History of Christianity*. Grand Rapids: Eerdmans, 2000.

Jenkins, Philip. *The New Faces of Christianity: Believing the Bible in the Global South*. New York: Oxford University Press, 2006.

———. *The Next Christendom: The Coming of Global Christianity*. New York: Oxford University Press, 2002.

"New Religious Movements." Hartford Institute for Religion Research. Accessed June 16, 2017. http://hirr.hartsem.edu/denom/new_religious_movements.html.

Offutt, Stephen. *New Centers of Global Evangelicalism in Latin America and Africa*. New York: Cambridge University Press, 2015.

Stiller, Brian C., Todd M. Johnson, Karen Stiller, and Mark Hutchinson. *Evangelicals around the World: A Global Handbook for the 21st Century*. Nashville: Thomas Nelson/World Evangelical Alliance, 2015.

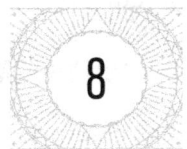

8

EVANGELICAL PROCLAMATION AND TEACHING IN THE TWENTY-FIRST CENTURY

DAVID WHEELER

"MILLENNIALS love Jesus but have issues with the church. The church is always looking for ways to judge somebody."[1]

Traditional Christians may bristle at such statements. But the undeniable truth is that the supremely attractive figure of Jesus stands above the "salad bowl" of global cultures and appeals to what is best and most noble and most hopeful in millions of people inside and outside the church.

Often as American believers we have tended to invite people into a Christian subculture containing a comprehensive worldview that must be swallowed whole. And in so doing we may not recognize the cultural conditioning of our own faith. Our contemporary encounters with "emissaries" from the global church, increasingly present here in the United States, remind us of the various expressions of authentic Christian faith that have blossomed in other times and places.

Thus evangelical proclamation and teaching in the twenty-first century must *begin* with the universal *story*—the story of Jesus Christ. Forming communities that attempt to live the Christian story, articulating coherent doctrines, and framing a worldview that connects the story with our experience and culture will follow.

"EVANGELICAL" CHRISTIANITY—SOME CONSIDERATIONS

As a term, "evangelical" has assumed various shades of meaning in church history—especially in recent decades. The term derives from the Greek word *euangelion*, the foundational "good news" of Christian proclamation. "The Word became flesh, and dwelt among us" (John 1:14, NASB). "God was in Christ reconciling the world to Himself" (2 Cor. 5:19, NASB). The foundational proclamation and experience is that God—the Divine Reality—became personally present in our midst in Jesus of Nazareth. Through him we can be transformed in the fullness of God's plan. This proclamation, this good news, sets the Christian faith apart from all other religious claims and philosophical systems.

In addition to denoting the foundational good news of Christian proclamation, the term "evangelical" has also been used to denote "Protestant," as in the "evangelical church" of the sixteenth-century Protestant Reformation. This happened because of the Reformation emphasis on *sola Scriptura* ("only the authority of the Scriptures," not humanly originated documents and doctrines), and *sola gratia* ("salvation by grace [through faith] alone," not by dependence on the practices and structures of the institutional church). More narrowly, in Anglo-American culture in recent decades, "evangelical" has often been associated with an understanding of Scripture as absolutely inerrant. This has been taken to mean that Scripture is accurate and truthful not only in matters of faith and practice but also in all its statements—whether historical, scientific, or moral.

In reaction against some of the currents flowing from the sixteenth-century European Renaissance and the eighteenth-century Age of Reason (Enlightenment), evangelicals and evangelicalism in Europe and North America came to be associated with a high view of biblical authority and with conservative moral and political convictions. Often in the twentieth century, evangelicals have been associated with a *propositional* understanding of Christian truth. This means that the Bible's teaching and Christian doctrine are primarily accepted as a body of truthful assertions.

That understanding of truth runs contrary to what is advocated in this chapter. Here we will maintain that the most effective evangelical proclamation for secular and unchurched persons is *invitational* in tone and content. "Come and see" (John 1:39, KJV). Come, hear the story of Jesus. Dare to follow him, to live his values as narrated in the Sermon on the Mount. Dare to look for signs of the in-breaking of God's righteous reign as he proclaimed it. Finally, dare to come alongside and join the community that anticipates Christ's reign. The sure promise is that whoever so dares will find himself or herself empowered by the Spirit of the risen Christ, just as did the first Christians who encountered him.[2]

So our understanding of "evangelical" and "evangelical proclamation and teaching" proceeds primarily from an *invitation* to come and hear the story of Jesus.

THREE STRATEGIC AFFIRMATIONS

Three strategic and practical affirmations follow from the stated understanding: (1) narrative takes priority over argument, (2) evangelical faith is faith grounded in and formed by Holy Scripture, and (3) evangelical proclamation is the fruit of a *free church* living and working in a *free society*.[3]

First, narrative (story) takes priority over argument. As the poet and songwriter Bob Dylan says, "You're gonna have to serve somebody."[4] Even in a broken world populated by universally flawed people—"For all have sinned and fall short of the glory of God" (Rom. 3:23, NIV)—

who live under the threat of death, we still bear our Maker's imprint, the *imago Dei* (Gen. 1:26-28). Thus most people arise each morning, prepare for the day, perhaps send their children off to school, and then take up their daily tasks *as if it matters*.

This principled, goal-directed behavior can be observed even among people living in poverty and under constant threat of violence. It is also witnessed among persons groaning under physical affliction or mind-numbing employment. Most people behave reasonably and with relative virtue most of the time. We believe in fairness, decency, and truthfulness, even when we repeatedly fall short. Why? Because *we believe it matters*. Theologian Hans Küng calls this "implicit faith."[5] And since we all must "serve somebody" or something, proclamation of the gospel begins not with *explicit* promotion of certain doctrines, but with a worthy object for our *implicit faith*.

Practically this is simply a matter of *telling the story*. But which story? Again, the answer is the supremely attractive story of Jesus, which can inspire and woo even the most secular and cynical among us. Jesus stands before all people, announcing a new world, a "new creation" (2 Cor. 5:17, NIV). This is a world where women and men, little children and foreigners, and the faithful remnant of Israel live together in humility, generosity, and mutual forgiveness; where health is restored and resources are shared and multiplied; and where even death itself will one day be vanquished. As has been true from the beginning, Jesus calls out, "Follow me" (Matt. 4:19; Luke 5:27, NIV). Do we dare?

In a very traditional way, we are affirming that evangelical faith is *personal*—a personal relationship with Jesus Christ. Such faith is not belief in a doctrine *about* Jesus but belief as "faithing," which is the correct meaning of the Greek verb *pisteuō* (I believe). This entails daring to leave behind all self-justification, self-sufficiency, and self-advancement, and daring *now* to live in and toward God's future of universal *shalom* (e.g., Isa. 11:1-10).

This is faith that "bears witness" (Greek, *martyreō*) in word and deed. It is faith expressed in the form of Koinonia Farm and the Habitat for Humanity movement born there.⁶ It is the active faith of the Sojourners Community⁷ and Prison Fellowship International (Matt. 25:36).⁸ Faith as "faithing" is observed among the evangelical minority in unlikely places such as Beirut, Lebanon,⁹ and the House for All Sinners and Saints in Denver,¹⁰ as diverse as these examples may be. A more or less coherent worldview and developed Christian doctrine follow rather than precede such decisions *to follow Jesus*.

Often the decision *to follow Jesus* entails great personal risk, as when in 1937 the young German pastor and theologian Dietrich Bonhoeffer established an underground seminary for the Confessing Church at Finkenwalde. This he did in the midst of "Hurricane Hitler." Later, although Bonhoeffer was a nonviolent follower of the Prince of Peace, he sacrificed doctrinal consistency to collaborate in a plot to assassinate Hitler. His decision to follow Jesus in this way cost him his life. Bonhoeffer thereby embodied his belief that "when Christ calls a man, he bids him come and die."¹¹ The original German title for Bonhoeffer's *The Cost of Discipleship* is *Nachfolge*, or "following after."

Usually the decision to follow Jesus is lived out quietly, away from the public eye. This is true of the Christian plumbers, auto-body workers, secretaries, and public schoolteachers who are role models and mentors to younger followers of Jesus. Whatever the form, the challenge for evangelicals in the opening decades of the twenty-first century is *to tell the story* and thereby create communities that *live the story*. Doctrine will catch up in due time.

Second, evangelical faith is faith grounded in and formed by Holy Scripture. This doesn't mean a collection of inerrant propositions, each carrying equal weight. Such a claim eventually ends in self-contradiction. Rather, "Holy Scripture" means a "great conversation" between God and God's people and among God's people across the generations. The psalmist illustrates this when he declares, "I have been young, and now am old, yet I have not seen the righteous forsaken or their children begging bread" (Ps. 37:25, NRSV). In contrast, hear the conversation in the book of Job as righteous Job mourns the death of his children and gropes toward some resolution beyond this life (19:25-27). Elihu, an accuser, mocks Job by saying, "The Almighty—we cannot find him" (37:23, NRSV). Before long, "the LORD answered Job out of the whirlwind" (38:1, NRSV).

The conversation between God and God's people that we hear in the Bible creatively continues today in intentional Christian communities that maintain the disciplines of Scripture study, worship, prayer, and advocacy for neighbors. This can include "radical" communities such as the Simple Way in inner-city Philadelphia[12] and the many Catholic Worker houses scattered across the United States.[13] But also the conversation is carried on in thousands of traditional churches worldwide, out of the limelight. Each week tens of millions of Christians gather worldwide for worship and annually provide billions of dollars' worth of diverse services to their communities.

Moreover, our conversational understanding of and approach to Holy Scripture must be Christ-centered. This means Jesus Christ as anticipated in the Law and the Prophets, present in our history, crucified, raised from the dead, present through the Holy Spirit, and returning at the end of the age. He is the axis running through all Holy Scripture. Indeed, the original meaning of "Word of God" is the creative Word spoken by God in the beginning (Gen. 1) that gave substance and shape to the primordial chaos. Or in the words of John's Gospel, "In the beginning was the Word, and the Word was with God, and the Word was God. . . . And the Word became flesh and lived among us" (1:1, 14, NRSV). Jesus Christ, the Word made flesh, is primarily what "Word of God" means.

The *written* Word is faithful testimony to Christ the *living* Word. When we encounter difficult texts in Scripture—texts of misogyny, violence, and seeming genocide (what Phyllis Trible calls "texts of terror"[14])—we carry those verses to the foot of the cross of Jesus; we acknowledge that while *many* have died because of sin, only the death of the Innocent One, Jesus the Messiah of God, can *resolve* our sins. And when we observe conflict or contradiction among Jesus's followers over contentious issues such as slavery or the role of women in church and society, we look to the practice of Jesus for instruction. And we turn to Jesus's promise that the Holy Spirit will lead us not into new truth but into "all the truth" as it is in Christ (John 16:13, NRSV).

The approach to and understanding of Holy Scripture that we are advocating here has a precedent in the teaching of Methodist founder John Wesley (1703-91). It is often referred to as the Wesleyan quadrilateral.[15] It involves (1) acknowledging *Scripture* as our primary source for faith and practice; (2) valuing Christian *experience*, personal and social; (3) affirming *tradition*, ecclesiastical and cultural; and (4) using *reason* as the God-given tool for analyzing and applying God's revelation. These four are what Methodist New Testament scholar Richard Hays calls "sources of authority."[16]

All four sources come into play in the way people hear and receive the story of Jesus. Two stories can illustrate this.[17] First, a young pastor was becoming bilingual in a congregation largely composed of Central American immigrants. The oldest daughter of a recently arrived Salvadoran family told the pastor that her two younger sisters wished to speak with him about accepting Christ. The family had been nominal Catholics in El Salvador and had been welcomed, encouraged, and assisted by the congregation. The sisters wanted to know more about this Christ the congregants believed in and served.

Arriving at their home, the pastor was greeted by the father, who spoke with him briefly. Then the father and his wife retired to the kitchen. From that vantage, the father could keep the two teenage daughters in his line of sight and within earshot. The pastor explained what it meant to accept Christ as one's personal Savior by using illustrations from Scripture. The two daughters listened intently. But when he sought their response, they looked at each other and were noncommittal. The pastor had mistakenly assumed that each sister would speak for herself.

Eventually, the father and mother and all three sisters *together* made professions of faith and were baptized as believers. The young pastor realized that contrary to the individualistic way Anglo-Americans tend to see things, these conversions were not instances of inauthentic groupthink. Instead, the family acted in harmony with the norms of their culture; they were making this life-changing decision communally. The teenage daughters had had the least face to lose in the family by expressing interest in becoming Christians. The pastor began to realize how much cultural traditions matter. This story is akin to the accounts in the book of Acts of both the households of Cornelius and the Philippian jailer becoming Christian at the same time as their household heads did (10:24-48; 16:32-34).

The second story happened in 1996. Due to the crash of the Russian ruble in post-Communist Russia, the Russian Baptists rented out much of their spacious building to American and other non-Russian mission agencies. Students were housed by twos and threes in small rooms on the dormitory floors. The dean's office, a faculty lounge, and a place for appointments with students occupied a single room. One afternoon a guest professor at the Moscow Theological Seminary of the Russian Baptist Federation unintentionally overheard a conversation between a Russian student and a visiting professor from Texas.[18]

The conversation was about what many Baptists call the perseverance of the saints, also known as once saved, always saved. The Texan pressed his doctrinal point, stressing such traditional proof texts as John 17:12: "I protected them in your name that you have given me. I guarded them, and not one of them was lost" (NRSV). By contrast, the Russian student pressed his belief in the possibility of defecting from one's relationship with Christ. The student did this in spite of the double discomfort of his desire to show traditional Russian deference to authority and his use of a second language. To support his position, the student cited Revelation 2:26: "He that overcome[s], and keep[s] my works [to] the end, to him will I give power over the nations" (KJV). But the Texan was unmoved.

Later the guest professor asked his friend Dean Gennadi to help him understand what he had overheard. Gennadi replied that Russian

Baptists, living for seventy years under Communism, sometimes on the fringes of legality and sometimes underground, had often experienced the trauma of discovering that a beloved pastor or deacon who might have sustained them through their suffering had become a KGB agent. He might even have baptized, performed marriages, and buried their loved ones. Surely, devout Baptists believed, it could not be that such a person had remained true to Christ!

This story keenly illustrates the impact context and experience can have on how we approach, understand, and teach Scripture. Rather than denying this, in conversation with our increasingly multicultural and global family of Christian brothers and sisters, we must seek understanding. As twenty-first-century teachers and evangelists, we must invite our neighbors to follow Jesus by how faithfully we tell and live the story, not by engaging in and winning cultural and doctrinal wars.

Third, evangelical proclamation in its most authentic and effective expressions is the fruit of a *free church* living and working in a *free society*. All attempts to use the power of the state to achieve the goals of the gospel, to use the powers of government to force people to comply with Christian norms, are doomed to failure. This error is often referred to as a Constantinian synthesis. It refers to the Roman emperor Constantine (ca. 272–337) and subsequent emperors who embraced Christianity as the empire's preferred and then official religion.[19] Being Christian became associated with political power and coercion. American evangelicals have sometimes sought to establish Christian practice in the nation by using the power of the state to force compliance. But selecting this route means following the same dead-end path that led to the failed state churches of the Old World.

Early Baptists such as John Smyth (ca. 1570–1612) and Thomas Helwys (ca. 1575–ca. 1616) lived and worshipped at the turn of the seventeenth century in their native England, and then as emigrants seeking protection in the Netherlands. They claimed absolute freedom of conscience based upon Scripture (e.g., Josh. 24:15; Isa. 42:2-3) and the illegitimacy of social or governmental coercion in matters of faith.

In 1636, Baptist minister Roger Williams founded Providence Colony (Rhode Island) and, in 1638, the First Baptist Church of Providence.[20] Williams prefigured the separation of church and state in the new American republic. He declared that "no civil magistrate, no king nor Caesar have any power over the souls or consciences of their subjects."[21]

Williams's declaration of independence that assures freedom for the gospel and the church's mission guards against evangelicals becoming identified with any state or political party, including political parties in the United States. God respects his creatures' freedom, including their political freedom. Jesus woos us by love, not by coercion, and rejoices when we follow him freely. And he grieves if we turn away (Mark 10:17-22; Luke 13:34-35). Jesus proclaimed and lived out the values of the kingdom of heaven. He performed works of liberating power and gathered an inclusive community that pointedly included the marginalized. Then and now, his redeemed community cuts across all political movements. His kingdom is distinct from the values of any political identification.

The values of the kingdom of God combine peacemaking (forgiveness of enemies), radical sharing, truthfulness, social transformation, purity, and fidelity in relationships. These values might be variously reflected by the political left and right. But they are never equivalent to, or in the possession of, either. Although Scripture calls on Christians to be engaged in public life (Jer. 29:7; Rom. 13:1-7; 1 Tim. 2:1-4), finally our dependence is upon the righteous power of God instead of political power.[22] American evangelicals in particular have sometimes lost sight of this truth and have placed too much trust in forming a political and cultural majority.[23]

Reminders of this danger are discernable in Central and South America, where surging evangelical commitments occur partly because evangelical churches constitute a countercultural reality through which people freely *choose* to follow Jesus. They do this as an alternative to a "cultural Catholicism" that has traditionally functioned as the religious expression of the social, political, and economic status quo.

In September 2014, a religious liberty conference organized by progressive legal scholars was held in Argentina. The conference was attended by representatives from the progressive wing of the Roman Catholic Church. It also included assorted religious minorities—Baptists, Methodists, Nazarenes, and other *evangélicos*. Adventists, Mormons, Jews, and Muslims were also present. The common goal shared by conference participants was what could be called a *free church* in a *free society*.[24] This is the posture par excellence for bearing witness to our faith in Jesus Christ. Too often we have dishonored our Lord and our mission by selecting deceptive political shortcuts for establishing "righteousness" in the land (Jer. 33:15).

Observing our third strategic affirmation—that evangelical proclamation in its most authentic and effective expressions is the fruit of a *free church* living and working in a *free society*—means that different cultures and different eras will discover, describe, and apply different perspectives of the gospel in their own contexts. Worldwide, faithful evangelicals will always wrestle with Scripture in the light of what the Holy Spirit teaches (John 14:26; 16:13). It is simply the case that the church has always read the Scriptures in changing contexts. That is no less true today. Even the first generation of Jewish Christ followers had to reinterpret messianic prophecy amid and for their Gentile neighbors, many of whom heard the story of Jesus gladly (Acts 8:4-8; 10:24-48), while Israel for the most part did not (Rom. 9–11).

Historian and interpreter of global Christianity Philip Jenkins illustrates my point by telling of a female preacher in Zimbabwe. Her sermon text was Jesus's command to his disciples to untie a donkey as part of Jesus's preparation for entering Jerusalem (Matt. 21:1-3). "I have," she said, "seen that we [women] are that donkey spoken of by the Lord. . . . Once we were not human beings. Some of us were even sold! To be married to a man was to be sold! . . . But with the coming of Jesus we were set free."[25] Most of us would likely never have had such an insight into the text. The preacher's sermon graphically illustrates the truth that wherever the gospel has gone, the good news has transformed people and cultures.

Many traditional societies of the Majority World (the Global South) "live in New Testament times" unknown to evangelicals in the West. These societies are marked by strict clan loyalties and gender roles. They have a lively awareness of the demonic. Christian believers in northern Nigeria, Iraq, and Syria, for instance, might see the curses and conflicts of the book of Revelation (the Apocalypse) as elements of their daily lives, instead of consulting "color-coded interpretations of prophetic passages" as some Christians in North America might do.

In 1998, similar differences and tensions came to light in Cali, Colombia. For a long time the Southern Baptists and the Colombian Baptists had a fruitful relationship. For instance, missionaries from the Southern Baptist Convention and their Colombian partners founded the Baptist seminary in Cali—the Seminario Teológico Bautista Internacional. But now, forty years later, the relationship between the Southern Baptist Convention and the Colombian Baptist Convention was fraying.

One of the pressing issues was the emergence of female pastors and leaders among Colombian Baptists. This was happening as the Southern Baptists were becoming more stringent about gender roles in the church. The question was, Would the Colombian Baptists be free to read Scripture and order their churches in harmony with their culture's matriarchal traditions, and with the groundswell of university educated women in urban churches?

Not only will observing our third strategic affirmation free other cultures to discover, describe, and apply different perspectives of the gospel in their own contexts, but also a second benefit is now unfolding. Christians coming from Majority-World cultures are positively influencing churches in Europe and North America.[26] While some parts of American evangelicalism struggle with division and decline, emissaries from the global church are pointing a way forward. For example, Rev. Doug Harris and Rev. Carol McVetty, former copastors (recently retired) of the North Shore Baptist Church in Chicago, led a team of pastors that served a congregation comprised of Anglo, African-American, Latino, and Japanese members. And Dr. Fred Lewis of the First Baptist Church of Indianapolis has witnessed the church's Sunday school and ministry to children and youth expand dramatically since the arrival of refugees from Myanmar (Burma). First evangelized two hundred years ago through the mission outreach pioneered by Adoniram and Ann Judson, upon arrival in America these Burmese Baptists sought out their spiritual forebears.

Similar scenarios are playing out in Europe. Many of the liveliest Anglican parishes in England are being revitalized by African and Caribbean believers. But their readings of Scripture and values are sometimes at odds with their English neighbors. The largest Christian congregation in Europe was founded in the Ukraine in 1993 by a Nigerian immigrant. Now, 98 percent of the worshippers are native Ukrainians.[27]

So in many ways the Majority World is coming to North America and Europe. Its representatives gladly gather wherever the story of Jesus is being faithfully told and where in Jesus's name the beloved community is being fostered. They are not preoccupied with the doctrinal disputes that have so often divided European and North American evangelicals.

Let us be clear. By applying the third strategic affirmation as we have, we are *not* advocating doctrinal or moral relativism. We are not saying that Scripture and historic Christian doctrine should be subject to changing cultural norms. Theologian Thomas Oden speaks of a "new ecumenism" emerging in the world of bankrupt secular ideologies.[28] The emerging ecumenism is founded upon the *ancient* ecumenism provided by the early ecumenical councils (the "conciliar consensus"), as discussed earlier in chapter 3. According to Oden, the emerging consensus is characterized by an "organic view" of historical change in the church overseen by a sovereign God.[29] It is (1) realistic about human sinfulness, (2) confident in the power of God, (3) engaging in cross-cultural listening to the Scriptures, and (4) expecting the emergence of a new consensus of

Christian conviction.[30] In the meantime we utter to the world "a gentle *no* on behalf of a greater *yes*" by affirming Jesus Christ as the only Lord and Savior of the world.[31] We make this affirmation against the grain of much contemporary teaching, even within the church.[32] Neither passively nor aggressively, we seek to tell the story clearly and practically and live it authentically and consistently.

The most compelling mandate for the church is simply to *tell the story*—the unique and compelling story of the One whom we believe to be the tangible, historic incursion of the Divine Reality into our shared history. The story is so beautiful and compelling that it overrides all culture-bound and institutionalized forms of Christianity.

Telling the story correctly includes living it in winsome communities that incarnate the values and the hope Jesus proclaimed, particularly among divided, disillusioned, and marginalized peoples. "Truly I tell you, just as you did it to one of the least of these who are members of my family, you did it to me" (Matt. 25:40, NRSV). Even for those whose perception of reality and life experiences may be crippled, the story of Jesus—rightly told and lived—will bring them into contact with the One who is the Good, the True, and the Beautiful. Living the story means living toward God's will.

Further, Thomas Oden's conviction holds true—that faithfully living the story will draw Christians into a renewed commitment to the foundational ecumenical creeds and doctrines of the church—the *ecumenical consensus*. However, doctrine doesn't come first; it follows committing to and living the story of Jesus. And Christlike conduct matures in the context of supportive, Christ-committed communities. To that end, the First Baptist Church in Portland,[33] Oregon, works in close cooperation with two rescue missions and with an Alcoholics Anonymous group that meets in the church building. Recovering alcoholics and addicts are welcomed into the traditional middle-class congregation. The church often includes their struggles and those of their friends in its prayers.

A striking incident that occurred in the Portola Church in San Francisco[34] further illustrates the point. An unmarried couple—already parents of a small child—was invited to worship with the congregation. They were welcomed into fellowship and Bible study. Soon they made professions of faith. As the pastor prepared to baptize them, some of the deacons protested: "But they're living in sin. They need to be married, and then they can be baptized." The pastor's response was, "Did Peter and the apostles vet the families of the three thousand on the day of Pentecost? No, the three thousand joyfully responded to the message about Jesus and were straightway baptized." So the church proceeded to baptize the couple. Before long the two said, "Pastor, we need to make our family like our faith. Will you marry us?"

Moreover, as we have seen, we must proclaim a faith and live lives informed by Scripture. Our reading of Scripture must be *dynamic* and *contextual*, informed first by the Holy Spirit (John 16:13) and second by Paul's conviction that in Christ, he was called to be "all things to all people, that [he] might by all means save some" (1 Cor. 9:22, NRSV).

Telling and living the story well will require that we avoid entangling our faith in political parties and agendas. We must be prepared to speak truth to power (Acts 4:19-20). The gospel of Jesus Christ is not an earthly political program or privileged nationality. Granted, in some instances there is no clear demarcation between the gospel and some culturally and linguistically identified churches that are to a large extent united with the political order in which they exist—an arrangement we have labeled "Constantinian." Some Orthodox churches can serve as examples. Nevertheless, historically the Jesus movement began and flourished among Palestinian Jews governed by a Roman power over which they had no control. For proclamation and expansion they effectively used synagogues of the Jewish Diaspora (dispersion) and the *Pax Romana* (Latin, "peace of Rome"). Since then, the church has always flourished best and been most true to its Lord as a *free church* in a *free society*—a truly countercultural movement.

The explosion of full-orbed Christian faith in the Majority World is good news for global evangelicalism.[35] It has given birth to indigenous churches large and small. Some are connected to historic global communions (denominations), while some are not. They are marked by uncompromising calls for faith in Christ as the only Savior. Committed to ministry to the whole person, they establish and support schools, medical institutions, and family life programs. Many of the churches enthusiastically accept Holy Spirit phenomena, something that hasn't characterized traditional American evangelicals. And as we have seen, this exploding global church is beneficially impacting European and North American evangelical churches. Its emissaries bring along their own Christian experiences and values. They challenge our old preoccupations and divisive doctrinal arguments.

For all of this we say, "To God be the glory!"[36]

For Further Study

Hauerwas, Stanley, and L. Gregory Jones. *Why Narrative? Readings in Narrative Theology*. Eugene, OR: Wipf and Stock, 1997.

Jenkins, Philip. *The Next Christendom: The Coming of Global Christianity*. New York: Oxford University Press, 2002.

Oden, Thomas C. *After Modernity—What? Agenda for Theology*. Grand Rapids: Zondervan, 1992.

Plueddemann, James E. *Leading across Cultures: Effective Ministry and Mission in the Global Church*. Downers Grove, IL: IVP Academic, 2009.

9

VOTING, VALUES, AND VOCATION
THE SHAPE OF EVANGELICAL POLITICS

TIMOTHY R. GAINES

NO BOOK on evangelicalism is complete until it gives attention to evangelicals and the political order. This is especially true, given how in recent decades evangelicals have been heavily involved in modern politics. With the rise of the religious right in the latter half of the twentieth century, evangelicals were vaulted to national attention in the United States and globally. Ironically, evangelical doctrine was often given little attention. Instead, political positions reflecting evangelical ethics attracted the most attention. Consequently, a public image for evangelicals that revolved around moral and social issues began to form. Championing the traditional family unit and opposing abortion were prominent among them. Bourgeoning evangelical parachurch organizations such as Campus Crusade for Christ were deployed to provide a "bulwark against secularism, moral decay, and communism."[1] They supposed they "could enhance America's ability to play a critical role in redeeming the world."[2] Certain moral norms and political alliances came to define evangelical belief and practice.

Given evangelicals' current political influence in the United States and elsewhere, considerable attention is being given to the question, Why are evangelicals so heavily engaged in politics?[3] Cable news pundits are amazed by evangelical influence as they discuss election results. Unmistakably, evangelicals constitute a powerful voting bloc capable of influencing public policy.

Here the question that calls for careful consideration is not, What are evangelicals doing to politics? but, What is politics doing to evangelicals? How is evangelical engagement in modern politics, perhaps especially in North America, shaping evangelicals?[4] The question is urgent because the content and range of evangelical faith must never be reduced to politics. Evangelical faith can be compromised and betrayed in many ways. Too closely aligning it with political interests and social issues is one dangerous and subtle form.

Recent polling data from the Public Religion Research Institute (PRRI; a nonpartisan, independent research organization) forcefully makes the point. In 2011, 30 percent of white evangelicals in the United States said that in order to elect political candidates who agree with them on political and social issues, they would be willing to ignore moral indiscretions in a candidate's or official's personal life. Furthermore, they maintained, moral failure would have no impact on a person's ability to execute his or her office. By 2016, that number jumped to 72 percent. Compared with a sampling of all Americans, evangelicals were 25 percent more likely to have changed their position on whether moral failure in an elected official's public life would impact his or her effectiveness. During that same period, the number of evangelicals who said a political candidate's religious beliefs are "very important" declined by 15 percent.[5]

The data seems to point to rapid and significant changes indexed to political interests instead of their traditional doctrinal convictions. The changes, and possible implications, require us to investigate what politics might be doing to evangelicals. Cable news outlets will likely not probe this question, but we who are committed to evangelical faith should. Possible implications must not be ignored.

A GOSPEL PEOPLE

Evangelicals claim to be gospel people. They claim a name given by the gospel itself—*euangelion* (Greek, "good news"). The gospel that names evangelicals is good news about God becoming flesh, incarnate, embodied in the person of Jesus of Nazareth, a peasant carpenter from the wrong side of the tracks. It is good news appearing in the person of someone who washed the feet of his followers, rode a donkey when a gallant horse was expected, associated with the "wrong" kind of people, touched untouchables, and shrugged off an opportunity to seize political power.

However, the political dimensions of this gospel cannot be denied. The gospel *is* political. Perhaps this strikes us as strange, even offensive. If so, that is likely because we have long associated the term "political" with shady figures vying for power in back rooms. Or we might have reserved the term for professional politicians willing to promise whatever it takes to be elected. When we hear "politics" we might imagine dishonest and deceitful practices. Or we might recall the political gridlock that too often chokes American political institutions. At any rate, this is not the gospel of Jesus Christ! The gospel, we say, is not supposed to divide people by party bickering. So what could justify speaking of the gospel as political?

To begin, the term "politics" has a long and rich history not necessarily associated with partisan prizefights. At its heart, politics is the art of creating a way of life that allows human collective life to flourish. It is the task of skillfully establishing a good and just order that benefits everyone. When understood in this way, the gospel of Jesus can be spoken of as political. It announces the arrival of a kingdom, governed by a good King, capable of establishing human relationships in which life can flourish.

Next, the gospel of Jesus is political because the inaugurated kingdom of God is even now becoming a reality on earth (Matt. 6:5-13; Luke 11:1-4; 17:20-21). Jesus's first words recorded in the Gospel of Mark announce good news to the world: "'The time has come,' he said. 'The kingdom of God has come near'" (1:15, NIV). This kingdom, Jesus tells us, grows as quietly as a plant, rather than through public displays of power (4:26-32).

Jesus doesn't simply talk about the kingdom. He inaugurates it, brings it near through his touch and presence. As seen in Mark's Gospel, Jesus, through his deeds and by parables, manifests the character of his kingdom. He manifests his kingdom by restoring the rejected to community, healing the sick, and strengthening the powerless (5:1-43). If his aim had been to score political points with the prevailing political powers, then restoring a dead child to life, conversing with Samaritan women of questionable character, and interacting with a demon-possessed outcast would have been a pointless waste of his time and effort. However, this is exactly how the kingdom of God comes and functions. And when the kingdom Jesus inaugurates eventually engages those in positions of political power, it results in a violent reaction. The powers display a radical departure from Jesus's kingdom activity of forgiving sin, feeding the hungry, and healing the sick (6:14-29).

When Satan tempts, or tests, Jesus (Matt. 4:1-11; Luke 4:1-13), he dangles before him a kingdom radically different from the kingdom Jesus was sent to inaugurate and proclaim. Matthew says Jesus is tempted to use his power to provide food for himself (Matt. 4:3), protection for himself (v. 6), and finally to reach for the "kingdoms of the world and their splendor" (v. 8, NIV). All he needs to do is abandon his mission of bringing a new kind of kingdom. Just grab the world's power already available and functioning (vv. 8-9). Jesus rejects these temptations without flinching. When he returns from his time of testing, his message is powerful and crystal clear: "Repent, for the kingdom of heaven has come near" (v. 17, NIV).

In the next chapter of Matthew, seated on a hill, Jesus presents to his listeners the "politics" of his kingdom. Astonishingly, he tells them "the meek . . . will inherit the earth" (5:5, NIV). "The merciful . . . will be shown mercy" (v. 7, NIV). Those who make peace will be God's heirs (v. 9). Enemies will be loved in the politics of the gospel (v. 44). "Those who hunger and thirst for righteousness," rather than for power and self-aggrandizement, will be satisfied (v. 6, NIV). Whatever primary loyalty we might have given to earthly kingdoms before, it will now be replaced by the new politics of God's kingdom.

What people had observed in politics is probably included in Jesus's words, "You have heard" (e.g., vv. 21, 27, NIV). Regrettably, in our day politics too often means infighting and exercising control over others. By contrast, the politics of Jesus's gospel blesses those who mourn, restores the fallen, and pronounces blessings upon the meek. Often we observe that in the world it takes wealth, money, and power to accomplish very much. But in the politics of Jesus, faithfulness to God carries the day. Many treat modern politics as a path for gaining one's own selfish way in the world. By contrast, the politics of Jesus transforms us into people who long and work for God's will to be done on earth, even as it is in heaven. The politics of Jesus contradicts what the world tells us about power, what we ourselves might even have believed, and upends it all. The politics of Jesus redeems the world by turning worldly values upside down.

Jesus's kingdom does not identify itself with the crafty patterns and manipulative schemes of worldly kingdoms. Instead, it quietly grows in hope, inching its way into the world like a plant sprouting from unseen seed. It is fertilized by God's faithfulness to the powerless and nurtured by Christ's refusal to deploy his power after the manner of earthly kings. The gospel of the kingdom and the politics of Jesus must give evangelicals their name, identity, and reason for being. Otherwise, evangelicals are indistinguishable from kingdoms desperately in need of a Redeemer and a redeemed people.

If the gospel is political as described, then so must those be who compose Christ's church. Evangelical life should announce that the kingdom of God is at hand! Otherwise, it fails to be evangelical life. This kingdom is not one in which citizens maneuver to become the greatest and most powerful—to elevate themselves above others—but to embody reconciliation by serving one another. "Church" should be the name we give to those who choose to live according to the values that mark the kingdom Jesus brings. It is a kingdom characterized by reconciliation, by doing nothing self-serving, and by valuing all others even as we value ourselves (Phil. 2:3).

The shape of Christ's gospel must shape evangelical life. This must not be limited to spiritual interests that exclude demands associated with our everyday life together. Rather, the gospel of Jesus is good news for all dimensions of human life. It lays claim to our time, our resources, and what we do with our bodies. It is political in the kingdom sense all the way down.

The good news is that the politics that characterizes the gospel is completely different from that offered by the world. Gospel politics has a different end in mind. Whereas the politics of the world too often seeks power for power's sake, the politics of the gospel seeks redemption and healing for all persons, regardless of party, ethnicity, or national identity. Because human life shaped by the gospel is so fundamentally different from the kingdoms of this world, we may be sure that a gospel-shaped life will not neatly comply with them.

And so our question is an important one. Given how vigorously evangelicals are engaging in the public political order, what impact is this making upon evangelicals? The question increases in urgency when churches appear to be too much shaped by values given to them by the kingdoms of this world, rather than by the politics of Christ's kingdom.

Sometimes churches and even denominations can come to be known by political labels used for national political parties. Some are known as "liberal" while others are "conservative." There are churches and denominations appropriately described as theologically conservative or theologically liberal. But the labels "conservative" and "liberal" become problematic when imported from this world's kingdoms. The gospel of the kingdom recognizes no such political labels. It recognizes only "faithful" and "unfaithful" disciples of Jesus Christ, being either "faithful" or "unfaithful" to kingdom politics, to its distinctive way of life.

No doubt those who adopt the political labels "conservative" and "liberal" do so because they think their political philosophy will help make the world a better place. While the two political philosophies share this much in common, they are in vigorous competition with each other over what "making the world a better place" requires. Each philosophy maneuvers to advance its own vision, its own causes, at the expense of the other. And each side believes itself superior to the other. Neither faction values the other above itself. They do not practice "foot washing" (Matt. 26:14-29; Luke 22:24-27; John 13:1-7).

When modern political patterns are permitted to take control of an individual church or a denomination, we begin to see the harm politics does to those who are supposed to be gospel people above all else. A politics foreign to the politics of God's kingdom moves in and dictates which one should be practiced. The distinctive pattern of God's kingdom—which seeks not self-interest but the interest of others (Phil 2:4)—is ignored or forgotten. To the degree that evangelicals narrowly identify themselves with the kingdoms of this world, they have forgotten the gospel that names them.

The challenge is to examine and correct this error so we might become a more faithful gospel-shaped people.

THE KINGS' SEDUCTIVE CALL

One of the things modern politics tempts evangelicals to do is join the political structures endorsed by this world's kings, rather than practice the political pattern of God's kingdom.[6] Think of this as an option between *the world of kings* and *the world of the kingdom*.[7] The world of kings operates according to the politics to which the world is accustomed—the politics of right vs. left, conservative vs. liberal, gaining power and using it to get our way.

The world of the kingdom, on the other hand, is a distinctly different world. "The purpose of political life is different in that world. Rather than overcoming the opposition for the sake of advancing our own agendas, the world of the kingdom understands that political life has much more to do with [being faithful] to a faithful God."[8] Trouble arises when the people of God hear and obey the seductive call coming from the world of kings. They proceed to align themselves with its political structures, rather than learning and walking according to the *way* of the kingdom God.

That is the damage modern politics is doing to evangelicals. When evangelicals submit to its seduction, when we begin to align primarily with the world of kings, we leave behind the good news of the entirely new kingdom God has given us in Jesus.[9]

This should not be taken to mean that Christians must refrain from participating in modern politics. Christians should vote and participate in ways their abilities offer, including elected office. But it does mean Christians must never elevate the world of kings above the gospel of Jesus and the kingdom he brings. The lives of gospel people must, above every other kingdom, announce God's good news that the kingdom of God is at hand.

In fact, Christians have been doing this for centuries. When Augustine (354–430), an early church leader, spoke of a Christian's relationship to politics, he pointed out that all political rulers rightly derive their authority from the only King to have ever been resurrected. When a mayor, judge, or magistrate exercises his or her authority, Augustine says, he or she must do so while recognizing that the resurrected and ascended Christ has been exalted "to the highest place" and has been given "the name that is above every name" (Phil. 2:9, NIV).[10] Christians are not required to withdraw from political life, but to engage in it while understanding their engagement should be shaped in accordance to the kingdom Christ is bringing (Rev. 11:15).

Gospel people are those who welcome, who embrace, the very different kind of politics given to us by the King of Kings, who was coronated in a Bethlehem stable. Only as we trust the good news of God's kingdom to shape our lives do we become evangelical.

VOTING OUR VALUES AND THE CALL TO DISCIPLESHIP

What else is modern politics doing to evangelicals? It threatens to replace the *vocation* of Christian discipleship. It tells evangelicals that politics is about having values that can be legislated, rather than Christian values being a *way* of life. The difference between the two is in how we relate to them. Values are stated ideals people hold in high regard. Discipleship, on the other hand, is a political reality that claims our whole life; it entails a relationship of following Jesus in loving obedience.

Consider Matthew's Gospel as it describes this relationship. Matthew says, "Jesus began to preach, 'Repent, for the kingdom of heaven has come near'" (4:17, NIV). In the next verse, Jesus walks beside the Sea of Galilee and spots men who would become his first disciples. What Jesus does next sets the kind of relationship his followers will have to his kingdom. "Come, follow me," Jesus says to Peter and Andrew (v. 19, NIV). Consider what Jesus did *not* say. He did not ask them to theoretically and mentally endorse a body of ideas about the kingdom he was bringing, and then move on to other things. He did not ask them to sign on to a package of beliefs, policies, and values. Instead, he called them to follow his *way*, and they did.

The vocation of discipleship is not primarily a matter of changing one's beliefs. It is primarily a call to follow Jesus as he establishes his kingdom. It is a call to align our entire lives with the kind of kingdom Jesus is bringing. Just as Peter and Andrew abandoned their nets, we, too, must abandon all allegiances—including political allegiances—that in any way compete with the gospel of Christ. Disciples relate to the kingdom Jesus brings by plunging into its way of life—into its politics—above all else.

The "gospel politics" Jesus proclaimed in his Sermon on the Mount are not inspiring ideas from which one can make selections. Jesus wasn't offering one ideology among others. Had that been the case, he would have just been one more politician among many. Rather, what he preached he also lived, and he calls his disciples to live with him by living as he lived. Jesus did not merely theorize about the meek inheriting the earth and then become a political lobbyist for them. He did not join Caesar's political system and use it to force his "politics," his values, on others. Instead, he inaugurated a new kind of kingdom in which the meek truly are blessed. He did not attempt to take over the Roman political system as though doing so was his only option. Rather, while Rome was busy catering to the powerful, Jesus established a mustard-seed kingdom that quietly does the work of redemption, of blessing those whom Rome would never bless. Blessing the poor, those who mourn, peacemakers, and the persecuted were not a social or political program Jesus hoped Rome would impose throughout the empire. Blessing those whom the kings of the world do not consider blessed is the very shape and content of the kingdom of God.

Jesus never strong-armed political powers into his kingdom. Nor did he try to overthrow them. Doing so would have required abandoning the kind of kingdom he was bringing, and joining Rome's fight for power. Instead, Jesus calls disciples to follow him by embodying a new kind of kingdom where strong-arming, coalition building, and power plays have no place.

Now, because the gospel is the good news of that kingdom, gospel people will not treat Jesus's kingdom as a set of ideals to be considered and occasionally practiced. No! Jesus's disciples—those gospel people—leave their nets and follow Jesus by living out the meaning of his kingdom. It is not enough to voice approval of the kingdom Jesus brings but then proceed to form one's life in Rome's image. That would reduce the gospel to an abstract ideology and the kingdom of God to a set of optional values.

Receiving the gospel of the kingdom of God excludes theoretical approval that leaves space for living as before. Rather, receiving the gospel entails following Jesus's way of life all the way to the cross and on to resurrection life. That is what it means to receive the gospel, to be gospel people, to be evangelicals.

Values and the way of Jesus are related, but they are importantly different. Values hold a place of importance in a belief system. They include cherished ideals, practices, and relationships.

Many evangelical churches now identify themselves by their core values instead of their articles of faith or statements of belief. Listed among their values may very well be things we associate with the kingdom that Jesus is bringing. There is certainly nothing wrong with naming our values. However, the danger lies in turning values into a collection of beliefs we affirm. Our challenge as Christians is not whether we can articulate a set of core values that align with God's kingdom but whether we are prepared to throw down our nets and obediently follow Jesus in his very particular way. Perhaps modern politics has conditioned us to be more concerned about *the ideals we value* than *the way we follow*.

An additional challenge is that if we settle for a body of core values, they may tell us nothing about how they should be lived or embodied. For example, a group of people may prefer chocolate over vanilla ice cream. But that "value" doesn't tell us how it is to be expressed. The "chocolate ice cream" people could quietly go about eating their ice cream. Or they could express their preference by forming a coalition to oppose or stamp out all "vanilla ice cream" people. Ice cream is not the point, but how the cherished value functions politically. Worthy kingdom values can be advanced in ways that are consistent with the kingdom politics of Jesus or that are quite contrary.

A young German philosopher named Friedrich Nietzsche (1844–1900) observed Christians filling German churches each week. They wanted to structure their society so that it would embody their values. But in the process, the way of Jesus took a back seat to the strategy those churchgoers chose. It wasn't that their strategy was necessarily bad, but that it was *theirs* and not *the way of Jesus*.[11] As if they were constructing a modern-day tower of Babel, they went about building the society they wanted without pausing to judge their plans against the way of Jesus, the pattern of life his kingdom brings. Eventually, for the German Christians the way of Jesus receded to become a quaint artifact. What they *valued* most was all that remained. Astonishingly, during World War II, many German Christians strongly supported Adolf Hitler. By contrast, German theologian and pastor Dietrich Bonhoeffer offered an uncompromising vision of the Jesus way, calling Christians to resist Nazi subversion of the gospel. He finally paid for his faithfulness at the hands of a Nazi execution squad in the early morning hours of April 9, 1945. Pastor Bonhoeffer both wrote and lived his famous discipleship charge, "When Christ calls a man, he bids him come and die."[12]

Someone might say that folks could still come together and affirm Christian values. True. But remember the chocolate ice cream. When *the way of Jesus* is reduced to a set of objective values, the door opens for advancing those values in ways inconsistent with *the way of Jesus*. Jesus did not initiate his kingdom by issuing a body of values his disciples were supposed to defend. Rather, he called them into a *vocation* called discipleship, which entails walking in Jesus's own way, comprehensively embracing gospel politics. Jesus did not enlist his disciples to make a political power play in the kingdoms of this world. Instead, he created the possibility for a different kind of kingdom altogether. In his kingdom, the meek shall inherit the earth, not those who are most successful in power politics.

Let's ask again, What has modern politics done to evangelicals? Too often it has convinced evangelicals that their most important contribution is to propose a set of values for legislative enforcement, rather than to model a *vocation to discipleship* that offers an altogether different kind of politics. If we evangelicals want to be gospel people, we must, above all else, live out the vocation of discipleship by shouldering Jesus's peculiar way of engaging the world. We must faithfully walk according to God's plan for redeeming his world and for achieving new creation. As gospel people, we evangelicals believe redemption is God's to bring, not ours. And it must arrive according to the way God has chosen. Following in the way of Jesus requires allowing God to redeem creation on his terms, not ours. Remember, God "tabernacled among us" (John 1:14, TLV; Luke 22:24-27) as a servant, not as a tyrant. Jesus is *how* God chooses to redeem the world. This is the gospel, the *euangelion*, upon which absolutely everything rests and upon which everything worthy of being called evangelical is founded!

Evangelicals must remain intensely aware of the idolatrous temptation to make something—anything—more important than the gospel of Jesus. As we have seen, the danger even applies to values associated with the gospel. They, too, can become more important than the gospel, that is, the announcement of a new kind of kingdom that forms a new kind of people. Gospel people forsake all other ways instead of trying to make Jesus fit into their own, or their political party's, way.

Embracing the politics of the kingdom, fully embracing Jesus's way, has from the beginning been a challenge for his disciples. Mark's Gospel, for example, shows the many ways Jesus's disciples tried to squeeze him into their political expectations. They were looking for a Messiah who would champion their inherited values—their ideology—at Rome's expense. As Jesus moves toward Jerusalem and all that will happen there, he repeatedly challenges his disciples' assumptions about how he will deal with the Romans, about how he will champion their political ideology. They want him to be a Messiah who will miraculously and decisively eliminate the oppressive Roman system and set up a heavenly reign on earth. Jesus does indeed establish a heavenly reign, but not according to the disciples' designs. When Jesus calls his disciples to pick up their crosses and follow him, he is calling them to align themselves with his way of self-sacrifice. The way of the cross will crucify the kind of kingdom they want to build. The way of the cross means that *the way of Jesus* would be *how* God's kingdom would be established and advance.

Today, many evangelicals seem to resemble those first disciples. They are committed to establishing a kingdom on earth consistent with Christian values and principles. But they seem to want to succeed by employing the kingdoms of this world to do so. Jesus's response remains the same today as it did on the shores of Galilee and the road to Jerusalem. Only the way of Jesus leads to things becoming "on earth as [they are] in heaven" (Matt. 6:10, NIV). As it did two thousand years ago, the Jesus way still includes foot washing, humility, and service. The Jesus way is lived out by a gospel people who trust that way enough to let it shape their lives, their kingdom politics. That is what the kingdom of heaven on earth looks like. That is the good news of Jesus Christ; that is what it means to be evangelical.

A TESTIMONY TO "OTHERWISE"

A phrase borrowed from Old Testament scholar Walter Brueggemann will highlight a final influence of modern politics upon evangelicals. From the lips of Israel's Old Testament prophets who declared the Word of the Lord, Brueggemann hears, "It could be otherwise!"[13] Woven through the ministry of Elijah, Elisha, and Israel's other prophets is a thread called "otherwise." It lies distinct in a field of options.

The world offers a plethora of options for how life should be lived. It urges us to decide between them. But what if there were an option the world does not know? That option is *otherwise*. *Otherwise* refuses to choose from among this world's options. It seeks another path. It rejects the claim that this world includes the entire package.

The book of 2 Kings provides an excellent example (2 Kings 4:8-37). It tells of a woman wrestling with options. She eventually lays "claim [to] invisible political options."[14] Her husband is soon to die, and she has no children—a bleak economic picture for a woman in ancient times. She receives an offer from Elisha to speak to the king on her behalf, probably a thinly veiled proposal that she become the king's wife.

Her options: destitution at home *or* provision with an unfaithful king. It was *either* stay with her people *or* go to the king and join his harem. But she saw *otherwise*. *Otherwise* was a political option invisible to her neighbors. When one has been as faithful to God as this Shunammite woman, faithfulness can open the eyes to possibilities others cannot see. In the end, her faith allowed the Shunammite to see a divine path forward, a beautiful example of *otherwise*. God gave her a son (v. 17).

Might it be that in a world with so many political options, our heavy reliance upon them restricts our evangelical voice and dims our testimony to *otherwise*?

Leading up to the 2016 US presidential election, many evangelical Christians expressed a desire for "better options." No matter how many political options there are, and no matter how preferable one might be to another, we must never forget that all of them represent the kingdoms of this world. All engage in power politics, practice self-assertion, and provoke conflict of some kind. Our hopes are that the winning party will to some extent represent our values.

But what if evangelicals were to refuse to identify with, or sponsor, any of this world's options? What if, instead, evangelicals as one voice were to announce their abiding allegiance to a kingdom that transcends this world's options? What if Jesus Christ and his kingdom politics were to become an uncompromising *otherwise* to which our lives and ministry bear witness?

The gospel calls Christians to see *otherwise*. Admittedly, in a world with so many options, *otherwise* can be difficult to see. Consider Mark's account of Jesus healing a blind man at Bethsaida (8:22-26). The blind man's friends lead him to Jesus, hoping he will be healed. At first, Jesus spits on the man's eyes, lays hands on him, and asks if he can see. "I see people; they look like trees walking around" (v. 24, NIV). Again Jesus placed his hands on the man's eyes, and this time he saw clearly. Why, we might ask, was Jesus's first effort not successful?

Mark wants us to ask that question as we encounter the next story.

"Who do people say I am?" Jesus asks of his disciples (v. 27, NIV). Eventually, Peter correctly confesses that Jesus is the Messiah. As soon as he does, Jesus begins to talk about how he will suffer and be rejected in Jerusalem. This upsets Peter so much he rebukes Jesus (v. 32). From Peter's perspective, the Messiah should not be one who suffers but one who makes others suffer—particularly Roman overlords! By Peter's partially restored way of seeing things, the Messiah should act in expected political ways. He should rise up against the Romans, overthrow them, and then install himself at the center of political and military power. Peter expected a Messiah who would act according to this world's political options. The problem was that Peter could only see the Messiah through lenses provided by the world's array of political options. He could see that Jesus is the Messiah. But he saw "trees walking." He needed a second touch before he could see clearly. He needed another option before his life could testify to *otherwise*.

All of us need a "second touch" when Jesus reveals what following his way requires. "If any want to become my followers, let them deny themselves and take up their cross and follow me" (v. 34, NRSV). This is the call to discipleship. It is the *way* of *otherwise*; it offers a political option seen only by those who choose the way of Jesus.

Surely, if as with Peter, all we are able to see is Jesus fitting into this world's political options (trees walking), then we need for him to lay his hands on us again. He must remind us again of the very *otherwise* kingdom he is bringing. He has left no doubt about how we are to respond to the gospel politics of his kingdom: "Whoever wants to be my disciple must deny themselves and take up their cross and follow me" (v. 34, NIV).

For Further Study

Bonhoeffer, Dietrich. *The Cost of Discipleship*. Translated by R. H. Fuller. 1959. Reprint, New York: Touchstone, 1995.

Gushee, David P. *The Future of Faith in American Politics: The Public Witness of the Evangelical Center*. Waco, TX: Baylor University Press, 2008.

Hoang, Bethany Hanke, and Kristen Deede Johnson. *The Justice Calling: Where Passion Meets Perseverance*. Grand Rapids: Brazos Press, 2016.

Hunter, James Davison. *To Change the World: The Irony, Tragedy, and Possibility of Christianity in the Late Modern World*. New York: Oxford University Press, 2010.

Moore, Russell. *Onward: Engaging the Culture without Losing the Gospel*. Nashville: B and H Publishing Group, 2015.

Palmer, Parker J. *Healing the Heart of Democracy: The Courage to Create a Politics Worthy of the Human Spirit*. San Francisco: Jossey-Bass, 2011.

Smith, James K. A. *You Are What You Love: The Spiritual Power of Habit*. Grand Rapids: Brazos Press, 2016.

10

EVANGELICALISM IN CATHOLICISM

JASON J. SIMON

MOST AMERICANS would not view Catholics as evangelicals. Most Catholics, in fact, would not *want* to be called evangelical. Because of how the media has commonly defined the word, Catholics usually see an unbridgeable gulf between their Catholic identity and what is commonly referred to as evangelical. But, in fact, to be truly Catholic is to be evangelical. For over fifty years popes and bishops have been leading a movement to build a bridge between this theological truth and mainstream Catholic life. Each one has endorsed what his predecessor taught about evangelical Catholic identity. They have exhorted the faithful and their shepherds ever more forcefully to live out an evangelical faith.

"Evangelical" simply means "of the gospel." Being "of the gospel" is to be wholeheartedly committed to Jesus Christ and the gospel. *Evangelical* Catholics, therefore, are singularly focused on living according to the truth and beauty revealed in Jesus Christ. They have a strong devotion to the Scriptures as the revealed Word of God, while also looking to the sacramental life, the hierarchy of the Catholic Church, and to God's revelation handed down in tradition (e.g., the Councils of Nicaea/Constantinople, Chalcedon, magisterial teaching,[1] etc.) as ways to encounter the truth and beauty of Jesus Christ. As an outflow of this devotion to Jesus Christ, evangelical Catholics long to draw more people into this life through the mission of evangelization. They strive to transform "all the strata of humanity" through the redeeming power of the good news.[2]

To believe and live this way is to be evangelical. To believe and live this way is also the essence of being Catholic. The term "evangelical Catholic" is actually redundant. Even so, following the unfortunate trend of so many peoples of faith, Catholic zeal for the Lord too often fades into mere weekly gatherings, cultural practices, and allegiance to particular leaders. Religious identity among many Catholics has too often been the end rather than the means. Too often Catholic communities of faith have turned away from the outward focus Jesus exemplified and have instead turned inward upon themselves. They have consequently created safe subcultures of unified belief and practice that shield themselves against outsiders.

However, at critical junctures in the church's history the Holy Spirit has inspired movements to awaken the church to its true evangelical identity and calling. Catholics are in the midst of just such a movement today. For the past fifty years the institutional authority of the Catholic Church has taken the lead to bring evangelical renewal to parishes, Catholic institutions, and movements around the world. Church leaders have used the magisterial teaching office to overturn the status quo. Their goal has been nothing short of reshaping mainstream Catholic life by encouraging a joyful embrace of evangelism and discipleship. Contemporary church renewal movements are responding joyfully: recharging parishes, youth ministries, Catholic universities, secular university campus ministries, and all aspects of church life through the purpose and power of the Great Commission.

In this chapter, we will examine some of the most consequential examples of this magisterial movement in order to show how the Holy Spirit is reinvigorating Catholic life. It will also explore the significant common ground between some of the core convictions of Catholics and evangelical Protestants.

LAUNCHING THE EVANGELICAL CATHOLIC MOVEMENT: POPE JOHN XXIII AND VATICAN II

In 1959, Pope John XXIII (r. 1958-63) called for the twenty-first ecumenical council (i.e., Vatican Council II). These councils are convened only when the church needs to address grave issues. Ecumenical councils gather ecclesiastical authorities and theological experts from around the world to settle important matters of church doctrine and practice. The commonly recognized ecumenical councils include the Councils of Nicaea (325), Constantinople (381), Chalcedon (451), and Trent (1545-63). These crucial councils brought together the highest church authorities and the sharpest theological minds to settle critical questions such as the relationship of the Son to the Father (Nicaea), the full deity and humanity of Christ in one undivided person (Chalcedon), and ecclesial issues raised by the Protestant Reformation (Trent).

Ecumenical councils are not convened lightly. Only very serious reasons justify a council. Pope John XXIII's grave reason for convening the Second Vatican Council in 1962 (1962-65) was to reclaim the Catholic Church's evangelical identity. In the opening address, he explained:

It is therefore an overwhelming source of grief to us to know that, although Christ's blood has redeemed every man that is born into this world, there is still a great part of the human race that does not share in those sources of supernatural grace, which exist in the Catholic Church. . . .

Such, venerable brethren, is the aim of the Second Vatican Council. *It musters the Church's best energies and studies with all earnestness how to have the message of salvation more readily welcomed by men.* By that very fact it blazes a trail that leads toward that unity of the human race, which is so necessary if this earthly realm of ours is to conform to the realm of heaven, "whose king is truth, whose law is love, whose duration is eternity."[3]

When Vatican II concluded in 1965, the church had refreshed its direction and revised its priorities. To express the mystery of the church, new language was used to give it a more evangelical disposition.[4] The council emphasized the universal call of all believers to holiness[5] and the missionary mandate of every Catholic to the world.[6] The council fathers sought to establish a new norm for lay prayer and devotion by urging every Catholic "to learn by frequent reading of the divine Scriptures the 'excellent knowledge of Jesus Christ' (Phil. 3:8). 'For ignorance of the Scriptures is ignorance of Christ' [St. Jerome]."[7]

These outcomes, and so many others, express the evangelical nature of this monumental council. George Weigel, Pope John Paul II's biographer, writes that Pope John Paul II (r. 1978–2005) saw the council as a "Spirit-led effort to renew Catholicism as an evangelical movement in history."[8] Vatican II did indeed spur an evangelical movement, and the popes that followed the council continued to build upon and expand its work.

ESTABLISHING THE PRIORITY OF THE MOVEMENT: POPE PAUL VI

In 1974, Pope Paul VI (r. 1963-78) convened a synod of bishops to continue exploring evangelization in light of the teaching of Vatican II. Following the synod he wrote an apostolic exhortation called *Evangelization in the Modern World* (*Evangelii Nuntiandi*). He boldly affirmed the conclusion of the bishops at the end of the synod: "Evangelizing all people constitutes the *essential* mission of the Church."[9]

The word "essential" carries heavy weight in Catholic tradition. It is used here as St. Thomas Aquinas (1225-74) employed the word, building upon Aristotle. Essence refers to that aspect of a thing that makes it what it is. To illustrate, a lamp has an essential quality that makes it a lamp. If its essential quality is removed by unscrewing its light bulb, breaking its stand, crushing it in a metal compactor, and melting it down in a furnace, at some point in this destructive process the lamp ceases to be a lamp. It will have lost its "lampness," its essence.

Pope Paul VI was reminding Catholic bishops, theologians, teachers, and laypeople that the church *has* an essence, a quality that is necessary for being the church. Its essence is a mission—evangelization. Without evangelization, Catholics could have a worldwide network of social gatherings, a structure of religious ritual, a cultural identity, or beautiful buildings, but they could not have the church: *churchness* equals *evangelization*. Without evangelization, the church ceases to be the church. To be evangelical, therefore, is inherent in the very nature of the church.

To expound on and strengthen this definition of the church's essence, Pope Paul VI wrote, "Evangelizing is in fact the *grace and vocation* proper to the Church, her *deepest identity*. She exists in order to evangelize, that is to say, in order to preach and teach, to be the channel of the gift of grace, to reconcile sinners with God, and to perpetuate Christ's sacrifice in the Mass, which is the memorial of His death and glorious resurrection."[10]

The literal meaning of the word "vocation" is "call." The church has a divine call to evangelize. Grace from God always accompanies a call from God. To take up this call and respond to this grace leads us into our deepest identity. God called Moses to free the Israelites. His grace, his presence and power, went with Moses. If he had not responded to this call and had instead continued to tend Jethro's flock, he would have missed out on his deepest identity. Not responding to our vocation and its accompanying grace leads to an incoherent life, a lack of meaning and purpose that results from failing to *be what we are*—Christian. On the other hand, by responding to this vocation and grace, we experience the power of God and our deepest identity as friends and colaborers with God.

Because the mission of the church belongs to each member of the body of Christ, Pope Paul VI made it clear that evangelizing is the essential mission, the grace, the vocation, the deepest identity of *all* Catholics, not just priests, religious, or professional missionaries. In other words, God is giving all Catholics the grace to evangelize their friends, families, and communities with the power of the good news of Jesus Christ. Catholics who feel no impulse to hope for, pray for, and work for the good news of the kingdom of God to come into the lives of their friends, family, and community are living incoherent lives. And they are missing out on the abundant life (John 10:10) that only comes from living their deepest identity in Christ (Phil. 3:7-11).

EXPANDING THE MISSION: ST. POPE JOHN PAUL II

The Catholic Church has been hesitant to apply the term "evangelization" very broadly. Baptized Catholics were not normally thought of as needing to be evangelized, but rather catechized or formed in the faith. Being Catholic is to be baptized into the fullness of faith. Catholics, therefore, were not thought to need evangelization; they had already been immersed into the good news and a life of faith.

The mission of evangelization was thought to be primarily directed toward the unevangelized people of the world. It was a mission *ad gentes*—"to the peoples." The exhortations to evangelize, expressed so forcefully at Vatican II and carried forward by Pope Paul VI, did not seem to apply to Catholics. Rather, the call was for Catholics to go outside their parishes to proclaim the gospel to unbelievers.

However, in the wake of the worldwide dissemination of the great teachings of Vatican II and Pope John Paul II, the impotence of many Catholics in the mission of evangelization became clear. Too many Catholics were unable, by their own lives and witness, to live the call to holiness and proclaim Jesus to unbelievers. First they needed more fully to experience the good news of Jesus Christ for themselves. They couldn't testify to what they hadn't experienced, and they lacked language for describing what they had known their whole lives.

This was especially true in the West—traditionally Christian nations. Many still self-identified as Catholics, still attended Sunday Mass, taught their children simple prayers, and even encouraged religious vocations. They lived in Catholic neighborhoods and attended Catholic schools. But for many, their religious affiliation was anchored more in the institutional reality of their Catholic faith than in their personal experience of Jesus. They lacked conviction about what Jesus meant in their lives. Often their lives, outside traditionally significant Catholic markers, did not evidence transformation by the gospel.

Reliance on the Catholic institution, ritual, and subculture for Catholic identity made parishioners vulnerable to emerging skepticism about institutional religion. They were also threatened by religious and moral pluralism instead of being able boldly to affirm their own faith. Simply put, the Catholic Church in the West was in trouble.[11]

Recognizing this growing weakness, at the 1968 Medellín Conference (in Colombia), Latin American bishops urged Catholic leaders to embrace evangelization. They voiced their urgency by employing what was at that time an unfamiliar term; they called for a "new evangelization." The bishops believed a new evangelization would "enable both the elite and the masses to achieve a more lucid and mature faith."[12]

Pope John Paul II, impressed by the thrust of the Latin American bishops' conferences, referred for the first time to a "new evangelization." He did this in a 1979 speech delivered to Polish workers oppressed under Communism.[13] Later he fully explained and promulgated "new evangelization" in his 1990 encyclical[14] on evangelization, *Mission of the Redeemer* (*Redemptoris Missio*): "There is [a] . . . situation, particularly in countries with ancient Christian roots, and occasionally in the younger Churches as well, where entire groups of the baptized have lost a living sense of the faith, or even no longer consider themselves members of the Church, and live a life far removed from Christ and his Gospel. In this case what is needed is a 'new evangelization' or a 're-evangelization.'"[15] Pope John Paul II repeatedly spoke of the urgent need for this new evangelization. In the same encyclical he wrote, "God is opening before the Church the horizons of a humanity more fully prepared for the sowing of the Gospel. I sense that the moment has come to commit all of the Church's energies to a new evangelization and to the mission *ad gentes* [to the peoples]. No believer in Christ, no institution of the Church can avoid this supreme duty: to proclaim Christ to all peoples."[16]

Even as John Paul II was watching the decline of Catholicism's strength in the West, the region of the church that had sent countless missionaries to the "ends of the earth," he also saw Eastern Europeans and others shaking off the atheistic grip of Communism. In the year prior to the publication of *Mission of the Redeemer*, the pope had watched millions march on Tiananmen Square in China, demanding freedom and democracy. He saw the desire of the human spirit for true freedom bubbling up all over the world. His writing seemed to be crying out: "If only we could strengthen the church in the West through a new evangelization, we could capitalize on the global opportunities to bring the gospel to places dramatically prepared to receive it."

The pope had a burning desire to reach the world with the gospel. He longed for the worldwide church to take up this call with equal zeal. In an apostolic exhortation dedicated to the Catholic Church in America, he passionately wrote, "The *burning desire* to invite others to encounter the One whom we have encountered is the start of the evangelizing mission to which the whole Church is called."[17]

This "burning" evangelical passion and impulse defined the pontificate of John Paul II. He traveled to more countries than had any previous pope. He visited over two-thirds of the world's countries to preach the gospel. He launched the World Youth Day phenomenon, drawing together millions of young people to encounter Jesus at international rallies. He sought to strengthen seminaries,[18] fostered evangelical movements in the church, and actively used the media to evangelize the world—Catholics and non-Catholics alike. His pontificate made the mission of the new evangelization a fixture in Catholic thought and a priority that could no longer be ignored.

POPE BENEDICT XVI AND THE YEAR OF FAITH

Pope John Paul II's successor, Pope Benedict XVI (r. 2005-13), took up the charge of making mainstream Catholicism evangelical. When he was elected, he had the reputation of being an inquisitor of doctrine. As head of the Congregation for the Doctrine of the Faith, he had worked under Pope John Paul II to rein in doctrinal abuses and establish a stronger orthodoxy. In some quarters he was called the Bulldog of Orthodoxy because of his doctrinal tussles with some Catholic thinkers. Many expected him to continue his bulldog ways once he became pope.

Imagine how surprised they were when Pope Benedict XVI's first encyclical was titled *God Is Love* (*Deus Caritas Est*). With a strong emphasis on the church's imperative to love above all else, the tone and content revealed a much larger goal for his pontificate than enforcing doctrinal rules.

In the first paragraph of this 2005 encyclical, Pope Benedict set the tone for his time as pope:

> *We have come to believe in God's love*: in these words the Christian can express the fundamental decision of his life. Being Christian is not the result of an ethical choice or a lofty idea, but the encounter with an event, a person, which gives life a new horizon and a decisive direction. . . . Since God has first loved us (cf. *1 Jn.* 4:10), love is now no longer a mere "command"; it is the response to the gift of love with which God draws near to us.
>
> In a world where the name of God is sometimes associated with vengeance or even a duty of hatred and violence, this message is both timely and significant. For this reason, I wish in my first Encyclical to speak of the love which God lavishes upon us and which we in turn must share with others.[19]

The emphasis on love and an encounter with Jesus as more primary than ethical debates or lofty theological ideas signaled that Pope Benedict's papacy would continue in the evangelical footsteps of his predecessor. His emphasis on loving God and neighbor, not as a matter of law, but as a response to God's love, became a consistent theme and hope of his pontificate.

Pope Benedict also made devotion to the Scriptures by all believers a pastoral priority. Shortly after his becoming pope, the fortieth anniversary of Vatican II's *Dogmatic Constitution on Divine Revelation* (*Dei Verbum*) occurred. Commenting on that sea-change document, Benedict said, "If [*lectio divina*][20] is effectively promoted, this practice will bring to the Church—I am convinced of it—a new spiritual springtime."[21]

As a theological advisor in the discussions leading to the drafting of *Dei Verbum*, Pope Benedict had long held the Scriptures in high regard, for the church and for himself. So it was no surprise when in 2008 he dedicated a synod[22] to the topic of the Word of God in the life and mission of the church. Based on the synod's conclusions, he wrote the apostolic exhortation *The Word of the Lord* (*Verbum Domini*). Its goal was to lead Catholics to meditate daily on the Scriptures and return frequently to the sacraments to renew their relationship with Jesus. He wrote as follows:

> Our own time, then, must be increasingly marked by a new hearing of God's word and a new evangelization. Recovering the centrality of the divine word in the Christian life leads us to appreciate anew the deepest meaning of the forceful appeal of Pope John Paul II: to pursue the *missio ad gentes* and vigorously to embark upon the new evangelization, especially in those nations where the Gospel has been forgotten or meets with indifference as a result of widespread secularism. May the Holy Spirit awaken a hunger and thirst for the word of God, and raise up zealous heralds and witnesses of the Gospel.[23]

Pope Benedict sought to restore the beauty of the church through a new, heartfelt participation in the Divine Liturgy, devotion to the Scriptures, and a loving proclamation of the gospel. A whole chapter could be written on the evangelical character of his three encyclicals, various apostolic exhortations, and his innovations such as the Year of

Faith, aimed at bringing unbelievers to faith in Jesus Christ. All this laid the groundwork for his successor, Pope Francis, who is working every day to make the Catholic Church more evangelical.

REACHING THE FRINGES: POPE FRANCIS AND THE EXISTENTIAL PERIPHERIES

Since becoming pope in 2013, Pope Francis has repeatedly emphasized the church's evangelical mission to the world. It is generally agreed that Cardinal Jorge Bergoglio, archbishop of Buenos Aires (1998–2013), was elected pope precisely because of his strong emphasis on reaching the "existential peripheries" with the gospel. He addressed his fellow cardinals as they were discerning who should succeed Pope Benedict XVI:

> Evangelizing pre-supposes a desire in the Church to come out of herself. The Church is called to come out of herself and to go to the peripheries, not only geographically, but also the existential peripheries: the mystery of sin, of pain, of injustice, of ignorance and indifference to religion, of intellectual currents, and of all misery....
>
> ... Thinking of the next Pope: He must be a man who, from the contemplation and adoration of Jesus Christ, helps the Church to go out to the existential peripheries, that helps her to be the fruitful mother, who gains life from "the sweet and comforting joy of evangelizing."[24]

Enough of the cardinals agreed with Cardinal Bergoglio's speech to choose him as the worldwide leader of Catholics.[25]

Since taking office, Pope Francis's teaching has a new, very practical tone in making the Catholic Church evangelical. Not only does he tell Catholics to evangelize, but he also tells them how! Hear his November 24, 2013, apostolic exhortation, *The Joy of the Gospel* (*Evangelii Gaudium*):

> Today, as the Church seeks to experience a profound missionary renewal, there is a kind of preaching which falls to each of us as a daily responsibility.... This is the informal preaching which takes place in the middle of a conversation.... Being a disciple means being constantly ready to bring the love of Jesus to others, and this

can happen unexpectedly and in any place: on the street, in a city square, during work, on a journey.

. . . In this preaching, which is always respectful and gentle, the first step is personal dialogue, when the other person speaks and shares his or her joys, hopes and concerns for loved ones, or so many other heartfelt needs. Only afterwards is it possible to bring up God's word, perhaps by reading a Bible verse or relating a story, but always keeping in mind the fundamental message: the personal love of God who became man, who gave himself up for us, who is living and who offers us his salvation and his friendship.[26]

Virtually every writing, speech, and homily coming from Pope Francis emphasizes a deep personal connection with Jesus, the richness of his revelation in the Scriptures, and the need sacrificially to bring his love to the world. Francis is working to lead the church into becoming a more structurally, doctrinally, and devotionally compelling evangelical witness in the world. He has been reforming the Vatican's staff, inspiring dialogue about a holy stewardship of the environment, prioritizing servant leadership as a criterion for bishops, and opening dialogue on aspects of Catholic practice that might be hindering people from experiencing Jesus in the church.

LOCAL BISHOPS CATCH THE FIRE

The work of Vatican II, Pope Paul VI, Pope John Paul II, Pope Benedict XVI, and now Pope Francis is having a powerful influence on the rest of the bishops throughout the world. Below are some illustrative recent writings by members of the hierarchy in the United States that show the rising tide of evangelical exhortation beyond Rome.

- *Disciples Called to Witness: The New Evangelization*
  Statement from the United States Conference of Catholic Bishops' Committee on Evangelization and Catechesis (2012)
- *Go and Make Disciples: A National Plan and Strategy for Catholic Evangelization in the United States*

Statement from the United States Conference of Catholic Bishops (2002)
- *"I Believed, Therefore I Spoke"*
Pastoral letter by Archbishop John C. Nienstedt (2012)
- *The Year of New Evangelization*
Pastoral letter by Bishop Sam G. Jacobs (2012)
- *Blest Are They Who Believe*
Pastoral letter by Bishops Thomas J. Olmsted and Eduardo A. Nevares (2012)
- "Why a 'New Evangelization' Now?"
Address by Cardinal Donald W. Wuerl (2011)
- "The Announcement of the Gospel Today, Between *missio ad gentes* and the New Evangelization"
Address by Cardinal Timothy M. Dolan to the College of Cardinals (2012)
- *A New Pentecost: Inviting All to Follow Jesus*
Pastoral letter by Cardinal Seán O'Malley, OFM Cap. (2011)
- *The Real Presence: Life for the New Evangelization*
Pastoral letter by Bishop Arthur J. Serratelli (2009)
- "The New Evangelization: Hospitality Is at the Heart"
Article by Reverend Monsignor Andrew Dubois (2012)
- "So That the World May Know New Hope"
Address by Cardinal Raymond L. Burke to the Knights of Columbus (2011)
- "Laity for the New Evangelization"
Article by Cardinal Stanislaw Rylko, president of the Pontifical Council for the Laity (2013)
- "Pope Francis, the Poor and the New Evangelization"
Article by Most Reverend Alexander Sample (2013)[27]

The Catholic Church is clearly in the midst of an evangelical movement, initiated by a hierarchy that promotes renewal at the parish level. The Holy Spirit has called specific popes, councils, and bishops to champion this movement and drive it deeper into the church's life.

Filled with zeal for our Lord Jesus Christ and compassion for the world, prominent Catholic leaders continue to spur the church to become a light to the nations (Isa. 49:6; Acts 13:47). They carry an evangelical burden for all persons everywhere to know the hope of Christ. They pray that the church will be seized by the fire of St. Paul seen blazing in 1 Corinthians 9:24-25: "Do you not know that in a race the runners all compete, but only one receives the prize? Run in such a way that you may win it. Athletes exercise self-control in all things; they do it to receive a perishable wreath, but we an imperishable one" (NRSV).

It is incoherent for the church, Jesus's body on earth, not to ache for people burdened by guilt, loneliness, insecurities, sadness, confusion, purposelessness, poverty, and wounds of oppression. These human ailments result from the fall and sin. They are wounds that only Jesus can heal, brokenness only he can mend.

The compassion of Christ sensitively speaks his hope and healing into all the world's dark places. And we are commissioned as his irreplaceable witnesses. "How can they believe if they have not heard?" (Rom. 10:14, GNT). Freely we have received forgiveness, friendship, confidence, joy, meaning, purpose, provision, and freedom. Now, freely we must give (see Matt. 10:8). Indeed, this has to be the essential mission of the ever-compassionate body of our risen Lord. This is what it means to be evangelical.

NEW EVANGELICAL MOVEMENTS AND ORGANIZATIONS

The Holy Spirit, who is inspiring this evangelical movement, is planting it in the hearts of millions of Catholics. Innumerable movements and organizations are now hard at work with the purpose of evangelizing and mobilizing Catholics to proclaim to the world the good news of Jesus.

More books, organizations, and ministries—too many to list here—are springing up to serve every area of the church and to evangelize every segment of society. A quick web search reveals a multitude of Catholic missionary organizations (domestic and international), leadership-consulting organizations (for priests, religious, and laity), retreat programs, youth programs and retreats, speakers' bureaus, radio and television stations, web-based informational resources, and learning management systems to prepare Catholics for evangelization.

Together they are making a profound impact. Nevertheless, the Catholic Church still has attrition problems. Catholic parishes are still not consistently evangelical. Indeed, evangelical Catholic parishes are still rare. Much work has to be done to train priests to preach evangelically, to reevangelize laity, and to form laity in basic practices of discipleship. But the Holy Spirit has provided the impetus through authoritative teaching that is necessary for evangelism to begin and spread worldwide. So the evangelical renewal for which popes and bishops long is spreading. Growing numbers of Catholics who would have otherwise left the church or who would have lived a nominal form of Christianity—unable to be evangelical witnesses—have experienced the good news of Jesus Christ. By the power of the Holy Spirit, they are now God's eager evangelical instruments in the world.

Let's listen to a story that illustrates the impact of the evangelical movement now spreading among Catholics. The story highlights many evangelical developments spurred by Vatican II and subsequent popes. Without these developments, Mike would likely be one of the many Catholics who say they have no religion.[28]

A CATHOLIC TESTIMONY OF THE NEW EVANGELIZATION

Mike grew up outside of Milwaukee in a family where the Catholic faith was very much part of life, even though sometimes in the background. His family went to church on Sundays and prayed before meals. However, like so many Catholic families, neither God nor the deeper questions of life were talked about very easily. His parents did, however, instill in him a belief and simple trust in God.

When Mike began high school, he was sucked into some common adolescent temptations. The faith he received at home was too simple to keep him strong in the face of serious testing. But the gift of his

Catholic faith did give him enough conscience to know when he was sinning. He didn't like choosing sin but was unable to resist.

The summer after his freshman year Mike's parents signed him up for a Catholic youth conference. Little did he know that this was a Catholic event with a purposeful evangelical emphasis. Contemporary worship songs helped open his heart to new expressions of God's love. Beautiful liturgies opened his eyes to rituals that had previously bored him. He came to know other Catholic high school students who were living completely for Jesus. He also heard great preaching that challenged him to leave his nets behind and follow Jesus. He remembers praying during the conference, "God, come into my heart. I have no idea what that means, but if you're there, please help me to know you."

When Mike went to confession, he was able to open his past to the Lord for healing. The priest's ministry made God's forgiveness powerfully and sacramentally present. When he received the Eucharist at Mass, for the first time in his life he felt intimately, even physically, close to the person of Jesus.

God blessed Mike with a profound encounter with Jesus Christ. At times he was overcome by a sense of God's presence and his very personal love. He cried tears of joy and knew that everything would change in his life because of this conference.

When Mike returned home, he longed for more time in prayer. His prayer was no longer defined by childish requests for help or by memorized prayers. He desired to commune with Jesus in his times of prayer. He began to read his Bible daily and to go to Mass and confession in order to connect with Jesus sacramentally.

When Mike arrived at college, he became part of an evangelical Catholic campus ministry. He joined a small-group Bible study in his dorm, joined the band that played praise and worship songs at the weekly large group, and began meeting one-on-one with a discipleship mentor. As he continued at the university, he soon led his own small group, became the worship music leader, and started being a one-on-one discipleship mentor to the younger students. He memorized Scripture voraciously in order to be more immersed in God's Word. He led many other young men to do the same.

After many years of being open to the call to the priesthood, today Mike is married and his wife loves Jesus as much as he. He has four children who know all of Chris Tomlin's worship songs and who are already learning to pray by using the Scriptures. Two of his children have received their first Communion. Because Mike and his wife have formed their children to love Jesus, they experienced first Communion (a Catholic rite of passage) as an encounter with the Lord and as a deeper connection with the church.

Mike works for a Catholic organization that leads Catholic parishes and campus ministries to launch evangelization small groups in their local communities in order to reach those who do not have faith in Jesus. Because of his story, he longs for the Catholic Church to fully embrace and express the evangelical spirit that reached him and changed his life. He is part of a growing movement of lay Catholics zealously responding to the evangelical call of the Scriptures and the last fifty years of evangelical magisterial writings.

Catholicism and evangelicalism fit together seamlessly as long as evangelicalism is not defined in a way that excludes Catholics. In fact, for the last fifty years the Holy Spirit has been inspiring a movement of renewal in the Catholic Church, championed and pushed forward by the highest authorities.

The Catholic Church is slow to reform. Popes can have a vision, and bishops can adopt these hopes, but moving a one-billion member church does not happen overnight. Neither does it happen outside of God's timing. As usual, our patient God is sowing seeds, watering them, and waiting for the plants to bear fruit. To be sure, there are weeds in the field that try to keep the growing number of evangelical seedlings from bearing fruit. However, as St. John Paul II optimistically proclaimed in 1990, "God is preparing a great springtime for Christianity, and we can already see its first signs."[29]

The number of evangelical Catholics is growing. Many are becoming priests. They are leading evangelical Catholic organizations. They are leading Bible studies at their law firms. They are starting moms' groups to support young mothers. They are visiting prisons. They are fostering children and advocating for foster kids. They are sharing their testimonies while working at food pantries. They are raising their children to love and experience Jesus in the sacraments *and* in the Scriptures. The evangelical movement in the Catholic Church—born of the Holy Spirit, launched by the seismic force of Vatican II, spurred on by subsequent popes and bishops—is cresting. By God's grace may it surge upon one billion Catholics. And through them and their evangelical brothers and sisters everywhere, may it surge upon the whole world, to the glory of our Lord and Savior Jesus Christ. Amen.

For Further Study

Allen, John L., Jr. *The Future Church: How Ten Trends Are Revolutionizing the Catholic Church*. New York: Doubleday, 2009.

Barron, Robert. *Bridging the Great Divide: Musings of a Post-Liberal, Post-Conservative Evangelical Catholic*. Lanham, MD: Rowman and Littlefield Publishers, 2004.

———. *The Priority of Christ: Toward a Postliberal Catholicism*. Grand Rapids: Brazos Press, 2007.

———. *Word on Fire: Proclaiming the Power of Christ*. New York: Crossroad, 2008.

Dulles, Avery Cardinal, SJ. *Evangelization for the Third Millennium*. Mahwah, NJ: Paulist Press, 2009.

O'Malley, Timothy P. *Liturgy and the New Evangelization: Practicing the Art of Self-Giving Love*. Collegeville, MN: Liturgical Press, 2014.

Sarah, Robert Cardinal, with Nicholas Diat. *God or Nothing: A Conversation on Faith*. Translated by Michael J. Miller. San Francisco: Ignatius Press, 2015.

Weddell, Sherry A. *Forming Intentional Disciples: The Path to Knowing and Following Jesus*. Huntington, IN: Our Sunday Visitor, 2012.

Weigel, George. *Evangelical Catholicism: Deep Reform in the 21st-Century Church*. New York: Basic Books, 2013.

CONCLUSION

THEOLOGIAN Rosemary Radford Ruether wrote that, paradoxically, the only legitimate way for the church to be "for itself" is to be "against itself." The church can be correctly "for itself" only by recognizing that it is *not* the kingdom of God. Though sanctified (1 Cor. 1:2), the church of God heralds and imperfectly embodies the inaugurated and arriving kingdom of God. The kingdom transcends the church, corrects it, introduces previously unrecognized vistas, and calls it forward in hope of the kingdom's consummation. The church will be unfaithfully "against itself" to the extent it minimizes the difference between church and kingdom.[1]

Applied more specifically, evangelicals can be correctly "for themselves" only as they are "against themselves." Evangelicals *as such* must never become a primary subject of interest; they must always be transcended and judged by the kingdom whose good news they proclaim. Being evangelical entails being constantly called forward by the gospel of the kingdom, understanding, living, and proclaiming it more joyfully, more creatively, and more convincingly than ever. King Jesus commissions his subjects to proclaim that he is now "scatter[ing] the proud in the imagination of their hearts, . . . putt[ing] down the mighty from their thrones, . . . exalt[ing] those of low degree . . . [and] fill[ing] the hungry with good things" (Luke 1:51-53, RSV).

Failure would invite a return of the oppressive powers and of the idolatry from which the crucified and risen Christ has set us free (Eph.

6:10-18; Col. 2:15). The threat respects no doctrinal or moral boundaries. It stalks incognito, even as "an angel of light" (2 Cor. 11:14, NRSV). It lurks in every ideology. One of its embodiments urges evangelicals to make "profitable" political alliances at the expense of downplaying or even ignoring morally troublesome questions. Such a failure comes at high cost to evangelical character and witness.

Evangelicals have one justifying identity: in the power of the Holy Spirit, to announce to the nations, as completely as possible, that in Jesus Christ, God's *revolution* that brings new creation has begun. In him, God has fulfilled all his covenant promises and met us as the world's Redeemer. He has unleashed a new kind of power into the world—utter gracious love named Jesus. In Christ, God has opened a path to repentance and reconciliation. He has broken the chains of sin's bondage in all its forms. He has set captives free. He has smashed all the idols that once demanded our worship and servitude. In the words of N. T. Wright, "Jesus' followers are now to go out into the world equipped with the power of his own Spirit to announce *that a new reality has come to birth.*"[2] This new reality is indexed to no political party, nation, or ethnicity. Through the Spirit, our priestly vocation is now to live as "rescued rescuers."[3]

Remaining diligently attentive and faithful to the revolutionary kingdom of God requires unrelenting fidelity to the Scriptures and apostolic faith. It also requires that evangelicals make sure the "mystery of godliness" (1 Tim. 3:16, KJV) remains an unfolding, judging, and inexhaustible mystery (Col. 1:26-27). Plumbing the "mystery of godliness" requires joyous submission to its prophetic as well as its redeeming quality.

Part of the gospel's joy is recognizing and fanning the *revolution* wherever it blazes—setting captives free and restoring them to community and worship of the true and living God.

Revolution is blazing in the costly witness of today's Christian martyrs. Rather than deny their Lord, they surrender their lives to their killers. On February 15, 2015, Islamist terrorists known as ISIS (or

Daesh) kidnapped and beheaded twenty-one Coptic Christians in Libya. As their executioners approached, some of the men—poor Egyptian farmers—were whispering, "Lord, Jesus Christ."[4]

According to Voice of the Martyrs, millions of Christians face intense persecution. Pastors are imprisoned or killed for proclaiming the gospel. Young people flee for their lives after their families discover they have embraced Christ as Lord. Believers are beaten, tortured, and pursued. Their homes and churches are burned. Bibles are burned, and businesses are destroyed. Christians are treated as criminals and rebels, forbidden to evangelize and forced to meet and worship in secret.[5]

The revolution blazes!

Anglican clergyman Rick Terry challenged the Episcopal bishop of southern Ohio to uphold sound Christian doctrine and moral standards. The bishop refused. Rick made a choice. After pastoring St. Paul's Episcopal Church in Chillicothe, Ohio, for eleven years, he resigned. With orthodox laypeople at his side, he rented space at a coffeehouse and began a mission church. Suffering financial hardship, and struggling to support two sons in college, Rick began painting houses to support his family while shepherding the mission church.[6]

The revolution blazes!

In the Kansas City Rescue Mission, Executive Director Joe Colaizzi and his staff are putting feet to the redeeming love of God. They are watching as men and women, whom life seems to have tossed aside, receive the good news that in Jesus Christ the old despair and bondage of addiction, abuse, and abandonment can be broken, replaced by new creation. Fellow agents of the *revolution* faithfully staff pregnancy resource centers throughout the United States, providing whole-life assistance as confirmation of God's forgiveness and promise.

The revolution blazes!

When Father Charles "Chuck" Pollak, retired nuclear submarine commander, now an Anglican priest, enters the Ridgeland Correctional Institution in Ridgeland, South Carolina, Chaplain Pollak tells incarcerated men that a powerful Liberator named Jesus is alive and present.

Because of him, their past failures need not dictate their future. Meet Father Pollak and you will encounter a joyous "revolutionary."

The revolution blazes!

And it *blazes* in the 178 Christian colleges and universities worldwide that compose the Council for Christian Colleges and Universities. Christian professors, administrators, and student service personnel are teaching students how to deploy their bright minds in the priestly vocation of Christian discipleship—whether in the sciences, education, public service, the arts, or parish ministry. In every sphere of life, may they commit to worshipping God faithfully by promoting human flourishing—"critically affirming and strengthening its healthy qualities and humbly criticizing and subverting its most destructive tendencies."[7]

What does it mean to be an evangelical?

It means celebrating the *revolution* that happened for all on Calvary, confirmed on Easter morning and unleashed at Pentecost. Everyone can join. It routs the powers, sets captives free, restores God's creation to rightful worship, and returns humankind to its glorious priestly vocation. It means letting the "joy of the gospel" fill our "hearts and lives," constantly being "born anew," being "set free from sin, sorrow, inner emptiness and loneliness."[8]

APPENDIX A
THE NICENE-CONSTANTINOPOLITAN CREED

(COUNCIL OF NICAEA, AD 325; REVISED, COUNCIL OF CONSTANTINOPLE, AD 381)

We believe in one God,
    the Father, the Almighty,
    maker of heaven and earth,
    of all that is, seen and unseen.

We believe in one Lord, Jesus Christ,
    the only Son of God,
    eternally begotten of the Father,
    God from God, Light from Light,
    true God from true God,
    begotten, not made,
    of one Being with [the same substance as] the Father.
    Through him all things were made.
    For us and for our salvation
        he came down from heaven:
    by the power of the Holy Spirit
        he became incarnate from the Virgin Mary,
        and was made man.
    For our sake he was crucified under Pontius Pilate;
        he suffered death and was buried.
        On the third day he rose again
            in accordance with the Scriptures;

he ascended into heaven
> and is seated at the right hand of the Father.
He will come again in glory to judge the living and the dead,
> and his kingdom will have no end.

We believe in the Holy Spirit, the Lord, the giver of life,
> who proceeds from the Father and the Son.
> With the Father and the Son he is worshiped and glorified.
> He has spoken through the Prophets.
> We believe in one holy catholic and apostolic Church.
> We acknowledge one baptism for the forgiveness of sins.
> We look for the resurrection of the dead,
>> and the life of the world to come. Amen.[1]

(Note: While this version is in the plural, the original Greek is in the first-person singular. Also, the phrase "and the Son," concerning the double procession of the Holy Spirit, was not included in the AD 381 version of the creed.)

THE DEFINITION (CREED) OF CHALCEDON

(AD 451)

We, then, following the holy Fathers, all with one consent, teach men to confess one and the same Son, our Lord Jesus Christ, the same perfect in Godhead and also perfect in manhood; truly God and truly man, of a reasonable [rational] soul and body; consubstantial [coessential] with the Father according to the Godhead, and consubstantial with us according to the Manhood; in all things like unto us, without sin; begotten before all ages of the Father according to the Godhead, and in these latter days, for us and for our salvation, born of the Virgin Mary, the Mother of God, according to the Manhood; one and the same Christ, Son, Lord, Only-begotten, to be acknowledged in two natures, *inconfusedly, unchangeably, indivisibly, inseparably*; the distinction of natures being by no means taken away by the union, but rather the property of each nature being preserved, and concurring in one Person and one Subsistence, not parted or divided into two persons, but one and the same Son, and only begotten, God the Word, the Lord Jesus Christ, as the prophets from the beginning [have declared] concerning him, and the Lord Jesus Christ himself has taught us, and the Creed of the holy Fathers has handed down to us.[2]

THE APOSTLES' CREED

(CA. MID-FOURTH CENTURY, LIKELY A MODIFICATION OF THE OLD ROMAN CREED)

I believe in God, the Father almighty,
> maker of heaven and earth;

And in Jesus Christ his only Son, our Lord;
> who was conceived by the Holy Ghost,
> born of the Virgin Mary,
> suffered under Pontius Pilate,
> was crucified, dead, and buried;
> He descended into hell.
> The third day he rose again from the dead.
> He ascended into heaven,
> and sitteth on the right hand of God the Father almighty.
> From thence he shall come to judge the quick and the dead.

I believe in the Holy Ghost,
> the holy catholic Church,
> the communion of saints,
> the forgiveness of sins,
> the resurrection of the body,
> and the life everlasting. Amen.[3]

THE ATHANASIAN CREED

(CA. FIFTH CENTURY)

Whosoever will be saved, before all things it is necessary that he hold the Catholic Faith.

Which Faith except everyone do keep whole and undefiled, without doubt he shall perish everlastingly.

And the Catholic Faith is this: That we worship one God in Trinity, and Trinity in Unity, neither confounding the Persons, nor dividing the Substance.

For there is one Person of the Father, another of the Son, and another of the Holy Ghost.

But the Godhead of the Father, of the Son, and of the Holy Ghost, is all one, the Glory equal, the Majesty co-eternal.

Such as the Father is, such is the Son, and such is the Holy Ghost.

The Father uncreate, the Son uncreate, and the Holy Ghost uncreate.

The Father incomprehensible, the Son incomprehensible, and the Holy Ghost incomprehensible.

The Father eternal, the Son eternal, and the Holy Ghost eternal.

And yet they are not three eternals, but one eternal.

As also there are not three incomprehensibles, nor three uncreated, but one uncreated, and one incomprehensible.

So likewise the Father is Almighty, the Son Almighty, and the Holy Ghost Almighty.

And yet they are not three Almighties, but one Almighty.

So the Father is God, the Son is God, and the Holy Ghost is God.

And yet they are not three Gods, but one God.

So likewise the Father is Lord, the Son Lord, and the Holy Ghost Lord.

And yet not three Lords, but one Lord.

For like as we are compelled by the Christian verity to acknowledge every Person by himself to be both God and Lord,

So are we forbidden by the Catholic Religion, to say, There be three Gods, or three Lords.

The Father is made of none, neither created, nor begotten.

The Son is of the Father alone, not made, nor created, but begotten.

The Holy Ghost is of the Father and of the Son, neither made, nor created, nor begotten, but proceeding.

So there is one Father, not three Fathers; one Son, not three Sons; one Holy Ghost, not three Holy Ghosts.

And in this Trinity none is afore, or after other; none is greater, or less than another;

But the whole three Persons are co-eternal together and co-equal.

So that in all things, as is aforesaid, the Unity in Trinity and the Trinity in Unity is to be worshipped.

He therefore that will be saved must thus think of the Trinity.

Furthermore, it is necessary to everlasting salvation that he also believe rightly the Incarnation of our Lord Jesus Christ.

For the right Faith is, that we believe and confess, that our Lord Jesus Christ, the Son of God, is God and Man;

God, of the Substance of the Father, begotten before the worlds; and Man, of the Substance of his mother, born in the world;

Perfect God and perfect Man, of a reasonable soul and human flesh subsisting;

Equal to the Father, as touching his Godhead; and inferior to the Father, as touching his Manhood.

Who although he be God and Man, yet he is not two, but one Christ;

One, not by conversion of the Godhead into flesh, but by taking of the Manhood into God;

One altogether; not by confusion of Substance, but by unity of Person.

For as the reasonable soul and flesh is one man, so God and Man is one Christ;

Who suffered for our salvation, descended into hell, rose again the third day from the dead.

He ascended into heaven, he sitteth on the right hand of the Father, God Almighty, from whence he shall come to judge the quick and the dead.

At whose coming all men shall rise again with their bodies and shall give account for their own works.

And they that have done good shall go into life everlasting; and they that have done evil into everlasting fire.

This is the Catholic Faith, which except a man believe faithfully, he cannot be saved.[4]

(The Athanasian Creed is also called *Quicunque vult* from its opening words, "Whosoever will/wishes." The creed is a brief and clear exposition of the doctrine of the Trinity and the incarnation. It briefly mentions other doctrines. The creed's language and structure point to a Western, rather than to an Alexandrian, origin, where Athanasius [ca. 296–373] was archbishop. The creed has never gained liturgical acceptance in the Eastern church.)

For a study of the creeds see Philip Schaff, *The History of the Creeds*, vol. 1 of *The Creeds of Christendom* (1876), Christian Classics Ethereal Library (CCEL), https://www.ccel.org/ccel/schaff/creeds1.pdf.

APPENDIX B
DOCUMENTARY RESOURCES

Amsterdam 2000. "The Amsterdam Declaration: A Charter for Evangelicalism in the 21st Century." *Christianity Today*, August 1, 2000. http://www.christianitytoday.com/ct/2000/augustweb-only/13.0.html?start=1.

First International Congress on World Evangelization. The Lausanne Covenant. August 1, 1974. Lausanne Movement. https://www.lausanne.org/content/covenant/lausanne-covenant.

International Conference for Itinerant Evangelists. The Amsterdam Affirmations. July 1983. Evangelical Ministries to New Religions. http://dev.emnr.org/the-amsterdam-affirmations/.

Ockenga, Harold John. "The Basic Theology of Evangelism." Paper presented at the World Congress on Evangelism, Berlin, 1966. http://www2.wheaton.edu/bgc/archives/docs/Berlin66/ockenga.htm.

Second International Congress on World Evangelization. The Manila Manifesto. July 20, 1989. Lausanne Movement. https://www.lausanne.org/content/manifesto/the-manila-manifesto.

NOTES

Introduction

1. Russell Moore, "Russell Moore: Why This Election Makes Me Hate the Word 'Evangelical,'" *Washington Post*, February 29, 2016, https://www.washingtonpost.com/news/acts-of-faith/wp/2016/02/29/russell-moore-why-this-election-makes-me-hate-the-word-evangelical/.

See Russell Moore, *Onward: Engaging the Culture without Losing the Gospel* (Nashville: B and H Publishing Group, 2015). Because of his opposition to Donald Trump as a presidential candidate, Mr. Moore has run into stiff opposition from some influential Southern Baptist leaders. See Jonathan Merritt, "Marginalizing Russell Moore Is Grave Mistake for Southern Baptists," *Religious News Service*, December 20, 2016, http://religionnews.com/columns/jonathan-merritt/.

2. Emily McFarlan Miller, "Russell Moore: Don't Call Me an 'Evangelical,'" *Religion News Service*, February 29, 2016, http://www.religionnews.com/2016/02/29/russell-moore-dont-call-me-an-evangelical/.

3. Thomas Kidd, "Polls Show Evangelicals Support Trump. But the Term 'Evangelical' Has Become Meaningless," *Washington Post*, July 22, 2016, https://www.washingtonpost.com/news/acts-of-faith/wp/2016/07/22/polls-show-evangelicals-support-trump-but-the-term-evangelical-has-become-meaningless/.

4. Erick Erickson, "I Will Not Vote for Donald Trump. Ever," *The Resurgent*, February 22, 2016, http://theresurgent.com/i-will-not-vote-for-donald-trump-ever/.

5. David Kirkpatrick, "The Evangelical Crackup," *New York Times Magazine*, October 28, 2007, http://www.nytimes.com/2007/10/28/magazine/28Evangelicals-t.html?_r=0.

6. Amanda Bennett, "Where Death Doesn't Mean Goodbye," *National Geographic*, April 2016, 53-67.

7. See Kate Bowler, *Blessed: A History of the American Prosperity Gospel* (New York: Oxford University Press, 2013), and Phillip Luke Sinitiere, *Salvation with a Smile: Joel Osteen, Lakewood Church, and American Christianity* (New York: New York University Press, 2015). To observe a radical contrast between the "gospel of riches" and the "gospel of the cross" read the epistle of St. Cyprian, bishop and martyr, to the North African martyrs and confessors who bore glorious witness to Christ during the persecution initiated by Emperor Decius in AD 250: "To the Martyrs and

Confessors," in *Ante-Nicene Fathers*, ed. Philip Schaff (1885; repr., Grand Rapids: Christian Classics Ethereal Library [CCEL], n.d.), 5:715, http://www.ccel.org/ccel/schaff/anf05.pdf.

See "The Guardian View on American Christianity: Change and Decay," *The Guardian*, January 15, 2017, https://www.theguardian.com/commentisfree/2017/jan/15/the-guardian-view-on-american-christianity-change-and-decay.

8. Søren Kierkegaard, "A Eulogy upon the Human Race, or A Proof That the New Testament Is No Longer Truth," in *The Attack upon "Christendom,"* in *A Kierkegaard Anthology*, ed. Robert Bretall (Princeton, NJ: Princeton University Press, 1946), 443.

9. Dietrich Bonhoeffer, *The Cost of Discipleship*, trans. R. H. Fuller (1959; repr., New York: Touchstone, 1995), 43.

10. Romano Guardini, *The Lord* (Washington, DC: Regnery Gateway, 1954), 228.

11. Cyprian, bishop of Carthage (d. 258), *On the Unity of the Church*, in *Ante-Nicene Fathers*, 5:1001. Cyprian referred to the church's unity as an inviolable "sacrament," a bond of concord "inseparably cohering" in Christ (996).

12. Admittedly, speaking this way fails to give due attention to the churches that compose Oriental Orthodoxy. They reject the "two natures" Christology affirmed at the Council of Chalcedon.

Chapter 1

1. David Bebbington, *Evangelicalism in Modern Britain: A History from the 1730s to the 1980s* (Grand Rapids: Baker Book House, 1989), 4. "Variations there have certainly been in statements by evangelicals about what they regard as basic. There is nevertheless a common core that has remained remarkably constant down the centuries" (4).

2. Among them are Lisa Sharon Harper, prolific author and senior director of Mobilizing for Sojourners; Doug Pagitt, founder and pastor of Solomon's Porch, Minneapolis; theologian Brantley W. Gasaway, associate professor of religious studies, Bucknell University; and Brenda Salter McNeil, associate professor of reconciliation studies in the School of Theology, Seattle Pacific University. See Doug Pagitt, "10 Things I Wish Everyone Knew about Progressive Evangelicals," OnFaith, https://www.onfaith.co/onfaith/2015/02/19/10-things-i-wish-everyone-knew-about-progressive-evangelicals/36195 and Open, http://www.theopennetworkus.org/about/.

See Tom Krattenmaker, *The Evangelicals You Don't Know: Introducing the Next Generation of Christians* (New York: Rowman and Littlefield, 2013).

3. Wes Granberg-Michaelson, "What Is an Evangelical?" *Sojourners*, January 6, 2012, https://sojo.net/articles/wes-granberg-michaelson-answers-what-evangelical. Granberg-Michaelson is former general secretary of the Reformed Church in America.

Some evangelicals find interesting ways to span doctrinal differences. Diarmaid MacCulloch tells of a large Presbyterian church in Korea that lectures Reformed Protestants in Europe on their responsibility to remain faithful to John Calvin. But its hymnody comes largely from Methodist sources. *Christianity: The First Three Thousand Years* (New York: Penguin Books, 2011), 10.

4. See Randall J. Stephens and Karl W. Giberson, *The Anointed: Evangelical Truth in a Secular Age* (Cambridge, MA: Belknap Press, 2011).

5. "Church Rites," sec. 10 in "The Epitome of the Formula of Concord," Book of Concord, BookofConcord.org, http://bookofconcord.org/fc-ep.php.

6. This phrase was widely circulated in English by Puritan Richard Baxter (1615-91), though its origins are debated (see https://en.wikipedia.org/wiki/In_necessariis _unitas,_in_dubiis_libertas,_in_omnibus_caritas). Baxter warned against pursuing orthodoxy in a manner that sacrifices Christian love and peace. "Pretend not to truth and orthodoxy against Christian love and peace." Richard Baxter, "Christian Ecclesiastics," chap. 7, direct. 9, in *A Christian Directory* (1673; repr., CCEL, 2006), http://www.ccel.org/ccel/baxter/practical.i.vi.vii.html.

7. Mike Pence, the current vice president of the United States, identifies himself as an "evangelical Catholic." Michelle Boorstein, "What It Means That Mike Pence Called Himself an 'Evangelical Catholic,'" *Washington Post*, July 18, 2016, https://www.washingtonpost.com/news/acts-of-faith/wp/2016/07/15/what-it-means-that-mike-pence-called-himself-an-evangelical-catholic/?utm_term=.1474abb63578.

Jay Michaelson, "Mike Pence, Postmodern Evangelical Catholic Conservative," *Daily Beast*, October 3, 2016, http://www.thedailybeast.com/articles/2016/10/03/mike-pence-postmodern-evangelical-catholic-conservative.html.

8. Bob Dylan, "The Times They Are A-Changin'," BobDylan.com, https://bobdylan.com/songs/times-they-are-changin/.

9. The question has been pointedly tackled by Mark A. Noll in "Noun or Adjective? The Ravings of a Fanatical Nominalist," *Fides et Historia* 47, no. 1 (Winter/Spring 2015): 73-82.

10. Mark Noll, "Into All the World," *Books and Culture*, May/June 2016, http://www.booksandculture.com/articles/2016/mayjun/into-all-world.html. Noll is reviewing *Evangelicals around the World: A Global Handbook for the 21st Century*, ed. Brian C. Stiller et al. (Nashville: Thomas Nelson/World Evangelical Alliance, 2015). The "old evangelical homelands" refer to Great Britain and North America.

11. Mark A. Noll, *The Scandal of the Evangelical Mind* (Grand Rapids: Eerdmans, 1994), 8. This book is an excellent source for learning the history of the evangelical movement in North America, complete with its flaws and commendations.

12. Bebbington, *Evangelicalism in Modern Britain*, 1.

13. Ibid.

14. Ibid., 3.

15. Bebbington, *Evangelicalism in Modern Britain*, 3.

16. Ibid.

17. Ibid., 4-5.

18. Ibid.

19. Ibid., 4. For example, in 1944, Max Warren, general secretary of the Church Missionary Society, gave priority to evangelism over everything else, even worship. For him, activism came first (5).

20. Ibid., 5.

21. Ibid., 3.

22. Kelly Cross Elliott, "The Bebbington Quadrilateral Travels into the Empire," *Fides et Historia* 47, no. 1 (Winter/Spring 2015): 46-53. Kelly Cross Elliot is assistant professor of history at Abilene Christian University. During the 2014 Conference on Faith and History at Pepperdine University, Bebbington observed that when writing *Evangelicalism in Modern Britain*, he did not realize he was breaking fresh ground by developing the quadrilateral. He was just "trying to capture the consensus of opinion among existing writers on the subject." David Bebbington, "The Evangelical Quadrilateral: A Response," *Fides et Historia* 47, no. 1 (Winter/Spring 2015): 87-96.

23. Noll, "Noun or Adjective?" 76-78.

24. Leith Anderson and Ed Stetzer, "Defining Evangelicals in an Election Year," *Christianity Today*, April 2016, 52-55.

25. For a most helpful discussion of a creative approach to the Bible for evangelicals see Mark A. Noll, *Jesus Christ and the Life of the Mind* (Grand Rapids: Eerdmans, 2013).

26. Anderson and Stetzer, "Defining Evangelicals in an Election Year," 55.

27. Ibid.

28. Ibid.

29. Timothy Larsen, "Defining and Locating Evangelicalism," in *The Cambridge Companion to Evangelical Theology* (New York: Cambridge University Press, 2007), 1-14. Thomas S. Kidd, professor of history at Baylor University, thinks omission of Larsen's fifth characteristic from Bebbington's quadrilateral is a serious error. "Belief in the active, immediate ministry of the Holy Spirit was precisely what made evangelical Christianity as novel and controversial as it was." Thomas S. Kidd, "The Bebbington Quadrilateral and the Work of the Holy Spirit," *Fides et Historia* 47, no. 1 (Winter/Spring 2015): 54-57. Bebbington disagrees. Over the course of the history of evangelicalism, the ministry of the Spirit was not consistently on par with the other "hallmarks." To be considered as a valid mark of the whole movement, a characteristic must have existed as prominent over time. Bebbington, "The Evangelical Quadrilateral," 87-96.

30. The NAE was founded in 1942 and serves as a united voice for millions of American evangelicals. The association represents more than forty-five thousand local churches from nearly forty different denominations. The NAE is headquartered in Washington, DC.

31. "Statement of Faith," National Association of Evangelicals, accessed April 28, 2016, http://nae.net/statement-of-faith/. Used by permission. A comparison of the characteristics stated by the NAE and the ten essential "hallmarks of evangelicalism" offered by prominent evangelical theologian Donald Bloesch (1928–2010) illustrates

how difficult it is to arrive at a uniform definition of evangelicalism. Bloesch: (1) the sovereignty of God, (2) the divine authority of Scripture, (3) total depravity, (4) the substitutionary atonement, (5) salvation by grace, (6) faith alone, (7) primacy of proclamation, (8) scriptural holiness, (9) the church's spiritual mission, and (10) the personal return of Christ. Donald Bloesch, *The Evangelical Renaissance* (Grand Rapids: Eerdmans, 1973), 48-79.

32. Noll, *Scandal of the Evangelical Mind*, 131.

33. Ibid., 211.

34. Ibid., 4.

35. Ibid., 9.

36. Ibid., 115.

37. Ibid., 62.

38. Ibid., 113.

39. Ibid., 115.

40. Ibid., 221.

41. "The four gospels are all about *the Kingdom of God*, a theme astonishingly muted to this day in much modern western preaching and teaching, even among would-be Bible Christians. . . . The good news [is] that the world's creator has rescued creation from disaster and established his Son, his true Image, at the centre of his remade world. . . . The dark powers have been defeated so that the power of love may flood the world and bring about the justice and peace which the secular world knows it wants but can't seem to find." N. T. Wright, "Saving the World, Revealing the Glory: Atonement Then and Now" (lecture, St. Mellitus College, London, October 17, 2016), NTWrightPage, http://ntwrightpage.com/2016/10/21/saving-the-world-revealing-the-glory-atonement-then-and-now/.

See N. T. Wright, *The Day the Revolution Began: Reconsidering the Meaning of Jesus's Crucifixion* (New York: HarperOne, 2016).

42. Theologian John Milbank accurately and succinctly joins "gospel" and "kingdom." In the New Testament, "Jesus's mission is seen as inseparable from his preaching of the Kingdom, and inauguration of a new sort of community, the Church. Salvation is available for us after Christ, because we can be incorporated into the community which he founded, and the response of this community to Christ is made possible by the response of the divine Spirit to the divine Son, from whom it receives the love that flows between Son and Father." John Milbank, *Theology and Social Theory: Beyond Secular Reason* (Oxford, UK: Blackwell, 1994), 387. Today, submission to the authority of Scripture as evangelicals claim requires that its entire agenda be mentored and, where needed, reconstructed by the current renaissance in biblical scholarship as exhibited in the work of Richard B. Hays, Ben Witherington, Luke T. Johnson, and N. T. Wright.

43. Only by restoring the kingdom of God as the point of departure for the gospel can we properly understand why and the extent to which the apostle Paul challenged the ascending Caesar cult, the worship of Caesar, and why the gospel

challenges all incarnations of empire ("blasphemous parod[ies] of Jesus' Lordship") as absolute, including absolutist secular ideologies of our day. N. T. Wright explains why Paul's proclamation of the gospel of the kingdom of the Messiah was a direct threat to the imperial cult. N. T. Wright, "Paul's Gospel and Caesar's Empire" (lecture, Princeton Center of Theological Inquiry, November 18, 1998), NTWrightPage, http://ntwrightpage.com/1998/01/01/pauls-gospel-and-caesars-empire/.

44. The gospel of the kingdom is the "gospel, the *euaggelion*, of the son of God, the Davidic Messiah, whose messiahship and divine sonship are validated by his resurrection, and who, as the Psalms insist, is the Lord, the *kyrios*, of the whole world." N. T. Wright, "Paul and Caesar: A New Reading of Romans," NTWrightPage, http://ntwrightpage.com/Wright_Paul_Caesar_Romans.htm.

45. N. T. Wright, *The Challenge of Jesus: Rediscovering Who Jesus Was and Is* (Downers Grove, IL: InterVarsity Press, 1999), 37.

46. Ibid.

47. N. T. Wright, "Imagining the Kingdom: Mission and Theology in Early Christianity" (inaugural lecture, University of St. Andrews, October 26, 2011), NTWrightPage, http://ntwrightpage.com/Wright_StAndrews_Inaugural.htm. "Israel's history, under the guidance of a strange and often opaque divine providence, had not come to a standstill, but was moving forward towards its appointed goal." For the Evangelists, Jesus is "the point at which the millennia-long narrative has reached its goal." In Jesus, the "story of all creation is reaching its decisive goal." According to all four Evangelists, in the person of Jesus Christ the long-anticipated Glory of God had returned to his people, to tabernacle among them (e.g., Matt. 1:23; Luke 19:11-42; John 1:14; Ezek. 10:18). The Evangelists tell the story of how in Jesus Christ, God becomes King of the whole world.

48. N. T. Wright says expectation of the end of exile marked the worldview of Second Temple Judaism: "We are Israel, the true people of the creator god; we are in our land (and/or dispersed away from our land); our god has not yet fully restored us as one day he will; we therefore look for restoration, which will include the justice of our god being exercised over the pagan nations." N. T. Wright, "Romans and the Theology of Paul," NTWrightPage, http://ntwrightpage.com/files/2016/05/Wright_Romans_Theology_Paul.pdf, originally published in *Pauline Theology, Volume III: Romans*, ed. David M. Hay and E. Elizabeth Johnson (Minneapolis: Fortress Press, 1995).

49. Wright, *Challenge of Jesus*, 35.

50. Ibid., 41.

51. Ibid., 42.

52. Ibid.

53. Wright says the end of exile is actually a new exodus "which has been accomplished in the death and resurrection of Jesus and the gift of the Spirit." N. T. Wright, "Paul and Caesar: A New Reading of Romans," NTWrightPage, http://ntwrightpage.com/Wright_Paul_Caesar_Romans.htm, originally published in *A Royal Priesthood:*

The Use of the Bible Ethically and Politically, ed. C. Bartholomew (Carlisle, UK: Paternoster Press, 2002).

54. Wright, *Challenge of Jesus*, 43.

55. Ibid.

56. Those who refused to join the remodeled covenant people were missing out on God's eschatological purpose. Wright, "Paul's Gospel and Caesar's Empire."

57. Guardini, *The Lord*, 460.

58. Ibid.

59. Ibid.

60. Ibid.

61. Wright, *Challenge of Jesus*, 47.

62. Ibid., 46.

63. Ibid.

64. Ibid., 47.

65. Ibid., 49.

66. Ibid.

67. Ibid., 50. In his message about God's kingdom, Jesus offered an alternative to the great disaster hanging over the heads of God's people. But their determination to resist the way of peace Jesus advocated would lead to nothing but ruin. Wright, *Day the Revolution Began*, 215.

68. Paul often refers to the "kingdom of God" in his epistles (Rom. 14:17; 1 Cor. 4:20; 6:9, 10; 15:24, 50; Gal. 5:21; Eph. 5:5; Col. 1:13; 4:11; 1 Thess. 2:12; 2 Thess. 1:5; 2 Tim. 4:1, 18).

69. John M. G. Barclay, *Paul and the Gift* (Grand Rapids: Eerdmans, 2015), 183.

70. Ibid., 72. Going forward, anyone who intends to take seriously grace in the New Testament must be mentored by Barclay's sweeping work. Not only does he examine "the gift" in antiquity, but he also extensively shows that throughout church history, theologians have often treated grace as univocal, without recognizing the important distinctions in its various forms or "perfections." Conflict has often resulted. When dealing with how the apostle Paul understood "the gift," it is imperative to understand the uniqueness in antiquity of the "perfection of incongruity."

71. In antiquity, gifts were always multifaceted relational things meant to generate social bonds. They were characterized by the dynamics of reciprocity, power, and obligation. They were usually given to create or reproduce social bonds, to foster mutuality. The rules of reciprocity raise expectations of return, even in unequal social relations. Barclay discovered six different possible "perfections" of grace (with "perfection" defined as "the drawing out of a concept to an end-of-the-line extreme" [*Paul and the Gift*, 4]) to define the essence of each in some "pure" or "ultimate" form (75). The six "perfections" of grace are distinct but overlap. They are (1) perfection in superabundance because of sheer scale or permanence; (2) perfection of singularity, showing that the giver is wholly benevolent; (3) perfection of priority, or when a gift is given freely, generously, before any claim to it can be made; (4) perfection of

incongruity, indicating the recipient does not deserve the gift as a reward for merit but instead receives the gift unconditionally, quite apart from his or her worthiness; (5) perfection of efficacy, or a gift that fully accomplishes its purpose; and (6) perfection of non-circularity, or a gift completely free of any need for reciprocation (70-73).

72. Ibid., 332.

73. Ibid., 73.

74. Ibid., 331.

75. Ibid., 333.

76. The atonement made by Christ on the cross should be understood as principally intended to restore or re-create community (*ecclesia*), as well as to transform individuals. In Christ, the triune God took the world's brokenness upon himself in order to "unite all things in him [Christ], things in heaven and things on earth," all "to the praise of his [God's] glorious grace which he freely bestowed on us in the Beloved" (Eph. 1:6, 10; see vv. 3-10, RSV; cf. Eph. 4:15-16; Acts 2:1-4).

77. John Milbank says God's grace manifest in Christ forges "one shared identity, one harmony, one tone, one flavor." John Milbank, *Being Reconciled: Ontology and Pardon* (London: Routledge, 2003), 77.

78. Barclay, *Paul and the Gift*, 355.

79. Ibid.

80. Ibid., 355-56. John Milbank has sketched the magnitude of what "realigning and recalibrating" all loyalties entails: fully telling the Christian story (*mythos*), proclaiming without reservation the meaning (*logos*) of Christian faith, embodying a comprehensive Christian practice (praxis)—all of which "[bear] the marks of the incarnation and Pentecost." *Theology and Social Theory*, 381.

81. Anything less, such as a Gnosticized Christianity, would not have threatened to subvert the "imperial cult and ideology which was part of the air Paul and his converts breathed." Paul was "ambassador for a king-in-waiting, establishing cells of people loyal to this new king, and ordering their lives according to his story, his symbols, and his praxis, and their minds according to his truth. . . . The resurrection has installed Jesus of Nazareth as the Messiah of Israel, and therefore also the Lord to whose allegiance the world is now summoned. That is the burden of his song, the thrust of his *euangelion*." Wright, "Paul's Gospel and Caesar's Empire."

82. Wright, *Day the Revolution Began*, 245.

83. Ibid., 199.

84. Ibid.

Chapter 2

1. The question of the Gospels as a genre of writing is not part of this discussion.

2. Graeme Goldsworthy, *Gospel-Centred Hermeneutics: Biblical-Theological Foundations and Principles* (Nottingham, UK: Inter-Varsity Press, 2006), 58.

3. Ibid., 58-59.

4. Ibid., 16.

5. Ibid.

6. C. C. Caragounis, "Kingdom of God/Kingdom of Heaven," in *Dictionary of Jesus and the Gospels* (Downers Grove, IL: InterVarsity Press, 1992), 417-30.

7. The period that began with the rebuilding of the temple in 515 BC and ended with its destruction in AD 70 is referred to as the Second Temple Period. While much of the literature composed in the latter period (300 BC–AD 70) is not part of the Protestant canon, it is vital in tracing the development of the idea of God's agency. Of particular significance are the Dead Sea Scrolls. See Herbert W. Bateman IV, Darrell L. Bock, and Gordon H. Johnston, *Jesus the Messiah: Tracing the Promises, Expectations, and Coming of Israel's King* (Grand Rapids: Kregel Academic, 2012), 212-13.

8. *Pss. Sol.* (*Psalms of Solomon*) 13:8-10; *Sib. Or.* (*Sibylline Oracles*) 3:704-6; *T. Job* (*Testament of Job*) 33:3ff.

9. For example, *Jub.* (*Jubilees*) 1:19.

10. *T. Jud.* (*Testament of Judah*) 24:6; *T. Levi* (*Testament of Levi*) 14:3-4; 18:3; *T. Naph.* (*Testament of Naphtali*) 8:3-4. All three references are part of the *Testaments of the Twelve Patriarchs*.

11. *Pss. Sol.* 17:30-31.

12. To name a few, 1QM, 4Q174, 4Q285, 4Q376. See further Bateman IV, Bock, and Johnston, *Jesus the Messiah*, pt. 2.

13. See discussion and conclusions in chap. 2 of Svetlana Khobnya, *The Father Who Redeems and the Son Who Obeys: Consideration of Paul's Teaching in Romans* (Eugene, OR: Wipf and Stock, 2013).

14. See Richard B. Hays, *Reading Backwards: Figural Christology and the Fourfold Gospel Witness* (London: SPCK, 2015), x, originally published by Waco, TX: Baylor University Press, 2014.

15. Kent Brower, *Mark: A Commentary in the Wesleyan Tradition*, New Beacon Bible Commentary (Kansas City: Beacon Hill Press of Kansas City, 2012), 45.

16. R. T. France, *Matthew*, Tyndale New Testament Commentaries (Nottingham, UK: Inter-Varsity Press, 1985), 76.

17. Graeme Goldsworthy, *Gospel and Kingdom: A Christian Interpretation of the Old Testament* (Exeter, UK: Paternoster Press, 1981), 89, now a part of *The Goldsworthy Trilogy* (Carlisle, UK: Paternoster Press, 2000).

18. Ibid.

19. N. T. Wright, *How God Became King: The Forgotten Story of the Gospels* (New York: HarperOne, 2012), 83ff.

20. Khobnya, *Father Who Redeems*, 77-80.

21. Barclay, *Paul and the Gift*, 567.

22. Ibid.

23. Christopher J. H. Wright, *The Mission of God: Unlocking the Bible's Grand Narrative* (Nottingham, UK: Inter-Varsity Press, 2006), 506.

24. Ibid.

25. Svetlana Khobnya, "Reconciliation Must Prevail: A Fresh Look at 2 Corinthians 5:14–6:2," *European Journal of Theology* 25, no. 2 (2016): 128-36.

26. Athanasios N. Papathanasiou, "Reconciliation: The Major Conflict in Postmodernity. An Orthodox Contribution to a Missiological Dialogue," *Greek Orthodox Theological Review* 58, nos. 1-4 (2013): 33.

27. C. Wright, *Mission of God*, 22-23, 29-32.

28. Ibid., 64-65.

29. Barclay, *Paul and the Gift*, 76.

30. N. T. Wright, *Paul and the Faithfulness of God, Parts I and II*, Christian Origins and the Question of God 4 (London: SPCK, 2013), 409.

31. C. Wright, *Mission of God*, 120.

32. George H. Guthrie, *2 Corinthians*, Baker Exegetical Commentary on the New Testament (Grand Rapids: Baker Academic, 2015), 246.

33. Ibid., 247.

34. I. Howard Marshall, *New Testament Theology: Many Witnesses, One Gospel* (Downers Grove, IL: InterVarsity Press, 2004), 34-35.

35. See the discussion of Christ's faithfulness in Khobnya, *Father Who Redeems*, chap. 4.

36. Marshall, *New Testament Theology*, 80.

37. Wright, *Paul and the Faithfulness of God*, 407.

38. Ibid., 407-8.

39. Ibid., 408.

40. Ibid.

41. Ibid.

42. Ibid., 409.

43. William M. Greathouse with George Lyons, *Romans 1–8: A Commentary in the Wesleyan Tradition*, New Beacon Bible Commentary (Kansas City: Beacon Hill Press of Kansas City, 2008), 182.

44. N. T. Wright, "The Letter to the Romans: Introduction, Commentary, and Reflections," in *The New Interpreter's Bible* (Nashville: Abingdon Press, 2002), 10:538.

45. Larry W. Hurtado, "YHWH's Return to Zion," in *God and the Faithfulness of Paul*, ed. Christoph Heilig, J. Thomas Hewitt, and Michael F. Bird (Tübingen: Mohr Siebeck, 2016), 434.

46. N. T. Wright, "Imagining the Kingdom: Mission and Theology in Early Christianity" (lecture, University of St. Andrews, St. Mary's College, Faculty of Divinity, October 26, 2011), http://ntwrightpage.com/Wright_StAndrews_Inaugural.htm.

47. Ibid.

48. C. Wright, *Mission of God*, 287.

49. Goldsworthy, *Gospel and Kingdom*, 99.

50. Jörg Frey, "Demythologizing Apocalyptic?" in *God and the Faithfulness of Paul*, 524.

Chapter 3

1. The word "creed" comes from the Latin word *credo*, meaning "I believe." In the Christian context it means far more than intellectual assent; it means submitting one's entire existence to the sovereign reign of Jesus Christ.

2. Richard B. Hays, *The Moral Vision of the New Testament: A Contemporary Introduction to New Testament Ethics* (San Francisco: HarperSanFrancisco, 1996), 210.

3. The importance and spirit of tradition is apparent in instruction given by Irenaeus of Lyons in *The Demonstration of the Apostolic Preaching* (usually called *Epideixis*): "We must . . . hold the rule of faith without deviation," what "the Elders, the disciples of the Apostles, have handed down to us" (sec. 3). Later, after extensively discussing the contours of the incarnation and redemption, Irenaeus says, "This, beloved, is the preaching of the truth, and this is the manner of our redemption, and this is the way of life, which the prophets proclaimed, and Christ established, and the apostles delivered, and the Church in all the world hands on to her children. This must we keep with all certainty, with a sound will and pleasing to God, with good works and right-willed disposition" (sec. 98). Armitage Robinson, trans. and ed. (New York: Macmillan, 1920; repr., Grand Rapids: CCEL, 2005), http://www.ccel.org/ccel/irenaeus/demonstr.iv.html.

See secs. 1-13 for Irenaeus's summary of the "order of the rule of our faith."

4. D. H. Williams, *Evangelicals and Tradition: The Formative Influence of the Early Church* (Grand Rapids: Baker Academic, 2005), 21.

5. Thomas Aquinas offers a clear statement of this principle: "Only the canonical scriptures are the standard of faith." Thomas Aquinas, *Commentary on the Gospel of John*, pt. 2, chap. 21, lecture 6, sec. 2656, Dominican House of Studies, http://dhspriory.org/thomas/John21.htm. The church's theologians, Aquinas says, have supported this principle; only that which agrees with Scripture is to be received as true. Brian Davies adds that for Thomas, the content of Scripture is "the content of the Christian creeds." They "amount to a restatement of what is in Scripture—a pocket Bible, so to speak." Brian Davies, *The Thought of Thomas Aquinas* (New York: Clarendon Press, 1993), 12.

The Second Vatican Council (1962-65) worked very carefully to articulate the relationship between the authority of Scripture and the authority of tradition. But finally the council assigned a place to tradition with which most Protestants disagree: "Both sacred tradition and Sacred Scripture are to be accepted and venerated with the same sense of loyalty and reverence." *Dogmatic Constitution on Divine Revelation* (*Dei Verbum*), chap. 2, sec. 9, http://www.vatican.va/archive/hist_councils/ii_vatican_council/documents/vat-ii_const_19651118_dei-verbum_en.html.

As important as tradition is, the Protestant doctrine of *sola Scriptura* does not permit the "same sense of loyalty and reverence." See "The Epitome of the Formula of Concord," secs. 1-8. On the other hand, Roman Catholics wonder how, in the absence of an authoritative magisterium that governs how Scripture should be interpreted, Protestants can avoid endlessly conflicting interpretations. Swedish Catholic theologian Mats Wahlberg explains that for Catholics the church's teaching authority "derives directly from Christ," not from Scripture. While the church is not "above" Scripture in any sense, the church and ecclesial tradition, unlike for Protestants, "provide an authoritative framework for the faithful reading of Scripture." Mats Wahlberg, "Reformed Ressourcement," *First Things*, February 2017, 63.

6. The classic Protestant formula has been that "Scripture is *norma normans* ('the norming norm'), while tradition is *norma normata* ('the normed norm')." Hays, *Moral Vision of the New Testament*, 210.

7. In his *Commentary on John*, John Calvin succinctly states what it means to be faithful to apostolic teaching: "If we do not wish to be ungrateful to God, let us rest satisfied with that doctrine of which the writings of the apostles declare them to be the authors, since in it the highest perfection of heavenly wisdom is made known to us, fitted *to make the man of God perfect* (2 Timothy 3:17.) Beyond this let us not reckon ourselves at liberty to go; for our *height*, and *breadth*, and *depth*, consist in *knowing the love of God*, which is manifested to us in Christ." *Commentary on John*, trans. William Pringle (1847; repr., Grand Rapids: CCEL, n.d.), 2:119, http://www.ccel.org/ccel/calvin/calcom35.pdf.

8. However, as John Calvin correctly warned, recognizing the Holy Spirit as teacher in the church must never be misconstrued as meaning that the Spirit is a "builder of new revelations. . . . The spirit that introduces any doctrine or invention apart from the Gospel is a deceiving spirit, and not the Spirit of Christ." The Holy Spirit instructs the church only in that which is faithful to Christ's revelation of the Father. Calvin, *Commentary on John* (comm. on John 14:26), 2:82.

9. A statement about John Wesley by Methodist theologian David Watson is equally applicable to Whitefield and Edwards: "Wesley . . . assumed the truth of the Church's great creeds, and he assumed other Christians did as well. He offered the right hand of friendship to Christians of many other traditions, and yet he most certainly held that 'primitive' Christianity—the Nicene-Constantinopolitan faith developed over the first five centuries of the Christian era—was key to understanding God's saving work in Jesus Christ." David F. Watson, "Was Wesley's Faith a Creedal Faith?" *Musings and Whatnot* (blog), April 8, 2015, https://davidfwatson.me/2015/04/08/was-wesleys-faith-a-creedal-faith/. Watson is professor of New Testament, United Theological Seminary, Dayton, Ohio.

10. Irenaeus said that John the Beloved lived in Ephesus and wrote his Gospel there: "Afterwards, John, the disciple of the Lord, who also had leaned upon His breast, did himself publish a Gospel during his residence at Ephesus in Asia." *Against Heresies* (hereafter identified as *AH*) bk. 3, chap. 1 sec. 1, New Advent, http://www.newadvent.org/fathers/0103301.htm. Eusebius says that John moved to Ephesus during the Jewish War (AD 66-73) and lived there until his death. *Church History*, bk. 3, chap. 1, sec. 1, New Advent, http://www.newadvent.org/fathers/250103.htm. However, there is good reason to think that John never lived in Ephesus. For example, when Ignatius of Antioch (ca. AD 35–ca. AD 107) wrote his letter to the church at

Ephesus a few years after John would have died there, he recalls the importance of Paul for the church but doesn't mention John once. *The Epistle of Ignatius to the Ephesians: Shorter and Longer Versions*, in *Ante-Nicene Fathers*, 1:138-63, http://www.ccel.org/ccel/schaff/anf01.pdf.

11. Irenaeus, *AH*, bk. 1, chap. 10, sec. 1, http://www.newadvent.org/fathers/0103110.htm.

12. Gnosticism was a highly complex and diverse religion/philosophy that posed a major threat to the young Christian faith in the second century. The name comes from a Greek word for knowledge (*gnōsis*). The Gnostics claimed to "know" the truth. Gnosticism viewed all material existence, including the human body, as deriving from an evil source and hence incurably evil. They resolutely denied that Christ was truly human.

13. For a printed translation of *Against Heresies*, see *The Ante-Nicene Fathers*, vol. 1, trans. Alexander Roberts and James Donaldson (1885; repr., Grand Rapids: Eerdmans, 1989), and John Behr, *On the Apostolic Preaching* (Crestwood, NY: St. Vladimir's Seminary Press, 1997). For partial translations of Irenaeus, see Dominic J. Unger, *St. Irenaeus of Lyons: Against Heresies*, vols. 1-3 (New York: Newman Press, 1992–2012); Paul Bassett, "From the Apostolic Fathers to Early Protestantism," in *The Historical Development*, vol. 2 of *Exploring Christian Holiness* (Kansas City: Beacon Hill Press of Kansas City, 1985); Paul Bassett, ed., *Holiness Teaching: New Testament Times to Wesley*, vol. 1 of *Great Holiness Classics* (Kansas City: Beacon Hill Press of Kansas City, 1997); and Robert M. Grant, *Irenaeus of Lyons* (London: Routledge, 1997).

14. Irenaeus, *Demonstration of the Apostolic Preaching*, sec. 1.

15. In the incarnation, through the Holy Spirit, God became visible. This is the rule of orthodox Trinitarian faith. Denis Minns, OP, *Irenaeus: An Introduction* (London: T and T Clark, 2010), 66. It is, says Irenaeus, central to the gospel. *AH*, bk. 5, chap. 15, sec. 2, http://www.newadvent.org/fathers/0103515.htm. "Proofs from the writings of St. Paul, and from the words of Our Lord" show that Christ did not become "man merely in appearance, but that He did so truly and actually." *AH*, bk. 3, chap. 18, introd., http://www.newadvent.org/fathers/0103318.htm.

16. God formed humans "with His own hands, taking from the earth that which was purest and finest, and mingling in measure His own power with the earth. . . . The image of God was man formed and set on the earth." Irenaeus, *Demonstration of the Apostolic Preaching*, sec. 11.

17. "And so fair and good was this Paradise, that the Word of God continually resorted thither, and walked and talked with the man, figuring beforehand the things that should be in the future, (namely) that He should dwell with him and talk with him, and should be with men, teaching them righteousness. But man was a child, not yet having his understanding perfected; wherefore also he was easily led astray by the deceiver." Irenaeus, *Demonstration of the Apostolic Preaching*, sec. 12.

For an excellent more recent treatment of this point, see Karl Barth's *Christ and Adam: Man and Humanity in Romans 5*, trans. T. A. Smail (1956; repr., Eugene, OR: Wipf and Stock, 2004).

18. Minns, *Irenaeus*, 13.

19. Irenaeus, *Demonstration of the Apostolic Preaching*, sec. 12.

20. "The Word of God was made flesh by the dispensation of the Virgin, to abolish death and make man live. For we were imprisoned by sin, being born in sinfulness and living under death. But God the Father was very merciful: He sent His creative Word, who in coming to deliver us came to the very place and spot in which we had lost life, and brake the bonds of our fetters." Irenaeus, *Demonstration of the Apostolic Preaching*, secs. 37-38.

21. Irenaeus, *Demonstration of the Apostolic Preaching*, sec. 5. "The Word of God, Son of God, Christ Jesus our Lord, who was manifested to the prophets according to the form of their prophesying and according to the method of the dispensation of the Father: through whom all things were made; who also at the end of the times, to complete and gather up all things, was made man among men, visible and tangible, in order to abolish death and show forth life and produce a community of union between God and man" (sec. 5).

22. Irenaeus means that by grace, Jesus's disciples are continuously transformed in holiness, not that they become God. Irenaeus's well-known statement comes from a note in a letter that refers to words written by Irenaeus. Taizé Community, "Saint Irenaeus of Lyons," Taizé, http://www.taize.fr/en_article6431.html.

23. Irenaeus, *AH*, bk. 2, chap. 22, sec. 4, http://www.newadvent.org/fathers/0103222.htm; cf. bk. 3, chap. 18, sec. 7, http://www.newadvent.org/fathers/0103318.htm. See also Irenaeus, *Demonstration of the Apostolic Preaching*, sec. 53.

24. "Just as through a disobedient virgin man was stricken down and fell into death, so through the Virgin who was obedient to the Word of God man was reanimated and received life. For the Lord came to seek again the sheep that was lost; and man it was that was lost: and for this cause there was not made some other formation, but in that same which had its descent from Adam He preserved the likeness of the (first) formation. For it was necessary that Adam should be summed up in Christ, that mortality might be swallowed up and overwhelmed by immortality; and Eve summed up in Mary, that a virgin should be a virgin's intercessor, and by a virgin's obedience undo and put away the disobedience of a virgin." Irenaeus, *Demonstration of the Apostolic Preaching*, sec. 33.

25. Ibid., sec. 38.

26. Irenaeus, *AH*, bk. 4, chap. 38, sec. 3, http://www.newadvent.org/fathers/0103438.htm; *AH*, bk. 5, preface, http://www.newadvent.org/fathers/0103500.htm (this type of description for holiness is uncomfortable for Western ears, but it is the gospel good news).

27. Colin E. Gunton, *Yesterday and Today*, 2nd ed. (London: SPCK, 1997), 225. "Never was there a writer more necessary to an understanding of the modern age than

Irenaeus of Lyons. He is a model of a theological integration of [Christ's] incarnation, saving death, resurrection and ascension" (225).

"The baptism of our regeneration proceeds through these three points: God the Father bestowing on us regeneration through His Son by the Holy Spirit. For as many as carry (in them) the Spirit of God are led to the Word, that is to the Son; and the Son brings them to the Father; and the Father causes them to possess incorruption. Without the Spirit it is not possible to behold the Word of God, nor without the Son can any draw near to the Father for the knowledge of the Father is the Son, and the knowledge of the Son of God is through the Holy Spirit; and, according to the good pleasure of the Father, the Son ministers and dispenses the Spirit to whomsoever the Father wills and as He wills." Irenaeus, *Demonstration of the Apostolic Preaching*, sec. 7.

28. Minns, *Irenaeus*, 100.

29. Ambrose, "O the divine mystery of that cross, on which weakness hangs, might is free, vices are nailed, and triumphal trophies raised." *On the Holy Spirit*, bk. 1, chap. 9, sec. 108, in *Ambrose: Selected Works and Letters*, trans. H. De Romestin, vol. 10 of *Nicene and Post-Nicene Fathers*, series 2 (1885; repr., Grand Rapids: CCEL, n.d.), https://www.ccel.org/ccel/schaff/npnf210.pdf.

30. "Arius's Letter to Eusebius of Nicomedia," in William G. Rusch, ed., *The Trinitarian Controversy* (Philadelphia: Fortress Press, 1980), 23.

31. In his *Thalia*, Arius says, "He who is without beginning made the Son a beginning of created things. He produced him as a son for himself by begetting him." *Thalia*, Fourth-Century Christianity, http://www.fourthcentury.com/arius-thalia-intro/.

Athanasius quotes from the *Thalia*: "Moreover he has dared to say, that 'the Word is not the very God;' 'though He is called God, yet He is not very God,' but 'by participation of grace, He, as others, is God only in name.' And, whereas all beings are foreign and different from God in essence, so too is 'the Word alien and unlike in all things to the Father's essence and propriety,' but belongs to things originated and created, and is one of these." Athanasius, *Against the Arians*, discourse 1, chap. 2, sec. 6, New Advent, http://www.newadvent.org/fathers/28161.htm.

32. Arianism prevailed in the East till the reign of Theodosius the Great (r. AD 379-95). The *Edict of Thessalonica* (AD 380), issued by Theodosius, Gratian, and Valentinian II, declared Nicene Christianity to be the only legitimate official religion. The Arians were not uniform in their teachings; Ambrose says that they fell "apart into several sects." Ambrose, *Exposition of the Christian Faith*, bk. 1, chap. 6, sec. 45, in *Ambrose: Selected Works and Letters*, https://www.ccel.org/ccel/schaff/npnf210.pdf.

33. For an excellent extended discussion of Arianism and its threat to the church, see Richard E. Rubenstein, *When Jesus Became God* (New York: Houghton Mifflin Harcourt, 1999).

34. Athanasius remained bishop for forty-six years although he spent seventeen of those years in several exiles; he was exiled five times. The charges brought against

Athanasius by his diverse opponents are given in a detailed account by Khaled Anatolios in *Athanasius*, The Early Church Fathers (London: Routledge, 2004), 12-33.

35. Both works are available online: *On the Incarnation of the Word*, CCEL, http://www.ccel.org/ccel/athanasius/incarnation.i.html, and *Four Discourses against the Arians*, New Advent, http://www.newadvent.org/fathers/2816.htm.

36. Athanasius scholar Khaled Anatolios says that for Athanasius "the notion that God needs any intervening mediator in order to relate himself to creation is repugnant." *Athanasius*, 54.

37. Athanasius affirms that "the Word of the Father is Himself divine, that all things that are owe their being to His will and power, and that it is through Him that the Father gives order to creation, by Him that all things are moved, and through Him that they receive their being." *On the Incarnation*, chap. 1, http://www.ccel.org/ccel/athanasius/incarnation.ii.html.

Athanasius asks, "What was God to do in face of this dehumanizing of mankind [by wickedness]?" He answers, "What else could He possibly do, being God, but renew His Image in mankind, so that through it men might once more come to know Him? And how could this be done save by the coming of the very Image Himself, our Savior Jesus Christ? Men could not have done it, for they are only made after the Image; nor could angels have done it, for they are not the images of God. The Word of God came in His own Person, because it was He alone, the Image of the Father Who could recreate man made after the Image." *On the Incarnation*, chap. 3, http://www.ccel.org/ccel/athanasius/incarnation.iv.html.

38. Athanasius, *On the Incarnation*, trans. John Behr (New York: St. Vladimir's Seminary Press, 2011), 16.

39. Ibid.

40. The term *perichoresis* (Greek, *perichōrēsis*) is commonly used to describe the relationship, the communion, the interpenetration, between the Father, Son, and Holy Spirit. Gregory of Nazianzus first used a related verb to describe the relationship between Christ's deity and humanity. Later, *perichoresis* was extended to speak of triune life.

41. For a detailed discussion of the conflict between Cyril and Nestorius see Justo L. González, *From the Beginnings to the Council of Chalcedon*, vol. 1 of *A History of Christian Thought*, rev. ed. (Nashville: Abingdon Press, 1970), 363-78.

42. Nestorius became bishop in 428 but was recognized as being less astute as a theologian than Cyril. Cyril was appointed bishop in 412. Norman Russell, one of Cyril's current interpreters, has given a brief account of Cyril's controversial life. Norman Russell, *Cyril of Alexandria* (London: Routledge, 2000), 2-11.

43. Cyril, *Commentary on John*, quoted by Russell, in *Cyril of Alexandria*, 18-19.

44. Eusebius, *Church History*, bk. 8, chap. 17, sec. 9, http://www.newadvent.org/fathers/250108.htm.

45. Those who succumbed to persecution were called "traditors." The term also applied to a bishop who surrendered the Scriptures. Mensurius, bishop of Carthage (AD 303), hid the Scriptures and instead surrendered heretical works.

46. The Macedonians were also known as Pneumatomachians (fr. Greek, *pneumatomachoi* [combatants against the (Holy) Spirit]).

47. The Oriental Orthodox Churches (e.g., the Christian Coptic Orthodox Church of Egypt) rejected the Definition of Chalcedon and instead insisted that in Jesus the divine and human natures are unified into one nature. However, the language can be puzzling: "Copts believe that the Lord is perfect in His divinity, and He is perfect in His humanity, but His divinity and His humanity were united in one nature called 'the nature of the incarnate word,' which was reiterated by Saint Cyril of Alexandria. Copts, thus, believe in two natures 'human' and 'divine' that are united in one *'without mingling, without confusion, and without alteration.'*" "The Christian Coptic Orthodox Church of Egypt," Coptic Network, http://www.coptic.net/EncyclopediaCoptica/.

48. In one of his sermons on Jesus's nativity, Pope Leo I (Leo the Great) affirms the confessional nature of Chalcedon's content: "When, therefore, we attempt to understand the mystery of Christ's nativity, wherein He was born of the Virgin-mother, let all the clouds of earthly reasonings be driven far away and the smoke of worldly wisdom be purged from the eyes of illuminated faith: for the authority on which we trust is divine, the teaching which we follow is divine. . . . Therefore in both natures it is the same Son of God taking what is ours and not losing what is His own; renewing man in His manhood, but enduring unchangeable in Himself. For the Godhead which is His in common with the Father underwent no loss of omnipotence, nor did the 'form of a slave' do despite to the 'form of God,' because the supreme and eternal Essence, which lowered Itself for the salvation of mankind, transferred us into Its glory, but did not cease to be what It was. . . . What mind can grasp this mystery, what tongue can express this gracious act?" Sermon 27, "On the Feast of the Nativity, VII," secs. 1-2, in *The Letters and Sermons of Leo the Great*, vol. 12 of *Nicene and Post-Nicene Fathers*, series 2, https://www.ccel.org/ccel/schaff/npnf212.pdf.

49. See Stuart Murray, *The Naked Anabaptist: The Bare Essentials of a Radical Faith* (Harrisonburg, VA: Herald Press, 2015).

50. J. N. D. Kelly, *Early Christian Creeds*, 3rd ed. (London: Longman, 1972), 378.

51. Ibid., 368-435.

52. Ibid., 434.

53. The controversy between East and West over this matter contributed to bitter division. The conflict is known as the *filioque* controversy.

54. Gillian R. Evans, Alister E. McGrath, and Allan D. Galloway, *The Science of Theology* (Basingstoke, UK: Marshall, Morgan and Scott, 1986), 117. The humanist movement is not the same as the modern humanist movement. It is a reference to the return to the study of original documents, including the Bible.

55. Quoted from Roland H. Bainton, *Here I Stand: A Life of Martin Luther* (1950; repr., Nashville: Abingdon, 1978), 49.

56. "God by a sudden conversion subdued and brought my mind to a teachable frame, which was more hardened in such matters than might have been expected from one at my early period of life. Having thus received some taste and knowledge of true godliness I was immediately inflamed with so intense a desire to make progress therein, that although I did not altogether leave off other studies, I yet pursued them with less ardor." John Calvin, preface to *Commentary on Psalms*, trans. James Anderson (1845; repr., Grand Rapids: CCEL, n.d.), 1:25, http://www.ccel.org/ccel/calvin/calcom08.pdf. Calvin's conversion happened sometime between 1552 and 1553.

57. John Calvin, *Institutes of the Christian Religion*, trans. Henry Beveridge (1845; repr., CCEL, 2005), bk. 3, chap. 2, sec. 24, http://www.ccel.org/ccel/calvin/institutes. Calvin began the development of the appropriation of salvation through Christ with the imagery of Christ as Prophet, Priest, and King in the *Institutes of the Christian Religion*, bk. 2, chap. 15, sec. 1. For Calvin, Christ's work as Prophet was his teaching ministry; the wisdom of God was exemplified in Christ. The priestly office revealed Christ's sacrifice for humanity, and we are brought into God's favor through Christ's priestly work. The kingly office was the triumph of Christ's kingdom and guaranteed the perpetuity of his church. All of this revealed God's grace and favor to humanity, which was effective in every aspect of life. John Wesley continued the language of Christ's three offices, which was grounded in John Calvin's model of salvation. David Rainey, "An Investigation: The Theological Relationship between John Calvin and John Wesley," in *Kálvin hatása Wesley munkásságára* (Budapest: Wesley Theological Association, 2010), 72-75. This set the foundation for justification by faith through Christ, who is our Representative before God and takes our place in the imagery of God's court in heaven.

It is important to understand that Christ stands in our place as complete humanity and, as our Representative, speaks on our behalf; this is substitutionary atonement. We might think of the Reformation as the rethinking of Christ as the sole Source of salvation, and through faith we are united with Christ. This is the good news!

58. To illustrate, in Calvin's comm. on 1 Peter 1:23, he gives his understanding of what it means to be born again of the Spirit: "The object, then, of Peter was to teach us that we cannot be Christians without regeneration; for the Gospel is not preached, that it may be only heard by us, but that it may, as a seed of immortal life, altogether reform our hearts." *Commentary on First Peter*, in *Commentaries on the Catholic Epistles*, trans. and ed. John Owen (1855; repr., Grand Rapids: CCEL, 2005), http://www.ccel.org/ccel/calvin/calcom45.pdf.

59. John Calvin, *Commentary on the Gospel According to John*, trans. William Pringle, vol. 2 (1847; repr., Grand Rapids: CCEL, 2005), comm. on 14:1, http://www.ccel.org/ccel/calvin/calcom35.pdf. He adds, "Whoever obtains Christ [lacks] nothing; . . . therefore, . . . whoever is not satisfied with Christ alone, strives after something beyond absolute perfection." Comm. on v. 6.

60. *A History of Christian Thought* by Justo L. González, 3 vols., rev. ed. (Nashville: Abingdon Press, 1987), is a good resource for gaining an understanding of how doctrine developed in the church.

Chapter 4

1. The "traditional Catholic" distinction between the *fides qua creditur* (faith by which it is believed) and the *fides quae creditur* (faith which is believed), often attributed to Augustine, seems actually to be a product of Augustine's Lutheran followers, who created the distinction precisely to make this point. See Olivier Riaudel, "*Fides qua creditur* et *Fides quae creditur*: Retour sur une distinction qui n'est pas chez Augustin," *Revue Théologique de Louvain* 43, no. 2 (2012): 169-94.

2. The five points are conveniently identified by the acronym TULIP. They are total depravity, unconditional election, limited atonement, irresistible grace, and perseverance of the saints. The five points are held to be the doctrine of salvation contained in the Bible.

3. This belief is known as deism.

4. Perry Miller, "Jonathan Edwards and the Great Awakening," in *America in Crisis*, ed. Daniel Aaron (New York: Alfred A. Knopf, 1952), 5-6.

5. Quoted in A. Skevington Wood, *The Inextinguishable Blaze: Spiritual Renewal and Advance in the Eighteenth Century* (London: Paternoster, 1960; repr., Eugene, OR: Wipf and Stock, 2006), 69-70.

6. Quoted in John Greenfield, *When the Spirit Came* (Minneapolis: Bethany, 1967), 12.

7. A Nonconformist, or Dissenter, was a Protestant who would not "conform" or submit to the governance and practices of the established Church of England. Nonconformists rejected the 1662 Act of Uniformity.

8. George Whitefield, *George Whitefield's Journals* (Lafayette, IN: Sovereign Grace, 2000), 21-26.

9. John Wesley, *The Works of John Wesley*, ed. Thomas Jackson (Kansas City: Beacon Hill Press of Kansas City, 1979), 1:103.

10. Ibid., 185.

11. Joseph Beaumont Wakeley, *Anecdotes of the Rev. George Whitefield, M.A.* (London: Hodder and Stoughton, 1872), 219-20. Wesley himself might have been aware of this anecdote because he used the exact same image when he related the story of the first Methodist preachers going to America to organize the work of Whitefield after his death so that the people would not be a "rope of sand." John Wesley, "The Late Work of God in America," in *The Sermons of John Wesley*, ed. Thomas Jackson (1872), *Wesley Center Online*, http://wesley.nnu.edu/john-wesley/the-sermons-of-john-wesley-1872-edition/sermon-131-the-late-work-of-god-in-north-america/.

12. Nigel Scotland, "Methodism and the English Labour Movement 1800–1906," *Anvil* 14, no. 1 (1997): 36-48.

13. "Romanticism was an artistic and intellectual movement that ran from the late eighteenth century through the nineteenth century." It stressed the importance of the individual and "strong emotion as a source of aesthetic experience. . . . [It] arose as a reaction against the excessive rationalism of the Enlightenment." *New World Encyclopedia*, s.v. "Romanticism," http://www.newworldencyclopedia.org/entry/Romanticism.

14. "Via media," or "middle way," refers to the Anglican Church's attempt "to occupy a middle ground between the polarizing positions of post-Reformation Roman Catholicism and the Protestant Reformation" in "doctrine, faith, and ecclesiology." Carl M. Leth, "Via Media," in *Global Wesleyan Dictionary of Theology*, ed. Al Truesdale (Kansas City: Beacon Hill Press of Kansas City, 2013), 556-58.

15. Whitefield died on Sunday, September 30, 1770, in Newburyport, Massachusetts. He is buried there beneath the pulpit of First Presbyterian Church.

16. For a detailed history of the New England revivals and a record of opposition to them, see George M. Marsden, *Jonathan Edwards: A Life* (New Haven, CT: Yale University Press, 2003), 150-252.

17. Ibid., 209.

18. Richard Cox, ed., "Stephen Bordley, George Whitefield, and the Great Awakening in Maryland," *Historical Magazine of the Protestant Episcopal Church* 46, no. 3 (1977): 297-307. Quote is on 307; spelling was modernized.

19. Benjamin Franklin, *The Autobiography of Benjamin Franklin* (New York: Henry Holt, 1916; repr., Project Gutenberg, 2006), chap. 11, http://www.gutenberg.org/files/20203/20203-h/20203-h.htm.

20. Charles Chauncy, *A Letter from a Gentleman in Boston to Mr. George Wishart, Concerning the State of Religion in New England* (Edinburgh, 1742), quoted in Alan Heimert and Perry Miller, eds., introduction to *The Great Awakening* (Indianapolis: Bobbs-Merrill, 1967), xxv.

21. As one may see in the shift in terminology in the early twenty-first century as more and more churches have "worship experiences" rather than "worship services."

22. Methodist New Testament scholar Richard B. Hays explains that experience refers not only to individual religious experience but also "to the experience of the community of faith collectively." This is what "John Wesley meant when he spoke of 'experimental religion': experience is the living appropriation of the [biblical] text, which becomes self-attesting as it is experienced in faith." *Moral Vision of the New Testament*, 210-11.

See also Timothy J. Crutcher, *The Crucible of Life: The Role of Experience in John Wesley's Theological Method* (Lexington, KY: Emeth Press, 2010). Although maintaining a proper tension or balance between theology and experience is "notoriously difficult," John Wesley "struck the balance well." "Divorced from human experience, theology becomes dry and bookish, an objective confession of orthodoxy with little connection to the way believers live their lives." But a "faith" derived solely from experience, unhinged from the Scriptures and Christian doctrine, reduces Christian faith to nothing more than anthropology (15).

23. Heimert and Miller, introduction to *The Great Awakening*, lxi.

Chapter 5

1. Candy Gunther Brown and Mark Silk, eds., *The Future of Evangelicalism in America* (New York: Cambridge University Press, 2016), 3.

2. As has been noted in this book, the definition of the word "evangelical" is still debated in many academic circles. Some groups generally considered "evangelical" were opposed to the revivals of the eighteenth and nineteenth centuries. This is especially true of the "Old School" Presbyterians.

3. "The Bill of Rights: A Transcription," National Archives, https://www.archives.gov/founding-docs/bill-of-rights-transcript.

4. Individual states were initially still allowed to have established religions or religious taxes that were used to support the faith of each individual's choosing. Massachusetts was the last state to have an established religion (Congregationalists); this was ended in 1833.

5. Nathan Hatch, *The Democratization of American Christianity* (New Haven, CT: Yale University Press, 1989); John Wigger, *American Saint: Francis Asbury and the Methodists* (New York: Oxford University Press, 2009).

6. Dickson D. Bruce Jr., *And They All Sang Hallelujah: Plain-Folk Camp-Meeting Religion, 1800-1845* (Knoxville, TN: University of Tennessee Press, 1981), 61-95; John B. Boles, *The Great Revival: Beginnings of the Bible Belt* (Louisville, KY: University Press of Kentucky, 1996), 37-40.

7. John McGee, "Letter," *The Methodist Magazine* 4 (1821): 190.

8. Charles G. Finney, *Memoirs of Rev. Charles G. Finney* (New York: A. S. Barnes, 1876), 24-40, 284-301.

9. Charles G. Finney, *Lectures on Revival of Religion* (New York: Leavitt, Lord, 1835), 232-55.

10. Nathan O. Hatch, "The Puzzle of American Methodism," *Church History* 63 (1994): 11; William M. Newman and Peter L. Halvorson, *Atlas of American Religion: The Denominational Era, 1776–1990* (Lanham, MD: Rowman and Littlefield, 2000), 39.

11. Paul E. Johnson, *A Shopkeeper's Millennium: Society and Revivals in Rochester, New York, 1815-1837* (New York: Hill and Wang, 1978), 118-25.

12. James Q. Wilson and Richard J. Herrnstein, *Crime and Human Nature* (New York: Simon and Schuster, 1985), 432.

13. Susan Hill Lindley, *"You Have Stept Out of Your Place": A History of Women and Religion in America* (Louisville, KY: Westminster John Knox Press, 1996), 90-134; Donald W. Dayton with Douglas M. Strong, *Rediscovering an Evangelical Heritage: A Tradition and Trajectory of Integrating Piety and Justice*, 2nd ed. (Grand Rapids: Baker Academic, 2014), 136-38.

14. George M. Marsden, *Understanding Fundamentalism and Evangelicalism* (Grand Rapids: Eerdmans, 1991), 13-15.

15. Henry Ward Beecher, "Preachers and Preaching: Henry Ward Beecher on the Study of Human Nature as an Indispensable Element," *The Phrenological Journal* 54 (1872), 397.

16. Ibid.

17. Charles Hodge, *What Is Darwinism?* (New York: Scribner, Armstrong, 1874), 177.

18. Marsden, *Understanding Fundamentalism and Evangelicalism*, 35-39.

19. George Marsden, *Fundamentalism and American Culture* (New York: Oxford University Press, 1980), 119.

20. Timothy P. Weber, "Premillennialism and the Branches of Evangelism," in *The Variety of American Evangelicalism*, ed. Donald W. Dayton and Robert K. Johnson (Eugene, OR: Wipf and Stock, 1997), 5-10; Randall Balmer, *The Making of Evangelicalism: From Revivalism to Politics and Beyond* (Waco, TX: Baylor University Press, 2010), 32-35.

21. Historian Sydney E. Ahlstrom says, "Nowhere did Darbyism fall on more fertile ground than when it reached Cyrus Ingerson Scofield . . . (1843–1921)." *A Religious History of the American People* (New Haven, CT: Yale University Press, 1973), 809. In his immensely influential *Scofield Reference Bible* (1909), Scofield advanced the normative form of American dispensationalism. For millions of people in many denominations, Scofield's dogmatic expositions of dispensationalism provided an indispensable pathway through the Scriptures.

22. Marsden, *Understanding Fundamentalism and Evangelicalism*, 57-59.

23. Edward J. Larsen, *Summer for the Gods: The Scopes Trial and America's Continuing Debate over Science and Religion* (New York: Basic Books, 1997), 170-196; Michael Kazin, *A Godly Hero: The Life of William Jennings Bryan* (New York: Anchor Books, 2007), 285-305.

24. Robert Watson Sledge, *Hands on the Ark: The Struggle for Change in the Methodist Episcopal Church, South, 1914-1939* (Lake Junaluska, NC: United Methodist Church, Commission on Archives and History, 1975), 140-45.

25. Benjamin T. Roberts, "New School Methodism," in *Benjamin Titus Roberts: A Biography by His Son*, ed. Benson Howard Roberts (North Chili, NY: "The Earnest Christian" Office, 1900), 113.

26. Ibid., 113-14, 119.

27. Several times Phoebe Palmer and her husband visited Britain, where they contributed to an evangelical awakening that added many members to British evangelical churches.

28. Vinson Synan, *The Holiness-Pentecostal Tradition: Charismatic Movements in the Twentieth Century* (Grand Rapids: Eerdmans, 1997), 16-18, 29-43.

29. Numerous holiness groups merged to form the Church of the Nazarene. The denomination marks 1908 as its official date of formation. For a brief history of the

denomination see "History: Who We Are," Church of the Nazarene, http://nazarene.org/history. Timothy L. Smith provides an excellent history of the nineteenth-century holiness movement and the formation of the Church of the Nazarene. Timothy L. Smith, *Called unto Holiness*, vol. 1 (Kansas City: Beacon Hill Press, 1962).

30. Ibid., 79-87.

31. Frank Bartleman, an "Azusa participant," called Los Angeles the "American Jerusalem." "The Azusa Street Revival: William Joseph Seymour," The Old Time Gospel, http://theoldtimegospel.org/revival/seymour.html.

32. Alma White, *Demons and Tongues* (Bound Brook, NJ: Pentecostal Union, 1910), 7.

33. Synan, *Holiness-Pentecostal Tradition*, 51, 90-106.

34. Barry Hankins, *American Evangelicals: A Contemporary History of a Mainstream Religious Movement* (Lanham, MD: Rowman and Littlefield, 2008), 35-38.

35. Balmer, *Making of Evangelicalism*, 51-52.

36. Riley B. Case, *Evangelical and Methodist: A Popular History* (Nashville: Abingdon Press, 2004), 27-35.

37. Synan, *Holiness-Pentecostal Tradition*, 220-27, 285-90.

38. Hankins, *American Evangelicals*, 137-44.

39. Robertson resigned as president in 2001 and was succeeded by Roberta Combs.

40. Ibid., 149.

41. Jim Wallis, *The Call to Conversation: Why Faith Is Always Personal but Never Private* (San Francisco: HarperSanFrancisco, 2005), xvii.

Chapter 6

1. "Public Praises Science; Scientists Fault Public, Media," Pew Research Center, http://www.people-press.org/2009/07/09/section-1-public-views-of-science-and-scientists/. Regrettably, these statistics are not broken out for evangelicals of other ethnic backgrounds.

2. Lee Rainie and Cary Funk, "An Elaboration of AAAS Scientists' Views," Pew Research Center, http://www.pewinternet.org/2015/07/23/an-elaboration-of-aaas-scientists-views/.

3. Ibid.

4. The Protestant Reformation was fueled by commitments to other *sola* statements too: *sola gratia* (grace alone)—justification is by God's gift of grace, not because of any merit on the part of humans; and *sola fide* (faith alone)—that gift of grace comes through faith, not by doing good works.

5. David B. Barrett, George T. Kurian, and Todd M. Johnson, eds., *World Christian Encyclopedia* (Oxford, UK: Oxford University Press, 2001), 18.

6. Peter Harrison, *The Bible, Protestantism, and the Rise of Natural Science* (Cambridge, UK: Cambridge University Press, 1998), 78.

7. See, for example, John H. Walton, *The Lost World of Genesis One* (Downers Grove, IL: InterVarsity Press, 2009).

8. Recent books from evangelical presses that discuss and endorse this approach include Deborah Haarsma and Loren Haarsma, *Origins* (Grand Rapids: Faith Alive Christian Resources, 2011); Karl W. Giberson, *The Wonder of the Universe* (Downers Grove, IL: InterVarsity Press, 2012); and Denis Lamoureux, *Evolution: Scripture and Nature Say Yes!* (Grand Rapids: Zondervan, 2016).

9. John Chrysostom, "Homily 9 on the Statues," sec. 5, New Advent, http://www.newadvent.org/fathers/190109.htm.

10. Francis Bacon, *The Advancement of Learning*, ed. Henry Morley (1893; repr., Project Gutenberg, 2014), bk. 1, sec. 1, para. 3, http://www.gutenberg.org/files/5500/5500-h/5500-h.htm.

11. This point is made nicely in Mary L. VandenBerg, "What General Revelation Does (and Does Not) Tell Us," *Perspectives in Science and Christian Faith* 62 (2010): 16-24.

12. Walton, *Lost World of Genesis One*, 118.

13. Ibid.

14. Wright, *Day the Revolution Began*, 76-77.

15. Walton, *Lost World of Genesis One*, 123.

16. Walton notes that "creation language is used more in the Bible for God's sustaining work (i.e., his ongoing work as Creator) than it is for his originating work" (*Lost World of Genesis One*, 121). He warns against a "practical deism" in which "God is seen as responsible for 'jump-starting' the evolutionary process and then letting it unwind through the eons" without his sustaining presence and activity. Some forms of "theistic evolution" are guilty of this (120).

17. These categories track fairly closely the standard typology developed by Ian Barbour in his *Religion in an Age of Science* (San Francisco: HarperSanFrancisco, 1990), but I'm using different labels for two. I give some extended discussion of Barbour's categories in the first three chapters of my *Science and Christianity: An Introduction to the Issues* (Chichester, UK: Wiley-Blackwell, 2017).

18. Many evangelicals continue to believe that the earth is six thousand years old and that the Bible supports this. Proponents are called young-earth creationists. For an example of how this claim is supported, see Lita Cosner, "How Does the Bible Teach 6,000 Years?" Creation Ministries International, http://creation.com/6000-years. A summary of the scientific conclusions about the age of the earth and universe can be found at "How Are the Ages of the Earth and Universe Calculated?" BioLogos, http://biologos.org/common-questions/scientific-evidence/ages-of-the-earth-and-universe.

19. Bernard Ramm, *The Christian View of Science and Scripture* (Grand Rapids: Eerdmans, 1954), 145.

20. Stephen Jay Gould, *Rocks of Ages* (New York: Ballantine Books, 1999), 65-67.

21. Pope Pius XII, *Humani Generis* (August 12, 1950), http://w2.vatican.va/content/pius-xii/en/encyclicals.index.2.html.

22. If you've not seen the image, type "old woman or young lady illusion" into an Internet search engine.

23. Mary Midgley, *Are You an Illusion?* (New York: Routledge, 2014), 114.

24. John Locke illustrated this point by describing a "studious blind man" who attempted to learn and understand the names of colors and claimed to be successful, "Upon which, his friend demanding what scarlet was? the blind man answered, it was like the sound of a trumpet." *An Essay Concerning Human Understanding* (Philadelphia: Kay and Troutman, 1846; repr., Google Books), bk. 3, chap. 4, sec. 11.

25. Bethany Sollereder, "Lost in a World of Maps: Relations between Science and Theology," October 7, 2015, Blogs, BioLogos, http://biologos.org/blogs/jim-stump-faith-and-science-seeking-understanding/lost-in-a-world-of-maps-relations-between-science-and-theology.

26. I recommend Alister McGrath's *Enriching Our Vision of Reality* (London: SPCK, 2016) as an excellent explanation and defense of science and theology as complementary visions.

Chapter 7

1. Kenneth S. Latourette, *Advance through Storm: A.D. 1914 and After, with Concluding Generalizations*, vol. 7 of *A History of the Expansion of Christianity* (New York: Harper and Brothers, 1945), 418.

2. Timothy L. Smith, "The Evangelical Contribution," in *The Evangelical Landscape: Essays on the American Evangelical Tradition*, ed. Garth Rosell (Grand Rapids: Baker, 1996), 69. Smith's student D. G. Hart questioned the adequacy of Smith's definition. Historians, he noted, have a way of projecting backward on the basis of a definition to create a historical movement. D. G. Hart, *Deconstructing Evangelicalism: Conservative Protestantism in the Age of Billy Graham* (Grand Rapids: Baker, 2004), 183, 187, 193-97.

3. Lian Xi, *The Conversion of Missionaries: Liberalism in American Protestant Missions in China, 1907-1932* (University Park: Pennsylvania State University Press, 1997).

4. Hilaire Belloc, *Europe and the Faith* (New York: Paulist Press, 1921), viii (italics added).

5. Martin Marty, *A Short History of Christianity*, 2nd ed. (Philadelphia: Fortress Press, 1987), 307.

6. *Atlas of Global Christianity*, ed. Todd M. Johnson and Kenneth R. Ross (Edinburgh: Edinburgh University Press, 2009), 267, 271, 279, 283, 287.

7. Philip Jenkins, *The Next Christendom: The Coming of Global Christianity* (New York: Oxford University Press, 2002), 57-71; Diarmaid MacCulloch, *Christianity: The First Three Thousand Years* (New York: Viking, 2009), 886. A variety of terms are used for these churches: non-Western, Two-Thirds World churches, and the Global

South—the term this paper will prefer. See also Dana Robert, "Shifting Southward: Global Christianity Since 1945," *International Bulletin of Missionary Research* 24 (April 2000): 50-58. On the epochal significance see Scott W. Sunquist, *The Unexpected Christian Century: The Reversal and Transformation of Global Christianity, 1900–2000* (Grand Rapids: Baker, 2015), 176.

8. "Status of Global Christianity, 2017, in the Context of 1900–2050," Center for the Study of Global Christianity, Gordon-Conwell Theological Seminary, http://www.gordonconwell.edu/ockenga/research/documents/StatusofGlobalChristianity 2017.pdf.

9. David B. Barrett and Todd M. Johnson, *World Christian Trends, AD 30–AD 2200: Interpreting the Annual Christian Megacensus* (Pasadena, CA: William Carey, 2001), 858.

10. *Atlas of Global Christianity*, 292.

11. Barrett and Johnson, *World Christian Trends*, 279.

12. Ibid., 27, 858; *Atlas of Global Christianity*, 99; Todd M. Johnson et al., "Christianity 2017: Five Hundred Years of Protestant Christianity," *International Bulletin of Mission Research* 41 (January 2017), http://www.gordonconwell.edu/ockenga/research/documents/IBMR2017.pdf. Methodist, Wesleyan, and holiness evangelicals are among the "Protestant" evangelicals. On the difficulties of counting evangelicals see Gina A. Zurlo, "Demographics of Global Evangelicalism," in *Evangelicals around the World*, 38-44.

13. Barrett and Johnson, *World Christian Trends*, 860.

14. Allan H. Anderson, "Pentecostals: Their Rise and Role in the Evangelical Community," in *Evangelicals around the World*, 94-95.

15. Ibid., 95.

16. Stanley M. Burgess, Gary B. McGee, and Patrick H. Alexander, eds., *Dictionary of Pentecostal and Charismatic Movements* (Grand Rapids: Zondervan, 1988), 818.

17. In 2010 there were 614 million "renewalists." The number is expected to rise to more than 1 billion by 2050 (*Atlas of Global Christianity*, 100-103, 328, 339, 343, 351-52; Johnson et al., "Christianity 2017").

18. Allan H. Anderson, "Types and Butterflies: African Initiated Churches and European Typologies," *International Bulletin of Missionary Research* 25 (July 2001): 107-13.

19. See Ussama Makdisi, *Artillery of Heaven: American Missionaries and the Failed Conversion of the Middle East* (Ithaca, NY: Cornell University Press, 2008). See also Joseph L. Grabill, *Protestant Diplomacy and the Near East: Missionary Influence on American Policy, 1810–1927* (Minneapolis: University of Minnesota Press, 1971).

20. Lamin Sanneh suggests one reason the missionaries downplayed the role of local leaders was their own prejudices toward persons of color. Jay Riley Case, "Interpreting Karen Christianity: The American Baptist Reaction to Asian Christianity in the Nineteenth Century," in *The Changing Face of Christianity: Africa, the West, and the World*, ed. Lamin Sanneh and Joel Carpenter (New York: Oxford University

Press, 2005), 135-57, and, in the same volume, Lamin Sanneh, "The Changing Face of Christianity: The Cultural Impetus of a World Religion," 13. Giving prominence to local missionaries, Charles Forman, *The Island Churches of the South Pacific: Emergence in the Twentieth Century* (Maryknoll, NY: Orbis, 1982).

Something similar happened in Brazil. The Assembleias de Deus began with Swedish Pentecostal missionaries in 1911. When American Assemblies of God missionaries arrived in the 1930s, they attempted to bring the group under their governance. Not all members of the Assembleias de Deus Brazilians agreed. The largest part, the General Convention of the Assemblies of God of Brazil (3.5 million members in 2001), affiliated with the American-based Assemblies of God. But the National Convention of the Assemblies of God (2 million members) did not (Sunquist, *Unexpected Christian Century*, 131-33).

21. David W. Bebbington, "Evangelicalism in Modern Britain and America: A Comparison," in *Amazing Grace: Evangelicalism in Australia, Britain, Canada, and the United States*, ed. George A. Rawlyk and Mark A. Noll (Grand Rapids: Baker, 1993), 185; David W. Bebbington, *The Dominance of Evangelicalism: The Age of Spurgeon and Moody* (Downers Grove, IL: InterVarsity Press, 2005), 21-23. Note that the bases for Bebbington's definition come from studies of English-speaking countries. Gina A. Zurlo makes the same point in "Demographics of Global Evangelicalism," 38. See Mark A. Noll, David W. Bebbington, and George A. Rawlyk, eds., *Evangelicalism: Comparative Studies of Popular Protestantism in America, the British Isles, and Beyond, 1700–1990* (New York: Oxford University Press, 1994).

22. Rawlyk and Noll, introduction to *Amazing Grace*, 20.

23. Sunquist, *Unexpected Christian Century*, 22-23.

24. See C. Peter Williams, "The Church Missionary Society and the Indigenous Church in the Second Half of the Nineteenth Century: The Defense and Destruction of the Venn Ideals," in *Converting Colonialism: Visions and Realities in Mission History, 1706-1914*, ed. Dana L. Robert (Grand Rapids: Eerdmans, 2008), 86-111; Paul Harris, "Denominationalism and Democracy: Ecclesiastical Issues Underlying Rufus Anderson's Three Self Program," in *North American Foreign Missions, 1810–1914: Theology, Theory, and Policy*, ed. Wilbert R. Shenk (Grand Rapids: Eerdmans, 2004), 61-85, and, in the same volume, Janet F. Fishburn, "The Social Gospel as Missionary Ideology," 218-42. See also William R. Hutchison, *Errand to the World: American Protestant Thought about Foreign Missions* (Chicago: University of Chicago Press, 1987), and Timothy Yates, *Christian Mission in the Twentieth Century* (Cambridge, UK: Cambridge University Press, 1994).

25. Cited in Sunquist, *Unexpected Christian Century*, 26.

26. Edward E. Andrews, *Native Apostles: Black and Indian Missionaries in the British Atlantic World* (Cambridge, MA: Harvard University Press, 2013), 7-10.

27. Ibid., 228. See Charles E. Farhadian, ed., *Introducing World Christianity* (Chichester, UK: Wiley-Blackwell, 2012), 1-3, and Dana L. Robert, introduction to Robert, *Converting Colonialism*, 20. For contrasting perspectives compare Irwin T.

Hyatt Jr., *Our Ordered Lives Confess: Three Nineteenth-Century American Missionaries in East Shantung* (Cambridge, MA: Harvard University Press, 1976), and Ryan Dunch, *Fuzhou Protestants and the Making of a Modern China, 1857–1927* (New Haven, CT: Yale University Press, 2001).

28. Wilbert R. Shenk, "Contextual Theology: The Last Frontier," in *Changing Face of Christianity*, 203.

29. Kevin Ward, "The East African Revival and the Revitalization of Christianity," in *Revitalization amid Diaspora. Consultation Three: Explorations in World Christian Revitalization Movements*, ed. J. Steven O'Malley (Lexington, KY: Emeth Press, 2013), 23; Adrian Hastings, *The Church in Africa 1450–1950* (Oxford, UK: Clarendon Press, 1994), 596-99.

30. John Mbiti, "Theological Impotence and the Universality of the Church," in *Mission Trends No. 3: Third World Theologies*, ed. Gerald H. Anderson and Thomas F. Stransky (New York: Paulist Press, 1976), 6-8.

31. Sarah E. Ruble, *The Gospel of Freedom and Power: Protestant Missionaries in American Culture after World War II* (Chapel Hill, NC: University of North Carolina Press, 2012), 2-3. Similarly, see Steve Brouwer, Paul Gifford, and Susan D. Rose, *Exporting the American Gospel: Global Christian Fundamentalism* (New York: Routledge, 1996).

32. Shenk, "Contextual Theology," 192-93, 206-7; Todd M. Vanden Berg, "Culture, Christianity, and Witchcraft in a West African Context," in *Changing Face of Christianity*, 46. See Rosemary Dowsett and Samuel Escobar, "Evangelicals, 1910–2010," in *Atlas of Global Christianity*, 97; and Julie Ma and Allan Anderson, "Pentecostals (Renewalists), 1910–2010," in *Atlas of Global Christianity*, 100-101.

33. Marthinus L. Daneel, "African Initiated Churches in Southern Africa: Protest Movements or Mission Churches?" in *Christianity Reborn: The Global Expansion of Evangelicalism in the Twentieth Century*, ed. Donald M. Lewis (Grand Rapids: Eerdmans, 2004), 182, 187, 193-94, 214-15. See, in the same volume, Allan K. Davidson, "'The Pacific Is No Longer a Mission Field?' Conversion in the South Pacific in the Twentieth Century," 146-47. See also David Martin, *Pentecostalism: The World Their Parish* (Oxford, UK: Blackwell, 2002), 74, 120-22, 130, 143, 174.

34. Ogbu Kalu, "West African Christianity: Padres, Pastors, Prophets, and Pentecostals," in *Introducing World Christianity*, 48. See B. G. M. Sundkler, *Bantu Prophets in South Africa* (London: Oxford University Press, 1948), 220-37; Philip Jenkins, *The New Faces of Christianity: Believing the Bible in the Global South* (New York: Oxford University Press, 2006), 17; Vanden Berg, "Culture, Christianity, and Witchcraft," 55; Paul Gifford, "A View of Ghana's New Christianity," in *Changing Face of Christianity*, 85-86.

35. Among the first to describe the separatist or independent churches were B. G. M. Sundkler, *Bantu Prophets in South Africa*, who provided a detailed description of a particular locality, and Vittorio Lanternari, *The Religions of the Oppressed: A Study of Modern Messianic Cults*, trans. Lisa Sergio (New York: Knopf, 1963), whose

work was broader. See also Kwame Bediako, "Christian Witness in the Public Sphere: Some Lessons and Residual Challenges from the Recent Political History of Ghana," in *Changing Face of Christianity*, 119.

36. Adrian Hastings, *A History of African Christianity 1950-1975* (Cambridge, UK: Cambridge University Press, 1979), 248-57.

37. Sheila S. Walker, *The Religious Revolution in the Ivory Coast: The Prophet Harris and the Harrist Church* (Chapel Hill, NC: University of North Carolina Press, 1983), 7, 16, 20, 37, 41, 54, 153, 158-60, 166.

38. Ibid., xv.

39. Ibid., 84, 87-89, 106-9, 121, 162.

40. Ibid., 124-31. See David A. Shank, *Prophet Harris: The "Black Elijah" of West Africa*, abr. by Jocelyn Murray (Leiden: E. J. Brill, 1994). Also see "Church of Christ—Harris Mission (Harrist Church)," World Council of Churches," https://www.oikoumene.org/en/member-churches/church-of-christ-harris-mission-harrist-church, and Cornelius Abiodum Olowola, "An Introduction to Independent African Churches," Biblicalstudies.org, http://biblicalstudies.org.uk/pdf/ajet/03-2_021.pdf.

In the Congo, another African leader, Simon Kimbangu (1887–1951), after being baptized by Baptists, began a ministry of healing. Though Kimbangu preached repentance, the sacrifice of Jesus Christ, and the necessity of removing fetishes, and though he spoke (unlike Harris) against both dancing and polygamy, he was known as the "healing prophet." The missionaries had Kimbangu arrested, and he spent most of his life imprisoned a thousand miles from where his ministry began. Yet his followers organized a church that became the largest church in the Congo and the first African Independent Church to join the World Council of Churches. Kimbanguism has an estimated 5.5 million members (Kalu, "West African Christianity," 48). See Sundkler, *Bantu Prophets*, 220-37; Jenkins, *New Faces of Christianity*, 17; Vanden Berg, "Culture, Christianity, and Witchcraft," 55; Gifford, "View of Ghana's New Christianity," 85-86.

41. Jonathan D. Spence, *God's Chinese Son: The Taiping Heavenly Kingdom of Hong Xiuquan* (New York: W. W. Norton, 1996).

42. Lian Xi, *Redeemed by Fire: The Rise of Popular Christianity in Modern China* (New Haven, CT: Yale University Press, 2010), 39-40, 155-78.

43. Ibid., 64-84.

44. Ibid., 42-63.

45. Ibid., 109-30. These positions would later lead Wang to reject the Three-Self Patriotic Movement. See Thomas Alan Harvey, *Acquainted with Grief: Wang Mingdao's Stand for the Persecuted Church in China* (Grand Rapids: Brazos, 2002).

46. Xi, *Redeemed by Fire*, 131-54. See also Daryl Ireland, "John Sung's Malleable Conversion Narrative," *Fides et Historia* 45 (Winter/Spring 2013): 48-75, and Ireland, "John Sung: Christian Revitalization in China and Southeast Asia" (PhD diss., Boston University, 2015). More generally, see Daniel H. Bays, "The Growth of Independent

Christianity, 1900-1937," in *Christianity in China: From the Eighteenth Century to the Present*, ed. Daniel H. Bays (Stanford, CA: Stanford University Press, 1996).

47. The three "selfs" of the Three-Self Movement are self-government, self-support, and self-propagation.

48. Xi, *Redeemed by Fire*, 7-8, 202-47; Johnson et al., "Christianity 2017."

49. John B. Carman and Chilkuri Vasantha Rao, *Christians in South Indian Villages, 1959–2009: Decline and Revival in Telangana* (Grand Rapids: Eerdmans, 2014), 113.

50. Ibid., 113, 116-23, 203, 212.

51. Katharine Wiegele, *Investing in Miracles: El Shaddai and the Transformation of Popular Catholicism in the Philippines* (Honolulu: University of Hawaii Press, 2005); Fred Maganua, "Jesus is Lord Fellowship," *Philippine Church Growth News* 9 (April-June 1987), 1-2; Michael Wourms, *The J. I. L. Love Story: The Church without a Roof* (El Cajon, CA: Christian Services Publishing, 1992); David S. Lim, "Consolidating Democracy: Filipino Evangelicals between People Power Events, 1986–2001," in *Evangelical Christianity and Democracy in Asia*, ed. David H. Lumsdaine (Oxford, UK: Oxford University Press, 2009), 240.

52. Sandra S. K. Lee, "Christianity by Major Tradition, 1910–2010," in *Atlas of Global Christianity*, 67.

53. Tan Kang San, "Will Asian Christianity Blossom or Wither?" in *Mission Round Table: The Occasional Bulletin of OMF Mission Research* 1 (January 2005), cited in Moonjang Lee, "Future of Global Christianity," in *Atlas of Global Christianity*, 104.

54. *Atlas of Global Christianity*, 352; Anderson, "Types and Butterflies," 108; Sunquist, *Unexpected Christian Century*, 151; Gifford, "View of Ghana's New Christianity," 94.

55. Sunquist, *Unexpected Christian Century*, 155-59.

56. See Arthur Leonard Tuggy, *Iglesia Ni Cristo: A Study in Independent Church Dynamics* (Quezon City, PH: Conservative Baptist Publishing, 1976), and Anne C. Harper, *Understanding the Iglesia Ni Cristo: What They Really Believe and How They Can Be Reached* (Baguio, PH: Asia Pacific Theological Seminary Press, 2014).

57. Joseph M. Kitagawa, *Religion in Japanese History* (New York: Columbia University Press, 1966), 298-300, 309-29; Sunquist, *Unexpected Christian Century*, 164-67.

58. Jenkins, *New Faces of Christianity*, 156, 160.

59. Ibid., cited by Jenkins, 55.

60. Ibid., 57, 60-61, 88-89.

61. Ibid., 67, 69, 72-73, 175. See Reynaldo C. Ileto, *Pasyon and Revolution: Popular Movements in the Philippines, 1840–1910* (Quezon City, PH: Ateneo de Manila University Press, 1979).

62. See Sundkler, *Bantu Prophets*, 139-44; Evelyn Cullamar, *Babaylanism in Negros: 1896–1907* (Quezon City, PH: New Day, 1986).

63. Compare Harvey Cox, *Fire from Heaven: The Rise of Pentecostal Spirituality and the Reshaping of Religion in the Twenty-First Century* (Reading, MA: Addison-Wesley, 1995), 218-41; G. Thompson Brown, *How Koreans Are Reconverting the West* (Bloomington, IN: Xlibris, 2008); and Timothy K. Park, "The Missionary Movement of the Korean Church," in *Mission History of Asian Churches*, ed. Timothy K. Park (Pasadena, CA: William Carey Library, 2011), 153-74. See also Lee Chung Soon, "The Pentecostal Face of Korean Protestantism: A Critical Understanding," *Asia Journal of Theology* 20 (October 2006): 399-417, and Boo-Woong Yoo, *Korean Pentecostalism: Its History and Theology* (Frankfurt: Peter Lang, 1987).

See Rebecca Y. Kim, *The Spirit Moves West: Korean Missionaries in America* (Oxford, UK: Oxford University Press, 2015).

64. MacCulloch, *Christianity*, 963, 965.

65. *The Whole Gospel for the Whole World: Story of Lausanne II Congress on World Evangelization, Manila 1989*, ed. Alan Nichols (Charlotte, NC: Lausanne Committee for World Evangelization, 1989), repeatedly affirmed evangelical social action and social involvement in order to address the world's poverty.

66. Jenkins made this point in *The Next Christendom*, 123.

67. David Martin, "Evangelical Expansion in Global Society," in *Christianity Reborn*, 293. See Gailyn Van Rheenan, *Communicating Christ in Animistic Contexts* (Pasadena, CA: William Carey Library, 1991). John Wimber and Kevin Springer, *Power Evangelism*, rev. ed. (San Francisco: Harper Collins, 1992), assumed that encounters with the spirit world were not simply a matter of non-Western churches, and Charles Kraft, *Christianity with Power: Your Worldview and Your Experience of the Supernatural* (1989; repr., Eugene, OR: Wipf and Stock, 2005), argued that the New Testament worldview, with its depiction of evil spirits as well as miracles, should be normative for all Christians. See also Julie C. Ma, *When the Spirit Meets the Spirits: Pentecostal Ministry among the Kankana-ey Tribe in the Philippines*, 2nd ed. (Frankfurt: Peter Lang, 2001); Martin, *Pentecostalism*, 157; and Jenkins, *New Faces of Christianity*, 98-127.

68. Paul Freston, "Contours of Latin American Pentecostalism," in *Christianity Reborn*, 255; see 221-70.

69. Samuel Escobar, "Christianity in Latin America: Changing Churches in a Changing Continent," in *Introducing World Christianity*, 171, and see R. Andrew Chesnut, "Brazilian Charisma: Pentecostalized Christianity in Latin America's Largest Nation," in the same, 186-200. See Lius N. Rivera-Pagán, "Pentecostal Transformation in Latin America," in *Twentieth-Century Global Christianity*, vol. 7 of *A People's History of Christianity*, ed. Mary Farrell Bednarowski (Minneapolis: Fortress Press, 2008), 190-210.

70. Cited in Sunquist, *Unexpected Christian Century*, 120. See also Philip L. Wickeri, *Seeking the Common Ground: Protestant Christianity, the Three-Self Movement, and China's United Front* (Maryknoll, NY: Orbis, 1988).

71. Luis Fontalvo, "Hispanic Pentecostals in a Canadian Anglo-Franco Environment," *Pneuma* 14 (Spring 1992): 74-79, cited in Martin, *Pentecostalism*, 45. See *Atlas of Global Christianity*, 267, 271, 279, 283, 287.

72. J. Steven O'Malley, introduction to *Revitalization amid Diaspora*, x.

73. Ibid.

74. GAFCON recognizes ACNA as an Anglican province, but the archbishop of Canterbury does not. Theologically orthodox, "The Anglican Church in North America unites 112,000 Anglicans in nearly 1,000 congregations across the United States, Canada, and Mexico into a single Church." Anglican Church in North America, http://www.anglicanchurch.net/index.php/main/About/. The large and theologically conservative diocese of South Carolina is currently considering membership in ACNA.

75. See the website maintained by the Global Anglican Future Conference: http://gafcon.org/.

76. Lamin Sanneh, "Conclusion: The Current Transformation of Christianity," in *Changing Face of Christianity*, 221.

77. Paul Joshua Bhakiaraj is also wrestling with these questions. Paul Joshua Bhakiaraj, "The Future of the Evangelical Movement," in *Evangelicals around the World*, 218-26.

Chapter 8

1. Otis Moss III, "Redeeming the Soul of America: Race, Justice, and Reconciliation" (Collins Lecture, Ecumenical Ministries of Oregon, Concordia University, Portland, OR, November 3, 2016).

2. John Calvin taught that "it was fitting that the new preaching of the gospel and the new Kingdom of Christ should be illumined and magnified by unheard of and extraordinary miracles" but that these miracles ceased when "the magnificence of his Kingdom and the dignity of his covenant had been excellently enough disclosed." *Institutes of the Christian Religion*, vol. 21 of *The Library of Christian Classics*, ed. John T. McNeill and trans. Ford Lewis Battles (Philadelphia: Westminster Press, 1960), bk. 4, chap. 19, sec. 6.

3. For a current African testimony to what I am advocating see the video statement by Olu Q. Menjay, president of the Liberia Baptist Missionary and Educational Convention: "Olu Menjay on Religious Freedom in Liberia," EthicsDaily.com, http://www.ethicsdaily.com/olu-menjay-on-religious-freedom-in-liberia-cms-23519.

4. Bob Dylan, "Gotta Serve Somebody," on *Slow Train Coming*, released August 20, 1979, Columbia FC 36120, 331/3 rpm.

5. Hans Küng, *Does God Exist? An Answer for Today*, trans. Edward Quinn (New York: Vantage Books, 1981), esp. 55-63, 425-77.

6. Koinonia Farm, https://www.koinoniafarm.org/history/.

7. Sojourners, https://sojo.net/about-us/our-history.

8. Prison Fellowship International, https://pfi.org.

9. For evangelicals in Lebanon, see "Dan and Sarah Chetti," International Ministries, https://internationalministries.org/teams/56-chetti, and Arab Baptist Theological Seminary, www.abtslebanon.org.

10. House for All Sinners and Saints, www.houseforall.org.

11. Bonhoeffer, *Cost of Discipleship*, 89.

12. See Shane Claiborne, Jonathan Wilson-Hartgrove, and Enuma Okoro, *Common Prayer: A Liturgy for Ordinary Radicals* (Grand Rapids: Zondervan, 2010).

13. The Catholic Worker Movement, www.catholicworker.org/communities/directory.html.

14. Phyllis Trible, *Texts of Terror: Literary-Feminist Readings of Biblical Narratives* (Philadelphia: Fortress Press, 1984).

15. *Theopedia*, s.v. "Wesleyan Quadrilateral," http://www.theopedia.com/wesleyan-quadrilateral.

See Don Thorsen, *The Wesleyan Quadrilateral: Scripture, Tradition, Reason, and Experience as a Model of Evangelical Theology* (Lexington, KY: Emeth Press, 2005).

16. Hays, *Moral Vision of the New Testament*, 208-11.

17. Both stories are firsthand accounts of the author's personal experience.

18. Although Anglophone visitors taught through interpreters, many of the Russian students spoke excellent English. So visitors enjoyed much direct communication with the students.

19. With the Edict of Thessalonica in AD 380, Emperor Theodosius I made Christianity the empire's sole authorized religion.

20. Almost 380 years later, the church is still in existence.

21. Roger Williams, *Bloudy Tenent of Persecution*, vol. 3 of *The Complete Writings of Roger Williams* (New York: Russell and Russell, 1963), 76, cited in Curtis Freeman, *Contesting Catholicity: Theology for Other Baptists* (Waco, TX: Baylor University Press, 2014), 72-74.

22. John Howard Yoder, *The Politics of Jesus* (Grand Rapids: Eerdmans, 1972), 78-90, 160-62.

23. This has been particularly problematic since the late twentieth century.

24. Congreso Internacional: La Libertad Religiosa en el Siglo XXI, Religión, Estado y Sociedad, September 3-5, 2014, Universidad Nacional de Córdoba, Córdoba, Argentina. On this topic, see also "Olu Q. Menjay: BWA Vancouver," *EthicsDaily*, July 7, 2016, https://vimeo.com/173793991.

25. Jenkins, *New Faces of Christianity*, 158.

26. In 2012, 12.9 percent of US residents were foreign born, the highest proportion since 1920. *The World Almanac and Book of Facts 2015* (New York: World Almanac Books, 2015), 616.

Hispanic evangelicals now compose 11 percent of the US evangelical population. According to Dr. Gabriel Salguero, president of the National Latino Evangelical Coalition, Hispanic evangelicals "tend to be socially conservative on issues of marriage and life and all that—but progressive on issues of economics, housing and immigration." Gabriel Salguero, as quoted by Laura Turner, "Know It All: The New and Complex Face of Evangelical Christianity in American Politics," *Pacific Standard Magazine*, June 19, 2016, https://psmag.com/news/know-it-all-the-new-and-complex-face-of-evangelical-christianity-in-american-politics.

27. Ryan Lenora Brown, "Pentecostal Christianity Is a Top Nigerian Export," *Christian Century*, September 30, 2015, https://www.christiancentury.org/article/2015-09/top-nigerian-export-pentecostal-christianity.

28. Thomas C. Oden, *The Rebirth of Orthodoxy: Signs of New Life in Christianity* (San Francisco: HarperSanFrancisco, 2003), 56.

29. Ibid., 57.

30. Ibid., 56-57, 117-26.

31. Ibid., 129, 147.

32. Ibid.

33. Chapter author is current pastor of this Portland, Oregon, church.

34. Chapter author is former pastor of Portola Church.

35. Jenkins, *New Faces of Christianity*, 9. Jenkins notes that the proportion of Christians in Africa grew from 10 percent in 1900 to 46 percent in 2000, and by 2016 there were more than 555 million African Christians, some 20 percent of them "independents," that is, not identifying with traditional Catholic, Protestant, or Orthodox bodies and not easily classifiable by their doctrinal emphases and practices.

36. Fanny Crosby, "To God Be the Glory," Hymnary.org, http://hymnary.org/text/to_god_be_the_glory_great_things_he_hath.

Chapter 9

1. William Martin, *With God on Our Side: The Rise of the Religious Right in America* (New York: Broadway Books, 1996), 28.

2. Ibid.

3. I am writing principally from an American context, though I hope this chapter will address how evangelicals should relate to a variety of political contexts.

4. Robert P. Jones, writing for *Time*, has asked this question in the wake of the 2016 presidential election. Robert P. Jones, "Donald Trump and the Transformation of White Evangelicals," *Time*, November 19, 2016, http://time.com/4577752/donald-trump-transformation-white-evangelicals/?xid=homepage.

5. Robert P. Jones and Daniel Cox, "Clinton Maintains Double-Digit (51% vs. 36%) Lead over Trump," Public Religion Research Institute (PRRI), October 19, 2016, http://www.prri.org/research/prri-brookings-october-19-2016-presidential-election-horserace-clinton-trump.

6. For a more complete exposition on these themes, see Timothy R. Gaines and Shawna Songer Gaines, *Kings and Presidents: Politics and the Kingdom of God* (Kansas City: Beacon Hill Press of Kansas City, 2015).

7. Ibid., 16ff.

8. Ibid., 16.

9. Methodist New Testament scholar Michael J. Gorman insists that "participation in a *cruciform* God of holiness requires a corollary vision of life in the world that rejects domination in personal, public, or political life." Christians who adhere to the God of holiness must reject the "normal sequence of piety, war, victory, and peace that pervaded ancient Rome." It is a sequence that plays out "in the minds and hearts of Christians who have found in the god of military power a seductive alternative to the cruciform God of Paul." Michael J. Gorman, *Inhabiting the Cruciform God: Kenosis, Justification, and Theosis in Paul's Narrative Soteriology* (Grand Rapids: Eerdmans, 2009), 128.

10. For a more complete exposition, see Augustine, *The City of God against the Pagans*, ed. and trans. R. W. Dyson (Cambridge, UK: Cambridge University Press, 1998), 909-49.

11. This is where Nietzsche's infamous proclamation "God is dead" is found. His point is not so much that God has actually ceased to exist as much as it is that God's followers have decided they don't need God to make the world of their own choosing. All that is left, then, is for humans to enter into a battle of wills in order to see which will come out on top. Those locked in such a battle fight for what they *value* most. The underside of a battle over "values" is that it relies upon power; one side wins by using its power to overcome the other. See Friedrich Nietzsche, *The Gay Science: With a Prelude of German Rhymes and an Appendix of Songs*, ed. Bernard Williams (Cambridge, UK: Cambridge University Press, 2001), 120ff.

12. Bonhoeffer, *Cost of Discipleship*, 89.

13. Walter Brueggemann, *Testimony to Otherwise: The Witness of Elijah and Elisha* (St. Louis: Chalice Press, 2001), 3.

14. Gaines and Gaines, *Kings and Presidents*, 59.

Chapter 10

1. In the Roman Catholic Church *magisterium* refers to the teaching office of the church. It consists of the pope and bishops. The magisterium is the church's divinely appointed authority to teach the Christian faith correctly.

2. Pope Paul VI, *Evangelization in the Modern World* (*Evangelii Nuntiandi*) (December 8, 1975), sec. 18, http://w2.vatican.va/content/paul-vi/en/apost_exhortations/documents/hf_p-vi_exh_19751208_evangelii-nuntiandi.html. Permission to quote granted: Vatican permissions for publication.

3. Pope John XXIII, "Address on the Occasion of the Solemn Opening of the Most Holy Council" (October 11, 1962), quoting St. Augustine, epistle 138, chap. 3. Permission to quote granted: Vatican permissions for publication (italics added).

4. Second Vatican Council, *Dogmatic Constitution on the Church* (*Lumen Gentium*) (November 21, 1964), chap. 1, sec. 1, http://www.vatican.va/archive/hist_councils/ii_vatican_council/documents/vat-ii_const_19641121_lumen-gentium_en.html. Permission to quote granted: Vatican permissions for publication.

5. Ibid., chap. 5, sec. 41. Permission to quote granted: Vatican permissions for publication.

6. Second Vatican Council, *Decree on the Apostolate of the Laity* (*Apostolicam Actuositatem*) (November 18, 1965), chap. 3, sec. 13, http://www.vatican.va/archive/hist_councils/ii_vatican_council/documents/vat-ii_decree_19651118_apostolicam-actuositatem_en.html. Permission to quote granted: Vatican permissions for publication.

7. Second Vatican Council, *Dogmatic Constitution on Divine Revelation* (*Dei Verbum*) (November 18, 1965) chap. 6, sec. 25, http://www.vatican.va/archive/hist_councils/ii_vatican_council/documents/vat-ii_const_19651118_dei-verbum_en.html. Permission to quote granted: Vatican permissions for publication.

8. George Weigel, "Papacy and Power," *First Things*, February 2001, https://www.firstthings.com/article/2001/02/papacy-and-power.

9. Pope Paul VI, *Evangelization in the Modern World*, sec. 14. Permission to quote granted: Vatican permissions for publication (italics added).

10. Ibid. (italics added).

11. William L. Portier, "Here Come the Evangelical Catholics," *Communio* 31, no. 1 (Spring 2004). Portier gives a detailed theological and sociological analysis of this phenomenon as well as a brief treatment of the phrase "evangelical Catholics" as it is used by various Catholic thinkers.

12. Second Generation Conference of Latin American Bishops, *The Church in the Present-Day Transformation of Latin America in the Light of the Council* (Secretariat for Latin America, National Conference of Catholic Bishops, 1979). The bishops of Latin America introduced the conclusions of the Medellín gathering in their letter "The Presence of the Church in the Present Transformation of Latin America" (September 6, 1968).

13. Pope John Paul II, "Holy Mass at the Shrine of the Holy Cross," Homily of His Holiness John Paul II (June 9, 1979), http://w2.vatican.va/content/john-paul-ii/en/homilies/1979/documents/hf_jp-ii_hom_19790609_polonia-mogila-nowa-huta.html.

14. An encyclical is a papal letter sent to all bishops and people of the Roman Catholic Church.

15. Pope John Paul II, *Mission of the Redeemer* (*Redemptoris Missio*) (December 7, 1990), chap. 4, sec. 33, http://w2.vatican.va/content/john-paul-ii/en/encyclicals/documents/hf_jp-ii_enc_07121990_redemptoris-missio.html. Permission to quote granted: Vatican permissions for publication.

16. Ibid., introd., sec. 3.

17. Pope John Paul II, *Ecclesia in America* (January 22, 1999), chap. 6, sec. 68, http://w2.vatican.va/content/john-paul-ii/en/apost_exhortations/documents/hf_jp-ii_exh_22011999_ecclesia-in-america.html. Permission to quote granted: Vatican permissions for publication (italics added).

Notes

18. Notice in this listing all the work that was done to teach on the priesthood and guide seminary education during the years (1978–2005) of Pope John Paul II's pontificate: "Church Documents for Priestly Formation," United States Conference of Catholic Bishops (USCCB), http://www.usccb.org/beliefs-and-teachings/vocations/priesthood/priestly-formation/church-documents-for-priestly-formation.cfm.

19. Pope Benedict XVI, *God Is Love* (*Deus Caritas Est*) (December 25, 2005), introd., sec. 1. Permission to quote granted: Vatican permissions for publication.

20. *Lectio divina* is an ancient practice of Scripture reading, meditation, and prayer.

21. Pope Benedict XVI, "Address of His Holiness Benedict XVI to the Participants in the International Congress Organized to Commemorate the 40th Anniversary of the Dogmatic Constitution on Divine Revelation 'Dei Verbum'" (September 16, 2005), https://w2.vatican.va/content/benedict-xvi/en/speeches/2005/september/documents/hf_ben-xvi_spe_20050916_40-dei-verbum.html. Permission to quote granted: Vatican permissions for publication.

22. Pope Benedict XVI, *The Word of God in the Life and Mission of the Church*, Twelfth Ordinary General Assembly of the Synod of Bishops, meeting in the Vatican, October 5-16, 2008, http://www.vatican.va/roman_curia/synod/documents/rc_synod_doc_20080511_instrlabor-xii-assembly_en.html.

23. Pope Benedict XVI, *The Word of the Lord* (*Verbum Domini*) (September 30, 2010), concl., sec. 122, http://w2.vatican.va/content/benedict-xvi/en/apost_exhortations/documents/hf_ben-xvi_exh_20100930_verbum-domini.html. Permission to quote granted: Vatican permissions for publication.

24. "Bergoglio's Intervention: A Diagnosis of the Problems in the Church," Vatican Radio, March 27, 2013, http://en.radiovaticana.va/storico/2013/03/27/bergoglios_intervention_a_diagnosis_of_the_problems_in_the_church/en1-677269.

25. In order to be elected pope, an individual has to receive over two-thirds of the voting cardinals' votes.

26. Pope Francis, *The Joy of the Gospel* (*Evangelii Gaudium*) (November 24, 2013), chap. 3, secs. 127-28, http://w2.vatican.va/content/francesco/en/apost_exhortations/documents/papa-francesco_esortazione-ap_20131124_evangelii-gaudium.html#Person_to_person. Permission to quote granted: Vatican permissions for publication.

27. This and a fuller listing can be found in the "Resources for the New Evangelization" section of the Catholic Apostolate Center's website: http://www.catholicapostolatecenter.org/new-evangelization.html.

28. Betsy Cooper et al., "Exodus: Why Americans Are Leaving Religion—and Why They're Unlikely to Come Back," PRRI, September 22, 2016, http://www.prri.org/research/prri-rns-poll-nones-atheist-leaving-religion/.

29. Pope John Paul II, *Mission of the Redeemer*, chap. 7, sec. 86. Permission to quote granted: Vatican permissions for publication.

Conclusion

1. Rosemary Radford Ruether, *The Church against Itself* (New York: Herder and Herder, 1967).
2. Wright, *Day the Revolution Began*, 384.
3. Ibid., 365.
4. Bishop Antonios Aziz Mina of Giza told the Fides news agency that "'in the moment of their barbaric execution,' . . . some of the Christians were mouthing the words 'Lord, Jesus Christ.' 'The name of Jesus was the last word on their lips.'" Leonardo Blair, "Heartbreaking: Egyptian Christians Were Calling for Jesus during Execution by ISIS in Libya," *Christian Post*, February 18, 2015, http://www.christianpost.com/news/heartbreaking-egyptian-christians-were-calling-for-jesus-during-execution-by-isis-in-libya-134340/.
5. "The Facts about Persecution," Voice of the Martyrs, https://vom.com.au/persecution/.
6. Thaddeus Barnum, *Never Silent: How Third World Missionaries Are Now Bringing the Gospel to Us* (Colorado Springs: Eleison, 2008), 260-61.
7. "Toward a New City Common[s]," abstract of chapter 6, from essay 3 of James Davison Hunter, *To Change the World: The Irony, Tragedy, and Possibility of Christianity in the Late Modern World* (New York: Oxford University Press, 2010), http://www.jamesdavisonhunter.com/to-change-the-world-abstracts.
8. Pope Francis, *Joy of the Gospel*, introd., sec. 1.

Appendix A

1. "The Nicene Creed," in *The Book of Common Prayer* (BCP) (New York: Seabury Press, 1979), 358-59.
2. "The Symbol of Chalcedon," in *The Greek and Latin Creeds, with Translations*, vol. 2 of *The Creeds of Christendom*, by Philip Schaff (1877; repr., CCEL, 2005), https://www.ccel.org/ccel/schaff/creeds2.iv.i.iii.html.
3. "The Apostles' Creed," in BCP, 66.
4. "Quicunque Vult," in BCP, 864-65.

www.ingramcontent.com/pod-product-compliance
Lightning Source LLC
Chambersburg PA
CBHW050858160426
43194CB00011B/2205